JEREMY TUNSTALL

The media in Britain

CONSTABLE

London

First published in Great Britain 1983
by Constable and Company Limited
10 Orange Street London WC2H 7EG
Hardback ISBN 0 09 464860 3
Paperback ISBN 0 09 465130 2
Copyright © 1983 by Jeremy Tunstall
Set in Linotron Times 10pt by
Rowland Phototypesetting Ltd
Bury St Edmunds, Suffolk
Printed in Great Britain by
St Edmundsbury Press
Bury St Edmunds, Suffolk

Contents

PART E: MEDIA POLICY

List of tables

List of figures

List of maps

Introduction

Britain's reputation and its image in the world are exceptionally bound up with British media; and yet Britain is also an extreme case of a country which is reluctant to face the need for policies covering the whole range of its media.

Beyond its shores, much information about Britain comes via Reuters news agency, the BBC external services, and two video news agencies – Visnews and UPITN. Yet none of these organizations is well known at home. More familiar within Britain are such media exports as zany comedies, drama classics, darts contests, and royal weddings. Its media exports seem to present an image of a country made up largely of economic disasters and costume grandeur – the two linked together by humour; London is a world champion at producing off-beat comedies and the outrageously whimsical story.

The British media industry can itself be fitted easily into Ealing comedy or hymns-ancient-and-modern views of Britain. *The Times* newspaper pioneered the steam printing press in 1814, and, ever since, British media have prided themselves on being attuned to 'new technology'. Meanwhile some of the practices of Fleet Street seem closer to the middle ages.

Some parts of the media – such as the BBC – really are deeply embedded in the national consciousness; the national newspapers also are so familiar that Britons do indeed make some kind of public statement by the choice of paper which they take to work in the morning. Yet beyond a few such familiar labels as the BBC or *Daily Mirror*, obscurity reigns. Take the BBC's competitors: how many Britons could even define what ITV is, let alone ITA, IBA, ITC, ITCA, or STV (three major organizations); or ABC, ABPC, ACC, AR, and ATV; or BMRB and BRMB?

This book, and its index, seek to explain the more significant of the proliferating organizations in independent broadcasting and beyond. The book also attempts to provide a broad *factual* account of British media – film, television, radio, newspapers and magazines. It summarizes the main published literature of books and official reports, plus some of the numerous unpublished surveys and research studies.

Facts, however, are not all and the book is also deliberately opinionated. For example:

- The British idea of the autonomous newspaper editor is largely a myth, but three or four thousand journalists and producers have an enormously powerful position throughout the media (pages 186–93, 212–17).
- Politicians and press leaders alike denigrate the common European idea of press subsidies; but in practice the tax concessions to the British press amount to a mammoth government under-writing not only of exotic trade union practices but of newspaper ownership by multi-national conglomerates (page 262).
- British tradition, law and practice favour national and international media and discriminate against the English regions; while sections of the Welsh and Scottish media prosper, the English regions suffer and the Midlands ITV contractor is used as a scapegoat (pages 218–34).
- Television is widely thought to constitute the dominant source of news, but British data suggest otherwise (pages 161–5).
- The Independent Broadcasting Authority when confronted with major decisions has usually managed to fall flat on its face; but the IBA reflects the inadequacies of British media policy and it remains a source of both media power and hope (pages 199–217).
- The British film industry has suffered from three great blights – Hollywood, television and (worst of all) British government policy (pages 54–68).
- British tradition frowns on the idea of a single media policy, media department or media minister. In consequence Britain has about thirty separate public agencies making media policy; one of the few beneficiaries is the Prime Minister who in practice plays the part of Media Minister (pages 238–9, 248 50).

Facts and *opinions* alone are not enough to encompass the British media. Dilemmas, paradoxes and *ambiguity* are also endemic. Many of the basic strategies of the media deliberately cultivate ambiguity – two-sides news, 'balance', the bigoted character who is presented as both stupid and loveable (pages 153–65).

The answers to many questions depend heavily on precise definitions. For example, how long does the average member of the great British public spend each week with the mass media? The answer can be as little as 25 hours per week, as much as 50 hours per week, or even as high as 75 hours per week, depending upon what exactly you mean by 'spend with' (pages 135–6).

This book deals primarily with the British media between the years 1945 and 1983. It does, however, occasionally look back to the 1930s or even earlier, and also sometimes attempts to peer forward. Three media revolutions confront British media and media policy:

First, the *old media* of over-the-air television and radio as well as home-delivered newspapers and magazines will experience large and painful changes. Secondly, the *new media* will, indeed, make enormous advances. Old categories such as 'news', 'entertainment' and 'advertising' many not survive the onslaught of electronic information technology. Thirdly, all countries will face a revolution of media *internationalization*. Britain is already unusual in the world as both a major importer and exporter of media, and Britain will face especially acute dilemmas. Britain at present is a four-television-network island anchored next to a European continent which has the world's richest concentration of major autonomous television networks. Will Britain, looking towards Brussels and Luxemburg, plug into the television network offerings of its European neighbours and will Britons thus become Europeans in front of the small screen? Or will Britain respond to multi-channel video by continuing to look towards Burbank and Los Angeles, making the now traditional – but still unacknowledged – assumption that The Media Are American?

However the media future develops, it will inevitably resemble the recent past in many ways. What is described in this book will remain relevant. Especially relevant may be the very simple point that the media do constitute a single coherent field for analysis – and for media policy.

PART A

Media myths, politics, policies

CHAPTER ONE

National myths, media myths

Britain, like other countries, has its supply of national myths and these myths are nowhere more evident than in the national mass media. Many countries have a mythology of the great national revolution, a revolution which is claimed to have seen the birth or re-birth not only of the modern nation but also its modern mass media. Britain's national mythology takes the reverse form – no national revolution in recent centuries, no revolution against domestic or foreign oppression – but instead a history of slow growth, of precedent broadening down to precedent. And Britain's press, broadening down from seventeenth- and eighteenth-century precedents, both exemplifies in its history this mythology as well as being a propagator and carrier of national self-imagery.

National celebrity, media celebrity

Personal celebrity pre-dates the modern media, but in recent years general and media celebrity have moved closer and closer and are now virtually identical. Media fame is general fame and vice-versa. In the nineteenth century national celebrity and press celebrity overlapped but were still far from identical. Politicians, the rich and titled, actors, singers and writers – all of these experienced press fame, as well as the somewhat separate celebrities of the live performance and of authorship, or the possession of wealth and the occupation of acres.

The television age took further something which radio had begun – the manufacturing of fame largely through appearances on the electronic media. From the late 1920s onwards radio made celebrities of bandleaders and comedians; but this celebrity creation was somewhat muted both by jealous theatrical interests and by BBC management. The BBC deliberately made news announcers anonymous to prevent the creation of expensive star personalities. It was only the war-time need to prevent German interventions on British wavelengths which led the BBC to identify its news presenters.

These radio newsreaders of the early 1940s were eminent examples of media celebrity. But the biggest radio celebrity of the early 1940s was Winston Churchill; his Prime Ministerial broadcasts did indeed achieve record audience levels.[1]

The television age has given fresh media opportunities to some of the main types of pre-television celebrities. Politicians can now become not merely household names but household faces, while actors can achieve an all-media celebrity never contemplated by the matinee idol. Comedians have perhaps benefitted the most because they – more than straight actors – are equipped to put on multi-media short takes; comedians are also more flexible, more script-able and better suited to the repetition of anecdotes. In Britain, as elsewhere, the current top comedians are television superstars.

But some other older forms of celebrity have become over-shadowed in the television age. No writers today can achieve the fame of Byron or even of George Bernard Shaw; Dickens – the all-media star of his day – would have trouble today in attracting the live audiences, although his histrionic gifts would be suitable for the occasional television short series. The rich and titled have also slipped back in terms of celebrity; these days celebrities need to perform. Some of Britain's idle rich have acknowledged this, by scattering their grounds with technicolor animals, and by develop-ing the guided tour of the family heirlooms into a new television form – part art lesson, part video gossip column. But wealth unvarnished by publicity or performance seldom now confers celebrity.

The television age has, however, created several major new sorts of celebrity. The leading example are the popular musicians; it is a curiosity that the superstar celebrities of the video age should have emerged from records, radio and live performance. Britain – es-pecially on a per-population basis – has been a world leader in the production of popular musicians; the Beatles, the Rolling Stones, the punk groups, of course conveyed much more than music. They built a new kind of group celebrity that was fiercely and rebelliously British, and yet which was too large, too wealthy, too celebrated to be contained within Britain.

Sports stars also existed previously, but television has enormous-ly increased their celebrity. Perhaps even more characteristic of the video age are the 'television personalities' – the disc jockeys or journalists – who became famous simply through a media version of everyday conversation.

Media celebrity in Britain seems to favour the integrated per-sonality – a real person with real teeth, a real accent and amusing prejudices – who can be presented in such varied settings as a talk show, an awards ceremony, a record request session, a quiz game, a newspaper interview. The celebrity should be capable of both gravitas and humour, of being flexible and funny without ceasing to convey an impression of having an integrated personality. Com-edians, disc jockeys, rock singers and journalists seem to fit these requirements. Politicians and actors on the whole less so. Who wants a humorous politician? The British Liberal party has specialized in politicians who make better comedians and mimics than politicians. Even straight actors seem to make insincere media personalities, sounding too reminiscent of product commercials.

Britain has one ancient category of celebrity which is well adjusted to contemporary media. The British Royal family have made many media mistakes, but their broad strategy is superb. They have identified themselves with the horse, which since the early years of the century has been the large and small screen's most riveting performer. The Royals have several different styles and acts, both with horses and without. They do things in boats, along with horses another hard act to follow. They have mastered both gravitas and after-dinner humour. They do a wonderful country house video guided tour. They know about avoiding over-exposure, but they also do the occasional special show – weddings and funerals mostly – that are top tear-jerkers world-wide. Above all they know the secret of not compromising yourself as a real person – their protruding teeth and ears are not smoothed away, while their crankily aristocratic – and often unworldly – opinions are seldom fully submerged. A new style of 'informal' television coverage can show the Royals at work and as approachable people.[2] The Royal family are certainly Britain's – and possibly the world's – number one long-lasting group of celebrities. Anyone who wants to observe the intermingling of Britain's national and media myths need only switch on to the next Royal occasion.

British ideals: freedom, objectivity, pragmatism, voluntarism
Such qualities as freedom, objectivity, pragmatism and voluntarism occupy prominent places in the national mythology and in Britain's media mythology. Many Britons would like to believe that their country is even freer – in some hard-to-define way – than the other great democracies such as France and the United States. A central place in this national freedom is taken up by the notion of press freedom, or (less familiarly) 'media freedom'.

Objectivity (or 'fair play') is another quality on which the British pride themselves – the ability to look facts in the face and to distinguish facts from emotions and opinions. The same quality, it is claimed, is to be found in British media. The formal distinction between fact and opinion was transferred from the press into radio and broadcasting, where it surfaces in the awkward British distinction between 'news' and 'current affairs' (in their BBC origins news came from news agencies and 'current affairs' from radio 'talks').

A related British virtue is pragmatism, common-sense, not getting too wound up in complicated theories or even complex detailed

legislation. The fewer theories and the fewer laws, the better Britain
– and Britain's media – will be.

One result is the national inability to define media 'freedom';
another is that Britain has less legislation specifically about the
media than does almost any other country.

Voluntarism is a further British virtue. Legislation and compul-
sion do not actually work half so well as a good voluntary agreement. Men and women of goodwill can solve it without the help of
the courts or Parliament. This attitude also applies to the media,
where some of the key institutions are entirely voluntary. Leading
examples are the Press Council and the Advertising Standards
Authority. The media censorship during the Second World War was
also operated on the voluntary principle. The 'D Notice' system of
today derives from this tradition – editors are told of certain military
secrets and asked voluntarily not to use them. This voluntary
approach was viable in the Second World War because the war was
a widely popular cause. The voluntary approach depends of course
on consensus, and would only be possible in a nation with a high
level of consensus and homogeneity of approach; these of course
have long existed – more or less – not least because of the strength of
Britain's national media.

The amateur principle

While the British tell each other about the need to be 'absolutely
professional' about this, that and the other, they still admire the
elegant amateur. The amateur principle exists far beyond the
media. For example senior civil servants in Britain continue to elude
the advice of successive committees and reports to the effect that
they should become more specialist and expert. Politicians are the
same. It is still assumed that a Member of Parliament supported by
one secretary and one research assistant can confidently take on the
massed forces of government. In the British system, Cabinet ministers play musical chairs between the great departments of state.
British actors have long been famous for wanting, like Bottom, to
play all the parts.

Among the last great refuges for the amateur are Fleet Street and
television. Journalists become instant experts as the result of news-
room shuffles paralleling those of the Cabinet. Television doctrine
has it that a good TV producer or presenter can produce or present
almost anything and is then capable of going on to become a senior
executive.

Underneath all of this 'amateurism' there is of course in reality a
lot of expertise, specialization, and burning of midnight oil.
Nevertheless the amateur principle carries weight and has consequences. There is, for example, a lot in common between the

gifted amateurs of the Whitehall Civil Service and the people who run television and the more serious bits of the press. Private school, Oxbridge, arts degrees, south of England origins, professional parents – all of these are common, although far from universal, in both cases.

Another consequence is that if the media practitioners themselves are somewhat amateur, there is little room for media expertise based outside the media. Journalism education as a university enterprise is not highly regarded; nor is the media industry as a field of specialized expertise either in academe or in the Civil Service. In British Civil Service and political approaches to the media, the amateur principle has double strength.

The American lure

A myth long favoured by Fleet Street was its claim to have the world's largest circulations (an indicator of performance not much more relevant than having the factory with the world's tallest chimney); this claim continued to be made long after the Japanese and the Russians had larger circulations.

Behind this and much other British media mythology was a veiled denial of American superiority. The British can still claim that *The Times* of London is the one after which the *New York Times* is named, that the popular London tabloids outsell all American daily newspapers, and that the BBC is the world's most respected broadcasting organization, while Reuters is the most respected international news agency. All of these claims may have some substance. But, as I have argued in *The Media Are American*, the media in their modern mass market – 'middle market' – forms were invented, or re-invented, in the United States. And having conquered the domestic USA market these continent-wide media formats went on to become world-wide. Through the export of both media products and also of models of media systems, American media profoundly influenced the media of all other nations in the world, almost without exception. Where is there a movie industry not influenced by Hollywood? Where in the world a popular newspaper untouched by Hearst?

In few nations in the world have these influences been greater than in Britain. In few nations should this account of world media prove more palatable because the American media in the world are more precisely 'Anglo-American' media. Britain is an active junior partner. In some respects – on a per-population, or economic product, basis – Britain's contribution to the partnership may be greater even than that of the United States. But this view of Britain – as both a big media exporter and also a major importer of American media – remains unfamiliar.

In the age of post-imperial decline, perhaps newspapers and television in Britain play the role of food and wine in post-1945 France. While the French could comfort themselves with the majesty of their cuisine, the British – more puritanically – decided to comfort themselves through the media with the consoling thought that although the news was bad the messenger who carried it was unbeatable.

A failure to acknowledge the significance of both British exporting and importing in the media results in a failure to understand how Britain's media differ from those both of the United States and the rest of Western Europe. Britain shares with Europe public sector, licence-financed broadcasting and other un-American activities. But Britain also favours certain typically Anglo-Saxon ideas which other Europeans find alien; one of these is the common law view that special bodies of legislation dealing with the media are undesirable.

In Britain there is little attempt (comparable to the American one) to examine the implications of a minimal intervention tradition – or to ask how this tradition can be squared with the fact of public sector broadcasting. British politicians are cautious about getting involved in such discussions; like democratic politicians elsewhere, they are reluctant to upset the media on issues which appear to be electorally unrewarding.

On the media side there are several quite sound reasons for leaving prevalent mythology undisturbed. Media imports are usually very *cheap* and the BBC – in view of its need to request licence fee increases – prefers to stress how *expensive* things are these days. Both BBC and ITV have long agreed to limit imports to 14% of programming; this low figure helps to support their desired image of production virtue and distracts attention from the fact that much 'TV violence' in Britain has either been violence originally produced for the American public or British imitations of Hollywood 'action' formats. *Imports* are a delicate matter also in industrial relations – public discussion of importing might lead to increased demands by trade unions.

Private publicity
All political systems include public relations. It is a peculiarity of the British system of political public relations that the mechanisms which generate the publicity are often remarkably secretive. Perhaps this is the amateur tradition again, or the cultivation at least of an appearance of amateurism: We simply tell the truth. That is the British tradition, but there are many ways both of telling the truth and of remaining silent. Central to the private operation of political publicity is the 'Lobby' – a system of publicity which until

around 1970 was little understood and is still not well understood now. One of the many peculiarities of the Lobby system is that the Prime Minister speaks to these journalists every day but nearly always through intermediaries.[3]

The major media organizations also are extremely concerned about their own media images, and the BBC – especially – devotes considerable quantities of senior executive time to discreet dining and discussing with the high and mighty, to public speeches, and to an endless round of anniversaries which stress the BBC's great traditions. The Royals, however, are perhaps the leaders in the private cultivation of discreet publicity. Royal public relations can be traced back some centuries. The first modern Royal PRO was appointed in 1947 and it was William Heseltine (1968–73) who dragged the Royals into the video age. Buckingham Palace has a press office of seven people – although all seven apparently insist that they do not engage in PR but merely tell the truth.[4] These PR persons were also sufficiently professional that when in 1981 they were planning Prince Charles' wedding, they chose Saint Paul's (superior to Westminister Abbey for cameras) and consulted the BBC as to the preferred day. The BBC strongly advised late July – after Wimbledon and the British Open Golf – and thus July 29th was reserved in the schedules. The live coverage of the wedding and later events found the BBC alone using some sixty cameras.[5]

But another event only ten weeks earlier had shown that the established forces of society are not alone in cultivating publicity in subtle and secret ways. The funeral of the IRA man Bobby Sands who starved himself to death in May 1981 was attended in Belfast by an estimated 300 TV reporters and cameramen. Many of them used a 25-foot-high structure of scaffolding and planking which had thoughtfully been placed in view of the grave by IRA publicity personnel.[6] Both mythology and counter-mythology can be propagated with discreet public relations.

CHAPTER TWO

Media-made politics, politically made media

This chapter and the next consider the connection between politics and media in Britain. Much of what happens in politics has media overtones; politics involve communication between politicians and public – communication which largely takes place through the media. It is incorrect to assume that media influence on politics is fairly recent or that somehow the media have 'altered' politics. Certainly at least since the early nineteenth century the impact of the press on politics was enormous.

But similarly politics has enormously influenced the media. There are the questions of political partisanship, bias, ownership, balanced reporting, equal time and so on – these issues are in practice under negotiation day-by-day in the output of the media and in the interaction between journalists and news sources, including politicians. But politics impinge on the media in another way – via deliberate policy decisions to legislate or not to legislate on for example issues such as new television channels. Media policy took on a new phase in the 1920s with radio and the problem of allocating radio frequencies. But media policy had been fairly active long before that. Early nineteenth-century examples in Britain included the policy of imposing penal newspaper taxes, a policy which was reversed in and around 1855. There is no such thing as a completely laissez-faire media system. In Britain, as elsewhere, the media which we see before us have been powerfully shaped by legislation and political decisions over many decades.

This chapter focuses on the two-way relationship between politics and the media; the next chapter considers the political forces which have shaped media policy and legislation in Britain.

Television revolution: decline of partisanship and bi-partisanship
Television's impact on politics – and television's influence also on press coverage of politics – dates in Britain roughly from the mid-1950s, around the time of the arrival of commercial TV in 1955. Indeed the whole post-Second World War period of British media divides itself fairly neatly into three periods – with 1955 (and

commercial TV) as one major divide, and with 1973 (and the oil price rise) as the second.

The media coverage of British politics was transformed in the second, 1955–73, period. A series of events in politics and in the press as well as in television, especially in the years 1956–60, can be summarized as the 'TV revolution' in media coverage of British politics.

Before 1955 there was very little coverage of politics on television. By 1960 there was a great deal of TV coverage; it was also much more aggressive and it affected the press as well. The traditional BBC radio approach to politics was extremely cautious and passive and initially it carried over into television. This passivity was exemplified by the '14 Day Rule' under which the BBC agreed not to broadcast discussions on any issues likely to be the subject of Parliamentary debate during the next two weeks; nor would any current legislation be discussed. Such a rule involved agreeing not to cover any of the major contentious issues of the moment. The BBC was itself partly responsible for this rule which began in 1944 and only ended in November 1956.[1]

1956 was also the year of Suez, when the BBC found itself in a major conflict with the Conservative government, which objected to the BBC's 'neutral' coverage of the British-French invasion of Suez. The BBC refused to back down, and continued to allow air time to criticisms of the government. This more vigorous coverage of politics was also evident in the news output of the commercial network which, when it began operations in 1955, attempted to escape from the BBC's passive and stilted approach. In 1958 Granada television gave the first extensive coverage to a by-election, in Rochdale. Another key event in this period was the 1959 General Election, the first one in which television took an active part and in which the politicians began to build their campaigning around the television coverage.[2]

The period 1956–59 saw an enormous increase not merely in the aggressiveness of TV coverage of politics but in its quantity. In 1955 the viewer could not find many minutes of politics on his screen each week; but by 1973 several hours a week of broadly political television were available.

In 1955–73 the overall media coverage of politics became very much less partisan. Television and radio continued studiously to cultivate political 'balance' and some of this seemed to rub off on to the press. A number of other factors were involved in the muting of press partisanship. Politics at this time tended towards the ('Butskellite') centre. The chief Conservative press Lords – Beaverbrook and the second Lord Rothermere – were past the vigour of youth and the *Daily Express* and *Daily Mail* were now comparatively mild in their Conservatism. The *Daily Mirror* (with the largest sale) was Labour, but right wing Labour – contributing powerfully to the moderate and bi-partisan tone.

By 1973 the bi-partisanship was itself in decline in the press – and after 1973 the press again became more partisan; notably in the case of *The Sun*, under Rupert Murdoch. Politics also were more partisan especially after the Thatcher election victory of 1979.

Television remains the main *mass* media source of political coverage and it attempts to remain neutral, although the rise of the SDP/Liberal alliance makes the simple Conservative-Labour balancing act now more complex.

Political crises have media sub-plots

Modern political crises normally have a media sub-plot.[3] This happens because a political 'crisis' can only be described as such if it threatens the government's (or the party's) electoral support. But since governments communicate with their supporters (and opponents) mainly via the media, the media tend to be sucked into the area of controversy. Government anxiety typically leads to accusations either of 'bias' and lack of neutrality, or – in case of military or security crises – the media are accused of bias exemplified by neutrality as between Britain and a foreign antagonist.

Examples of the latter kind include the Suez crisis of 1956 and the Falklands crisis of 1982 – in both cases there were bitter accusations addressed at, and exchanged between, newspapers. In both cases the government accused the BBC of treating the domestic opposition and the foreign enemy with excessive neutrality and objectivity. The same thing occurs in other, more domestic, political dramas – including major strikes and general elections.

The political parties get weaker, the media get stronger

British political parties have in the twentieth century grown steadily weaker in relation to the media.[4] In contrast, in much of western Europe, political parties still directly command press support, although to a diminishing extent. In the United States the media's independence from party has been one factor in the decline of party discipline and the emergence of 'personal parties' built around individuals with the ability to attract votes and (consequently) to attract the money required to fight elections. But in Britain this latter American pattern has not occurred, with the partial recent exception of the Social Democratic Party.

In Britain in 1900 there was a considerable party and partisan involvement in press ownership, and the decline of the Liberal press in the early decades of the century was partly balanced by Labour Party and trade union control of the *Daily Herald*, which was briefly the national circulation leader in 1930. Even by 1920 the British press was owned largely on commercial lines with the party element declining. Nevertheless the direct party linkage did not finally disappear until the 1960s.

Perhaps more important than the loosening grip of the parties on the press has been the fact of the emergence of television, where the parties have no control, but only an entitlement to 'balance'. It may be more accurate to say that the parties have stood still, while the media have grown both larger and more fully removed from party control. From the party point of view, the civil servants and the bureaucratic machinery of government have also grown stronger and larger.

Media shape elections
In the period up to 1955, television played very little part either in election coverage or in the coverage of politics. Radio was more important and it retained the extreme caution which Reith had initiated. There was one exception to this: the ministerial broadcast, to which there was often no opposition reply — a form which had become common in the Second World War and which the Labour governments of 1945–51 continued much to the fury of the Conservatives. Labour relied on these because the press was still the main political medium and to them it seemed very pro-Conservative. As Table 1 shows, of the four elections from 1945 onwards, the 1945 election was the one in which the press was most pro-Conservative. In 1955 the circulation strength of the *Daily Mirror* and the *Daily Herald* brought Labour almost up to the pro-Conservative circulation level. At this point Labour politicians had little to complain about and the probable increase of 'balanced' television coverage made it look as though the earlier pro-Conservative bias of the media was at an end.

From 1955 to the early 1970s there were important changes in political coverage. In this period the press also adjusted itself to television and paradoxically the probably less partisan news coverage was marked (Table 1) in the 1959, 1964 and 1966 elections by a resurgence of the anti-Labour press majority in terms of editorial support. Labour Party anxiety about this certainly continued – focusing especially on the *Daily Herald*'s re-launch as the unsuccessful IPC *Sun* – mitigated, however, by Labour's winning the 1964 and 1966 elections.

A new period is marked by the two elections of 1974, the first of which saw a massive anti-Labour circulation majority. This was largely due to *The Sun* which 'voted' in the first 1974 Election for the Conservatives. Labour party anxiety at this was behind the quick setting up in 1974 of a Royal Commission on the Press. Labour fears

TABLE 1

CONSERVATIVE AND LABOUR SHARE OF NATIONAL DAILY NEWSPAPER CIRCULATION'S EDITORIAL ENDORSEMENT AND SHARE OF NATIONAL VOTES IN GENERAL ELECTIONS, 1945–79

General Election of year	Conservative			Labour			Conservative difference excess over Labour difference
	(a) Share of circulation	(b) Share of votes	(a) - (b) Difference	(a) Share of circulation	(b) Share of votes	(a) - (b) Difference	
1945	52	40	+12	35	48	−13	+25 } Av = 19
1950	50	43	+ 7	40	46	− 6	+13 }
1951	52	48	+ 4	39	49	−10	+14 } Av = 11
1955	52	50	+ 2	40	46	− 6	+ 8 }
1959	54	49	+ 5	38	44	− 6	+11 }
1964	57	43	+14	42	44	− 2	+16 } Av = 14
1966	55	42	+13	43	48	− 5	+18 }
1970	55	46	+ 9	44	43	+ 1	+ 8 }
1974 Feb.	71	38	+33	31	37	− 6	+39 } Av = 31
1974 Oct.	47	36	+11	31	39	− 8	+19 }
1979	65	44	+21	27	37	−10	+31 }
1983	74	44	+30	22	28	− 6	+36 }

Sources: Colin Seymour Ure, (1977) *Studies on the Press*, HMSO for the Royal Commission on the Press, pp. 172–3; for 1979: David Butler and Dennis Kavanough, *The British General Election of 1979*, London: Macmillan, 1980. p. 232. Audit Bureau of Circulations figures for Jan–June 1979.

of press hostility deepened further in the run-up to, and coverage of, the General Election of 1979; four of the five largest sale national dailies (*Express*, *Sun*, *Mail*, *Telegraph*) 'voted' Conservative – against the pro-Labour *Daily Mirror*. The 1979 General Election was an important one in several respects. The Election followed the 1978–79 'winter of discontent' – a period of strikes in which, in Labour eyes, the popular press (knowing an election to be imminent) abandoned any pretence of fair coverage. The Conservative election campaign sought to remind voters of these events. It did so with a kind of media campaign not previously seen in Britain. Whereas all national elections for twenty years had been focused on television, the Conservatives in 1979 ran their campaign as a single integrated advertising campaign – modelled on the way in which a consumer product would be sold via television commercials, with closely orchestrated support in other media. Saatchi and Saatchi, an advertising agency, was involved in the entire campaign including the 50 minutes of free network television time (five party political broadcasts of ten minutes each) which were built around the format of an ITV news show with commercial interruptions. Advertising in women's magazines and newspapers, television broadcasts, and the letter-box leaflets were all designed in the advertising agency.[5] A major theme was to entice working-class housewives to vote differently from their Labour husbands – a theme also used in 1959 and reminiscent of a typical advertising strategy for almost any packaged food or soap product.

Politicians had become used to the idea that the general election campaign focused largely on a succession of morning press conferences designed for television coverage; but these press conferences at least took place in the parties' London headquarters. In 1979 the election receded further into media land – from the party HQ press conference to the advertising agency's 'creative' department.

Few things could be better calculated to induce Labour anger, than a victorious Conservative election campaign conceived in an advertising agency and dedicated to attacks on trade unions.

Public and private publicity: Lobby correspondents

The national nature of both politics and the media in Britain, and the peculiarities of an unwritten Constitution, in which the respective roles of Parliament and Cabinet are somewhat unclear, has led to a peculiar set of arrangements for political journalism. Lobby journalism was, until recently, a very *secretive* system of publicity;[6] since the late 1960s it has become the focus of fierce public debate. The Lobby correspondents normally have these types of access:

1. They may stand in the Lobby of the House of Commons and talk to members.
2. They receive early 'embargoed' copies of the full flood of official documents, before publication and before ordinary MPs.
3. They may attend regularly scheduled 'briefings' by the Prime Minister's press staff and by other politicians, such as the Leader of the House of Commons and the Opposition leader.
4. They have offices at Westminster under 'Big Ben'.

Two apparently contradictory criticisms are made of these journalists. One criticism (often made by other journalists) is that these Lobby correspondents are the tame lapdogs of the government of the day, happy to be fed on government handouts and harmless trivialities, incapable of discovering what is happening to the government of Britain. The second criticism (usually made by Cabinet ministers) sees the Lobby correspondents as remorseless bloodhounds from whom no Cabinet discussion can be kept secret for more than a few hours, before it is barked forth to a waiting nation of political cynics.

These two critiques appear contradictory, but they are not. The lapdog critique is broadly true of the Lobby correspondent's weak coverage of the civil service and the government bureaucracy. But the remorseless bloodhound critique is truer of the Lobby correspondent's strong coverage of the *political* running of the government and of Cabinet-Parliament relations in particular.

The Lobby correspondents are much too busy, and there are too few of them (three for a typical national daily) to cover the government machine of Whitehall. They do not claim even to attempt this; numerous other specialists cover subjects such as Finance, Defence, Education, Labour, Transport and the appropriate ministries.[7] The Lobby correspondents claim to cover Parliament (Westminster), the Cabinet (Downing Street), and the connections between the two. The key point about competition is not that the correspondents compete to get stories (although they do), but that politicians compete to *give* stories away.[8] Since a British Prime Minister must include in the Cabinet some of his (or her) main political rivals, in the nature of competition for resources (for their departments), for preferment generally and for publicity, some Ministers must win and others must lose. One of the key weapons in this competition is the resort to publicity. Richard Crossman is only one of several Cabinet ministers who have recorded their amazement at the consistency with which Cabinet documents and discussions appear in the press – sometimes before the relevant Cabinet meeting even takes place.[9] In leaking, the first

suspect is the person at the top – in a company or University the
chief executive or Vice Chancellor, in a department the senior
minister, in the Cabinet the Prime Minister.

None of this means that the often quoted legal restrictions on the
British media do not exist. D Notices, Official Secrets, Libel,
Contempt and Parliamentary Privilege all do exist[10] – but these
restrictions all affect Whitehall more than Westminster. The real
constraints of these laws are greatly alleviated by the other reality
that British governments leak heavily at the centre. However, this
does indeed raise the question of issues which do not reach the
Cabinet, but which are decided in the bowels of Whitehall. These
kinds of stories are often (but not always) of less potential interest in
news value terms than the stories which do appear from the Lobby
men. Moreover there is a good deal of fairly penetrating reporting –
for example of the Treasury and economic policy generally by the
Financial Times and other media. Many British 'secrets' cannot be
kept secret because they involve consultation with so many other
governments and foreign companies. There is many a leak 'twixt
London and Brussels, Paris, Bonn and Washington. There was for
example much leaking of information about delays and overspend-
ing in the construction of the Concorde aircraft: there were four
main sorts of sources – French and British government departments
and French and British companies – a multiplicity of sources, one of
which often wanted to spread the blame elsewhere. The same
pattern now applies to an increasing number of economic, defence
industrial and agricultural policy issues.

The Cabinet minister and the media

The Lobby system has emerged as a 'private' form of publicity
which focuses on the Cabinet and the Cabinet's relationships with
Westminster. A big emphasis is upon information which comes
indirectly – at one remove – from the Cabinet; much Cabinet
information which reaches Lobby journalists is sieved through
official documents, briefings, conversations with MPs who have
talked to ministers, and with junior ministers who work for senior
ministers.

This system undoubtedly gives enormous advantages to the
Prime Minister, the only person who has a potentially inexhaustible
daily supply of high grade political gossip and information. This is
especially noticeable in the 'honeymoon' period during a new Prime
Minister's first year. A steady stream emerges of plans, advance
gossip on appointments, news of forthcoming legislation, and personal tittle-tattle about the new Prime Minister's dynamic work
style and life style; all of this almost entirely positive information

surges through the various publicity sluices and into the Lobby correspondents' stories, day after day – typically for the first year of the prime ministership and perhaps into the second year. Such 'extra fair' treatment was certainly accorded to Harold Wilson in 1964–5, to Edward Heath in 1970–71 and to Margaret Thatcher in 1979–80. At this stage the 'tame lapdog' critique of the Lobby looks valid.

During this honeymoon phase comparatively little is heard from other Cabinet ministers – the senior ones are, of course, grappling with the mammoth and detailed concerns of the major departments of state. But, usually somewhere around the start of the second year, all this changes. The Prime Minister continues to command the lion's share of attention, but by now it includes some criticism. Some of this more critical coverage derives from other Cabinet ministers who now come more fully into the publicity picture. Ministers are now 'read into' their departments and are manoeuvring to obtain more finance or favourable slots in the legislative schedule; they are also competing to obtain the friendly media coverage which will act as a fair wind for their department plans and their own political careers.

In the middle phase of a typical British government two or three senior ministers may in effect have become rivals to the Prime Minister in the field of publicity and leaking. And while in the first year 'Prime Minister prepares plans' headlines predominate, by around the third year of a government's life headlines of a 'Cabinet conflict' kind are more common.

The Prime Minister can make a formidable number of publicity moves on a single day – quite apart from Prime Minister's questions in the Commons and speeches in major debates. On a single day in sheer publicity terms a not unusual tally might be: morning and afternoon briefings by press secretary to the Lobby; two or three government publications – over which the PM will have had veto power – may be published on a single day; a Cabinet sub-committee, parts of which will leak to journalists by the next day; a meeting with a delegation of backbenchers, selected accounts of which will be repeated to journalists within minutes or hours; short meetings with other prominent figures which also may surface in the media; perhaps a request via the press staff to a loyal backbencher to ask a friendly Parliamentary Question which will enable a positive answer to achieve publicity; and a similar hint by the press office on the telephone to a friendly journalist that a senior ministerial briefing is available. This amounts to perhaps a dozen separate publicity initiatives on a single day; and of these half or more might appear as stories, some overtly linked to the Prime Minister, some not.

TABLE 2

A CABINET MINISTER'S ACTIVITIES IN THE YEAR 1977
(Mr Tony Benn, Secretary of State for Energy)

1. *Member of Parliament for Bristol S.E.*	50 public engagements 12 general speeches in the city 16 surgeries
2. *Work with constituency party*	4 General Management Committee meetings 20 ward meetings
3. *House of Commons*	129 votes registered (House sat 149 days)
4. *Parliamentary Labour Party*	12 PLP meetings 14 speeches to PLP sub-groups
5. *Secretary of State for Energy*	3 Energy Bills 59 Statutory instruments, 33 memoranda 8 speeches to Commons on energy 5 Parliamentary statements 51 Oral Parliamentary Questions answered 171 Written questions answered 154 meetings with non-Governmental groups
6. *Member of the Cabinet*	42 Cabinet meetings 106 Cabinet committee meetings 49 Cabinet and committee papers submitted
7. *International work*	19 visits abroad (including USA, USSR) 32 visits by foreign ministers and ambassadors 6 meetings as chairman of the EEC Energy Council 6 other major EEC meetings
8. *National Executive Committee of the Labour Party*	15 NEC meetings 62 NEC committee meetings
9. *General political work*	80 speeches 83 radio interviews 57 television interviews 34 press conferences 16 articles 30 interviews with individual journalists

Source: Malcolm Dean, 'The Nine Lives of a Cabinet Minister', *The Guardian* 11th February, 1978.

However, the publicity-seeking senior Cabinet minister has another formidable array of publicity outlets which also allow the firing of many publicity salvoes per week. Table 2 is based on the activities of one such minister, Mr Tony Benn, during the year 1977 when he was Secretary of State for Energy in the Labour government. Mr Benn's publicity activities were not confined to direct media appearances and political speeches (often mainly aimed at journalists) – although heading (9) indicates some 300 of these in the year. Constituency engagements are typically aimed at least in part at the local press; Parliamentary Labour Party meetings often produced big stories (with Mr Benn well to the fore); the 148 Cabinet and Cabinet committee meetings doubtless produced many hundreds of leaks, large and small; the 19 visits abroad in a year and visits to the minister by foreign politicians and diplomats are occasions both for public publicity (handshakes at the ministry, statements at the airport) as well as more private publicity – conversations with journalists on the plane to Saudi Arabia, advance briefings to the specialist energy press, and so on. The National Executive Committee of the Labour Party (77 meetings and committees) is one of the leakiest of London's many leaky political forums, with Mr Benn again not shirking publicity. This list, while showing how busy some Cabinet ministers are, still omits many other brief publicity opportunities that a prominent publicity-seeking minister has – telephone calls from individual trusted journalists (for example the Lobby man needing a quick story on Sunday for Monday), brief exchanges with Lobby men at the Commons, and with other journalists in and around meetings, plus conversations with other politicians which will probably be repeated to journalists. Over a somewhat narrower range of issues a prominent Cabinet minister can mount a publicity barrage almost equal to that of the Prime Minister, adding up to numerous separate publicity shots per day, continuing at least for a succession of days.

After the first 'honeymoon' year there are usually publicity battles of this kind underway between the Prime Minister and one or more senior Cabinet ministers. Just as 'Cabinet Conflict' is something for which London political correspondents often have daily, even hourly evidence, it is also true that 'publicity conflict' is a major force in shaping the conduct of Cabinet ministers; it even encourages British Prime Ministers to conduct much sensitive Cabinet business through Cabinet sub-committees, whose members the Prime Minister can select and whose leaking propensities are more controllable. The minutes of sub-committees are also less revealing and less widely distributed that those of full Cabinet meetings.[11]

Parliament, Whitehall

Even most Cabinet ministers are much less active in terms of publicity than the Prime Minister and the two or three most prominent and most publicity-seeking ministers of the moment. For the typical backbench member of parliament the flow of both publicity and early or sensitive information is much less active. Many backbench MPs have very little that they can tell a journalist, but on most topics there are a few key backbenchers – such as former ministers, chairmen of backbench specialist committees or the leaders of significant political factions – who have the ear of Cabinet ministers and other highly placed persons. Such backbenchers seek out, and are sought out by, journalists when relevant topics are politically salient. But for most backbenchers most of the time the media are of more significance as their main source of information – the raw material of much of the MP's basic concerns. MPs are, not surprisingly, most aware of television as a politically potent source of publicity, while the serious newspapers and weeklies such as *The Economist* are the most important media source of information.[12]

While the Opposition relies especially heavily on the media for information, the journalists are much more interested in the governing party – where the action, events, news values are – than in the opposition, unless the opposition is engaged in some entertaining intra-party civil war. Only the leader of the Opposition can normally be sure to get a regular – almost day-to-day – coverage. Thus the Opposition leader may well be relatively satisfied with his personal media coverage while being unhappy about the media's lack of interest in the Opposition in general and its constructive far-seeing new policies in particular. (There is a close analogy with the case of the national trade union leader.) The Opposition leader is relatively well reported and his greatly superior access to publicity is one of his few resources in trying to impose his will on the party (as the trade union). Needless to say, not all the followers share the leader's views; backbench MPs of the Opposition party depend upon the media for information and for the occasional crumb of publicity and must often feel relatively impotent in relation to what, from this perspective, looks like an over-powerful media machine.

The view as seen by civil servants in Whitehall is different again. A criticism of the Lobby correspondents is that they are bad at covering Whitehall. This, they would broadly admit, is true – but is only relevant when 'departmental' stories are covered by the Lobby correspondents who as political specialists are inevitably ignorant of the details of agriculture, education or defence. More usually, however, departmental stories are covered by correspondents who specialize in those topics. As seen from Whitehall there must be plenty of examples of stories which are successfully manipulated into either favourable coverage or no coverage at all, in keeping with the departmental public relations people's wishes.

However, there are undoubtedly many cases of highly critical coverage by specialist correspondents, whose sources – like Lobby men's – include 'opposition' elements, factions, leaks and the like. Government departments also try to attract the attention of the Lobby correspondents because the ensuing publicity attracts Cabinet and other highly placed attention. However such attempts must often fail. The dilemma as elsewhere is that Whitehall best matches news values when it is in trouble. There is a great deal of critical coverage of 'Whitehall'. Some of this may be journalists working out their frustrations at secretive bureaucrats by condemning the entire bureaucratic species.

CHAPTER THREE
Politically made media policy

The main texts which constitute the bible of British media policy since 1945 are a large shelf-full of Stationery Office publications. There have in particular since 1945 been three Royal Commissions on the Press and three Committees on Broadcasting:

Royal Commissions on the Press		Broadcasting Committees	
Ross Commission	1947–49	Beveridge Committee	1949–51
Shawcross Commission	1961–62	Pilkington Committee	1960–62
McGregor Commission	1974–77	Annan Committee	1974–77

There were three major rounds of policy-making between 1945 and 1982. Each of the rounds concluded with a Broadcasting Act – in 1954, 1964, and 1980; and each of these Acts led to a new TV channel – ITV in 1955, BBC2 in 1966 and the second IBA channel in 1982.

The Press Commissions – without anything like new TV channels and new technologies to dispose of – have been much less significant in policy outcomes. But the 1947–49 Commission originally recommended the Press Council (which came into existence in 1953); the second, Shawcross, Commission made recommendations which led to the major innovation of special anti-monopoly press legislation

In addition there is a history of film industry enquiries and legislation – which, together with press and broadcasting enquiries and legislation make up the 'public' mode of British media policy.

But the media go on all the time and not everything can be fitted into a policy cycle of some twelve years on average; the time-lag from the setting up of a broadcasting committee to the appearance of a new TV channel alone averages around seven years. There is also a 'private' mode of media policy-making – short, sharp and more private enquiries into some specific urgent problem often leading to policy implementation in a matter of months, not years. In addition there is much other legislation – especially legal issues such as libel, contempt of court and privacy – which heavily affects the media.

There are some long 'public' documents on the media policy-making shelf, such as the McGregor Royal Commission on the Press (1974–77) which produced 13 HMSO Volumes totalling 2,645 pages, and few other visible consequences. Some of the documents are short, such as *Cable Systems* (1982), a 54-page report from a short sharp 'private' enquiry of great policy consequence.

Among the jumble of documents on the media policy-making shelf are many Parliamentary Debates on Press, Broadcasting and Film – some of the debates are major ones, on for example Broadcasting legislation, some are more discursive ones on the press, and there are also many shorter debates on more specific or short-term issues.

Very noticeably there are no reports, no debates and no legislation on British media in general. There are several different policy fields and policy traditions presided over by different government departments and ministers. Broadcasting was traditionally under the Post Office, but now the Home Office; the Department of Industry watches over the press; Trade is responsible for Films and Press Monopoly; the Foreign Office for the BBC's external services and the Central Office of Information.

These several different strands of media policy each have their own quite different history and traditions. There are some obvious points in common, drawn from the past. Present-day British media are the inheritors of an imperial tradition. *The Times* and Reuters were the leading press voice and the news agency of an Empire; much film policy was set with imperial objectives in mind – British films must not needlessly stir up the colonial audience. The BBC was establishing a world-wide imperial influence – setting up All India Radio in 1935 – before it grappled with Hitler, or launched television.

British media policy is also conducted against a background of the Second World War – this was the finest hour not only of the BBC and the British film industry with its war documentaries, but also of the popular Fleet Street press. There is an unspoken but powerful note of nostalgia in British media policy-making – how can we get back to those days of immensely serious yet popular media output (without the restrictions of pages and hours and without the advantage of a popular war)? But few people ask whether we should return to the war-time device of a single Ministry of Information. It is widely believed in Britain that a single media policy or government ministry would be contrary to democratic ideas of diversity and freedom.

Not operating a single media policy inevitably produces anomalies and inconsistencies. At worst official media policy is naive, chaotic and self-defeating and leaves effective media policy to be made by such interested parties as trade unions and multi-national corporations.

Some of the most elementary principles – such as freedom – are not defined and some of the simplest available policy devices, such as taxation, are not co-ordinated. Discussions of media 'freedom' implicitly make quite different assumptions about quite similar situations. In films 'freedom' is seen as a problem for one individual, the director, against largely commercial forces. In the press the focus is again on an individual, the 'editor', but he is seen as resembling an airline pilot who ought to be in sole charge of his craft but who is buffeted by pressures from customers, crew, airline and weather. In broadcasting the public discussion of freedom tends to focus on the position of the chief executive of the BBC, or of an IBA company, trying to resist outside political pressures. With such varied conceptions of media freedom, an effective policy to protect it is scarcely feasible.

Taxation (and subsidy) is the most obvious existing instrument in the hands of government through which it could fashion a comprehensive media policy. But the possibility of operating a policy through this mechanism is never discussed.

Partisanship, bi-partisan consensus, conservatism

In the formal and 'public' mode of media policy-making it is, of course, politicians who make the decisions. In practice in British media policy, legislation is almost invariably enacted by the Conservative party, and sometimes in a highly partisan atmosphere.[1] The Labour party opposed both the 1954 and 1980 Broadcasting Acts which awarded the first and second commercial television channels.

The Labour party has often set up committees to look into media questions, but has usually been too internally divided to be able to agree on enacting major legislation. The Labour party in office, has however engaged in many 'private' media policy decisions. Harold Wilson as Trade Minister, 1947-51, in relation to the film industry and as Prime Minister (1964–70, 1974–76) – in allowing several major newspaper takeovers – has had a bigger say in media policy than has any other Labour politician. The only common theme in the Wilson decisions appears to be the protection of employment.

The Conservative party has in practice made most key media decisions – it set up all three new TV channels since 1954, as well as obtaining a 'voluntary' Press Council. But the Conservative party has also tended to be internally split over media issues. For example, while many radical Tory voices have called for extensions to commercial television and radio, there has also long been a strong element of senior Conservatives who have wanted to protect the survival of the BBC and also to see the BBC innovating new services (such as the BBC's second TV channel and the first British Direct Broadcast Satellite channels).

While there is thus indeed a large measure of inter-party conflict

on media policy, and while governments invariably seek their own
partisan advantage in media policy, the element of intra-party
conflict also leads to a largish measure of bi-partisan consensus.
Labour party fears have typically been loudly voiced, and partly
because the same fears also exist among Conservatives, they have
usually been in part built into the legislation – for example into tight
controls on TV commercials. Consequently when the next Labour
government has come to power it has not attempted to undo recent
Conservative media policies.

This powerful element of political consensus underlies widespread agreement at Westminster that the government should limit
itself to laying down strategic financial guidelines, but that detailed
operations – including all editorial questions – should be left to the
'professionals' directly involved.

Bi-partisanship has also been an essential aspect of the curious
political fiction by which the government of the day makes key
appointments of public figures – governors and members, who
preside respectively over the BBC and IBA – who then somehow
miraculously become independent guardians against political pressures. Bi-partisanship makes this more than a fiction; the miracle
really does happen in at least some cases because the appointees
tend to be politically moderate individuals who are genuinely
hostile to both political and commercial interference.

Indeed several prominent ex-politicians have been involved in
some of these 'independent' positions; most notably the task of
presiding over commercial broadcasting – chairman of the Independent Broadcasting Authority – has been carried out by a succession
of elder statesmen politicians – Lords Hill (Conservative) and
Aylestone and Thomson (both ex-Labour). A comparable figure in
the press has been the ex-Labour Minister, Lord Shawcross, who
chaired a Royal Commission on the Press and later the Press
Council. With the possible exception of the last-named, none has
been widely accused of partisanship.

The policy-making cycle
1982 saw the birth of the fourth major policy-making cycle in the
British media since 1945. In 1982–83 major decisions were taken –
once again by a Conservative government – on the two related
issues of Direct Broadcast Satellites and Cable. These initiatives
followed the 'private' mode of small quick committees and reports
leading to rapid decisions.

1982 also marked the end of the third major policy-making cycle
in the British media, with the launch of the fourth channel in
November. This completed three such cycles in 35 years (1947–82).
A dozen years is, indeed, a lengthy policy cycle for such a fast

moving field. This pace derives from the broadcasting enquiries of the 1920s and 1930s and fits into the nineteenth-century tradition of decisions about newspaper taxes, the electric telegraph and the establishment of radio. It matches the characteristic British media tradition of slow, gradual change.

Apart from its slowness the traditional policy cycle has other common characteristics, especially its three marked phases. First there is the *enquiry phase* – in this the 'public interest' is to the fore, reflecting the consensus of the Committee members who are the usual selection of public persons from the law, the universities, big business, the trade unions, Scotland and Wales. From their consensual focus on the public interest and from their scanning of the evidence and the old reports of previous policy cycles, they go for proposals which indeed stress the 'public interest', which are expressed in a-political terms, are a trifle unworldly and rather lacking in financial realism. Recommendations for new TV channels, for example, tend to be short on financial detail.

The second is the *political phase*. The report goes to the relevant government minister and department. A White Paper may follow, then a Bill and, after the usual Debates, an Act is finally enacted. The Act may reflect only quite a small part of the public committee's recommendations, and even these may be adopted in altered form. In keeping with the political nature of this phase the neutral media coverage of politics and politicians tends to be prominent, with the financial details and also the 'public good' aspects more vague.

The third is the *operational phase*, which puts the legislation into effect. In practice the legislation has said very little about what a new TV channel, for example, will carry; not only a programming policy and the crucial financial details still need to be decided, but many major institutional/organizational details have to be worked out from scratch because they were little considered in the several previous years of 'debate'. Evidence that the operational planning was hurried and unrealistic seems to be provided by the fact that each of the new television channels – in 1955–6, in 1964 and in 1982–3 ran into immediate major and foreseeable, but unforeseen, difficulties. The same was true of the launch of commercial radio in 1973 and even the allocation of new television licences by the IBA which came into existence in 1968 and 1982.

A somewhat similar set of phases has occurred with press policy-making. For example the Press Council was the main recommendation of the 1947–9 Ross Royal Commission – and it was conceived of as a very broad-ranging protector of the public interest. The second phase consisted not of legislation but a threat of legislation. When the Press Council was finally established it covered only a narrow segment of the territory initially mapped out by the Royal Commission.

The fact that policy proposals have to pass through these three phases – the public interest enquiry, the political phase of legislation and the third operational phase – demands enormous stamina. Moreover each of the phases itself requires a consensus to emerge. The surviving proposal must pass through a consensus on the committee of enquiry, a consensus in Parliament, and yet another consensus among those – such as the IBA members – who are operationally responsible.

The kind of proposal which has sufficient consensual stamina seems to be one which is specific as an idea – such as another TV channel or a Press Council – but which is also fuzzy at the edges (making consensus easier). Ideally it should be capable of summary in terms of some abstract but empirically grounded proposition – 'choice', a 'responsible' press, more 'minority' programming.

The fourth television channel was an obvious idea with obvious stamina. Important in building consensus for it was the notion of 'independent producers', an idea which a group of would-be such producers managed to endow with an aura of responsibility, creativity, enterprise and public interest.

The 'private' non-partisan civil service tradition

The model and imagery of the civil service is important in British media policy-making in many ways. The BBC was, in practice, one of the first state-owned industries (along with London Transport and pre-dating the airlines, coal and the railways). The BBC was also the first of the great cultural bureaucracies (pre-dating the Arts Council, and the British Council).

The civil servant provided a model for the political neutrality of the BBC producer, which has gone on to influence all of the British media. Paradoxically but importantly, the British media had their finest hour during 1939–45, when government regulation of course existed but operated despite many muddles with considerable delicacy and finesse.

Although it can truly be said that BBC producers, IBA bureaucrats and even the more serious journalists in some respects model themselves on the Whitehall bureaucrats, it is also true that all of these categories are highly suspicious of Whitehall which in their eyes stands for secrecy and 'bureaucracy'. They may also suspect that Whitehall in general and in particular the Treasury – where Britain's public finances are privately[2] governed – has a bigger say in media policy than at first meets the eye.

Private: the Treasury

The Annan Committee listed eight government powers in broadcasting, five of which are financial powers in some sense:

1. Powers in technical areas including broadcast coverage. For example, all UHF transmission facilities are built on common BBC and IBA sites.
2. Powers to set the BBC licence fee and the levies on ITV and commercial radio.
3. Powers to fix levels of capital expenditure.
4. Powers to inspect BBC and IBA accounts.
5. Powers to direct the BBC and IBA to publish details of their finances in their annual reports.[3]

The strategic importance of the Treasury is further illustrated by the way in which it has influenced the entire pattern of finance. For example the Treasury does not allow the BBC to accumulate reserves; and until 1963 it took a slice off the licence fee before allowing what was left to go to the BBC.

Treasury rules have played a big part in BBC reluctance to drop the licence-fee system. The Treasury told Annan that if the licence fee were abolished and the BBC became taxation-financed, then much more detailed scrutiny and control of its operations would have to follow. The Treasury does not allow 'hypothecating' – a special tax to be used solely for the financing of broadcasting would not be allowed. A tax-supported BBC would be dependent on general taxation and hence the inevitability of detailed scrutiny. For example the BBC's buildings, employment and pay practices would have to conform to Whitehall guidelines. In other words the Treasury forces the BBC to be an exception, because of the radical consequences of not being one.

Media policy – substance and image

The most obvious weaknesses of British media policy are two-fold. It does not concern itself sufficiently with what is happening in other countries, and secondly the political/civil service/'public interest' strains in policy-making are so strong as relatively to obscure the financial and technological aspects – and the crucial part played by popular taste.

The taste of British audiences for American programming and formats has been long feared, but it has not been well understood and still is not; this leaves many question marks over the detailed outcome of multi-channel cable and satellite television. British policy-making has also been remarkably inept in not adequately understanding what is going on in western Europe, where, although the details are different, the basic policy dilemmas have long been broadly similar.

The importing of television programming and films from the United States has long been a delicate topic and has long been a ghost – more feared than discussed – at the policy-making feast. This issue brings into conflict two other delicate issues in media policy-making. Trade unions are against such imports as a threat to employment; obviously Hollywood and other companies favour such imports, which symbolize the fact that the most dynamic force in media policy-making internationally are the great Hollywood, New York and European multi-national media companies.

But in concluding this part of the book let us mention again mythology and imagery. In media policy-making the image may be more important than the substance. For example the image of the BBC as 'bureaucratic'. Advertising expenditure, television franchises and channels, monopoly decisions, BBC licence-fee increases – all of these things may be influenced by images of reality. In building consensuses and evolving policies with consensus stamina, imagery is again vital.

Finally imagery is important because quite a lot of the people who make media policy – Royal Commission members, Members of Parliament, Treasury civil servants – are too busy to pay much attention to those very sectors of the media which dominate the leisure time of the British people.

PART B

British media since 1945

CHAPTER FOUR

Television

A truly British compromise?
Britain's mixed system of part 'public service' BBC and part commercial television can be seen as a truly British compromise. The mixture of licence-financed and advertising-financed television may be a sensible half-way house if only evolved after some painful trial and error in the 1950s and 1960s. In contrast to some other national systems this is not (like France) a state-dominated system with a commercial element tacked on, nor is it a commercial system with a small public service sector.

The British system does produce 'serious' television in peak viewing hours notably the main news, original single dramas by celebrity writers, documentaries, and other non-fictional programming. But the system also has in peak hours large quantities of the most popular material – variety shows, comedies, long running serial soap operas, sport and feature films.

In terms of scheduling there is indeed the most brutal kind of direct competition in which similar popular programmes compete head-to-head in the same time slot. However, complementary scheduling also exists. At any evening hour there is usually a choice between two or three different types of programming.

Hollywood is also the subject of another compromise. A basic tenet of British television since it began in 1936 has been that it should indeed be *British* and not deluged with American imports. Britain thus appears to achieve the internationally unusual feat of making about 85% of its own television while still running four networks of decent quality. However this 85% includes a fair amount of programming which although made-in-Britain is based on a Hollywood format. Leading examples are the game shows and quizzes which helped commercial television to survive its difficult early months in 1955–56. But such format imports were still there a quarter of a century later as the second commercial channel was being legislated into existence. In 1980 three of British TV's top twenty were *Blankety Blank* (BBC), *Play Your Cards Right* (London Weekend) and *Family Fortunes* (ATV) – all three based on successful American game shows (*Match Game*, *Card Sharks* and *Family Feud*) from a single Hollywood production house.[1] Another American format still going strong was *This is Your Life* – which in 1980 had its 21st anniversary on British television.

British television over much – even most – of its output is a
compromise between highbrow and lowbrow, between educated
and uneducated tastes, between entertainment and information/
education. The BBC has long proudly claimed that its popular
programming is 'good of its kind', for example comedy built around
talented writers and comedians; the BBC has also pointed out that
its more ambitious programming – public affairs, documentaries,
and single dramas – often (with the help of friendly scheduling) gets
audiences of 10% or 15% of the entire adult population. The main
commercial network similarly boasts of prestige drama, that its
News at Ten has often been in the week's top twenty and that
televised opera is usually followed by a little over one per cent of all
British adults.[2]

In this compromise system it is possible for programmes to be too
popular as well as not popular enough. Grand opera and other
prestige things are acceptable a few times a year, but any serious
show which routinely gets an unexpectedly small audience will
either be taken off or re-scheduled outside the prime audience
evening times. Similarly any programme which is very popular – but
also totally lacking in artistic pretensions or undeserving of the
accolade 'good of its kind' – is suspect. Quiz and game shows, soap
operas, and variety formats have been taken off by both BBC and
IBA command despite – or some would say because of – their
massive audiences.

This compromise system of television clearly can claim several
advantages. It mildly flatters public taste; somewhat ambitious or
demanding matter may achieve a goodish audience, especially if
scheduled against weak opposition and between popular programmes and aided by publicity packaging. This policy of having four
national channels – all of them programmed along non-specialized
lines – does indeed tend to minimize differences in social class
background. Although there are some differences (more educated
people do watch more BBC and working-class people watch more
ITV), nevertheless most British adults watch some programmes
across three or all four of the channels. Popular comedies or football
and more demanding drama or documentaries alike all attract
remarkably widely spread audiences.

But there are some penalties attached to these advantages. These
four national channels are indeed *national*; with the major exception mainly of some local news/weather/sport all four channels are
national and London dominated. Secondly the urge to limit imports, while it allows in quite a large slice of Hollywood direct
imports and another indirect slice of Hollywood formats and imitations, has had the effect of largely shutting out non-English-
speaking programming. Germany, France and Italy are major

forces in world television but Britain's compromise on imports allows in very little from those countries. European Common Market programming supposedly counts as domestic, but there is still little such importing.

A third penalty – or critique – is that nearly all British television is neither one thing nor the other. Serious programming must have its popular gimmicks – classical drama often is heavily cut, political programming must be garnished with film of blood-on-the-streets, dramatic music and studio 'confrontations'. But popular programming must be contrived to seem 'good of its kind'; popular sports must be shown as edited 'highlights'; even comedy shows – having built a huge audience – must be carefully rationed so as not to strain the artistic integrity of the scriptwriters. All shows, it is said, must be built around popular-but-reliable, serious-but-amusing, respectable-but-cheeky personalities. Over three hundred hours a week of national television, dominated by three hundred celebrity faces.

1936–55 The BBC television monopoly

Commercial television commenced operations in 1955, while BBC television had begun in 1936. But pre-war television had been a London-only, primarily experimental service, in fact subsidized by radio licence revenue; and between 1939 and 1946 there was no television service.

In the late 1940s the BBC did not give a high priority to television. It was still a period of general rationing, and shortages – not least for building materials and electronic equipment. Radio had emerged from the war triumphant and the BBC in 1946 was more interested in the launch of its third – unashamedly highbrow – radio channel, than in its TV channel. Producers in TV were starved of funds, equipment, and – some claimed – understanding.

In 1954 some 3·2 million television licences were paid for, indicating television in about 20% of all British households. This was a low level of TV penetration compared with the United States, and this comparison was made by those within the BBC television operation who saw themselves discriminated against by the radio establishment. But compared with the rest of Europe and the world, 20% household penetration by 1954 was extremely high.[3]

During the year 1954 the BBC's TV staff grew from 1,320 to 1,700. It was putting out about six hours of TV per day on one channel. Most programming was 'live', either from the studio or from outside broadcasts. Television still occupied only a small part of the BBC's programme guide, *Radio Times* – which claimed the world's largest magazine sale (8·2 million in 1954).

In 1954 the BBC was shaken not only by the passage of legislation establishing commercial television, but by the defection of almost

all of its 'Light Entertainment' television producers to join the new
commercial companies. These producers felt frustrated by what
they doubtless saw as the BBC's restrictive attitude to television in
general and 'Light Entertainment' TV in particular; the defectors
included Bill Ward, Brian Tesler, Francis Essex and Bill Lyon-Shaw
– all of whom later headed ITV companies.[4]

The BBC's development of television was another compromise.
It was quite fast in view of equipment shortages and governmental
restrictions on capital spending; quite fast also in view of the fact
that the masses (paying radio licence fees) were subsidising those of
above average income who predominated amongst the first purchasers of television sets. However, the development was too slow
to contain the external criticisms of monopoly and dullness which
had been appearing in *The Economist* since 1945.[5]

One senior BBC personality who saw problems was Lord Simon
of Wythenshawe, chairman of the BBC 1947–52. Quoting BBC
research evidence, Simon recognised that the appeal of television
was stronger than that of radio; people who had television sets in
1950 watched them longer than those in radio-only households
listened to radio – and more TV viewers gave the TV their undi-
vided attention.[6]

The economics of television

Television is an expensive medium, especially compared with radio.
Figure 1 shows that the BBC's popular TV channel costs five times
as much as the two popular radio channels combined. In 1980–81
BBC expenditure went roughly 70% on two TV channels and 30%
on four radio channels plus local radio.

Some television programming resembles radio in costs, but this is
the most simple 'talking heads' interview or discussion programme
unrelieved by original video material. At the other end of the scale
single television dramas are really films made for showing on
television; they typically involve big production staffs, sizeable casts
of expensive actors, and fairly lavish provision of days (and colour
film) for outside filming. Most television falls somewhere in between and, very roughly indeed, in Britain *an hour's networked
television costs about ten times as much as an hour's networked
radio*.

Some of the high expense of television lies in the basic technology
of cameras (as well as sound), the larger studios, the costumes and
make-up, the need to build sets and scenery, the hiring of performers, the cost of colour film and video-taping, the more elaborate
(than radio) technology of transmission. But some of the expense of
television comes also from its being *competitive*. Within any one
type of programming there is a general correlation between expen-

FIGURE 1: BBC EXPENDITURE 1980-81 (when total expenditure was running at £500 million per year)

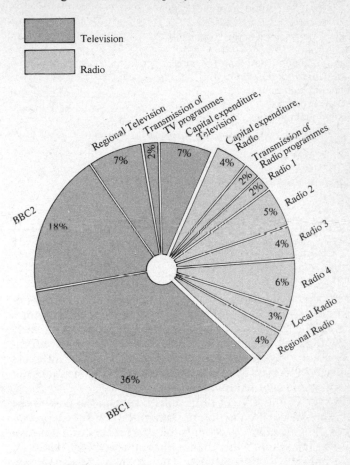

Television

Radio

Source: BBC

diture and audience appeal. There is also the simple fact of competitive bargaining, and a long history of commercial television enticing executives, technicians and star comedians away from the BBC with higher cash offers. For some big sports occasions and feature films there is competitive bidding.

However, as Table 3 shows, there are very big differences in costs between different types of programming, only some of which are

TABLE 3

TYPICAL BBC TELEVISION PRODUCTION COSTS PER HOUR
(Based on single dramas = 100)

Single Dramas, mini-series drama	100
Serial drama	55
Major documentaries, features, music	55
Current affairs, weekly	45
Light entertainment	35
Outside broadcasts	30
Lesser documentaries, features, music	18
Current affairs, daily	15
Religion	15
Schools, further education	15
Sports	12
Children's	8
Regional	8
'Bought in' series and feature films	8

Source: Author's estimates based on various BBC statements.

reflected in bigger audiences. But to justify higher costs programming must either attract big audiences or big prestige. Programmes transmitted in peak times normally get the largest budgets; early and late evening get budgets roughly half as big; daytime, educational, religious and regional programming costs significantly less again – and could cost still less, were the television organizations not dealing with strong national trade unions.

The domestic colour TV set represents a substantial cost to the consumer. One calculation is that in Britain the TV set (depreciation or rent, and electricity) accounts for 70% of the total national cost of having television; while the total revenues of BBC and ITV account for only 30% of the real cost.[7] The expensive set can thus be seen as a subsidy to the television networks. On the other hand, consumers – aware that they are paying a lot for the set and the licence – may raise their demands in terms of programming.

BBC finances depend on the licence fee which is vulnerable to the whims of governments and to inflation. Increased output does not increase BBC revenue. ITV finances are perhaps even more bizarre. The difficulty arises because ITV is solely dependent on advertising expenditure which is sensitive to general economic conditions and the trade cycle.

ITV in its early years showed a chronic tendency first to make embarrassingly large losses, and then to make embarrassingly large profits. The 'licence to print money' days around 1960 led to the introduction in 1963 of a government levy on profits. This levy was based on *revenue*, took no account of costs, and when it siphoned off substantial sums to H. M. Treasury it also made ITV finances even more unpredictable than before. Since 1974 the levy has operated on a sliding scale based not on revenue, but on profit; after a small initial levy-free slice, the levy is two-thirds of profit.

The financial underpinnings of BBC and ITV are very different. But both are entirely dependent upon a single source of revenue, the BBC on licence fees and ITV on Net Advertising Revenue After Levy (NARAL). Both sorts of revenue are highly vulnerable to changes in the national economy. In both cases there is relatively little scope for cutting costs in the short term (because the networks have commitments to put on programming). And in both cases the source of revenue comes under the strong influence of the government of the day. Governments control BBC licence fee increases, they control the IBA's future destinies and they have a say in ITV's raising its advertising rates. In times of inflation these points are increasingly salient. The BBC television licence fee was increased only twice in the 1950s and three times in the 1960s, but no less than five times in the 1970s. There were licence fee increases in 1977, 1978, 1979 and 1981 more than doubling the colour licence fee in just four years (Table 4). This inevitably made the economics of British television an even more politically charged field.

TABLE 4

TELEVISION AND RADIO LICENCE FEES

	Television		Radio
	Mono-chrome	Colour	
Nov. 1, 1922			10s (50p)
June 1, 1946	£ 2		£1
June 1, 1954	£ 3		£1
Aug. 1, 1957	£ 4		£1
Aug. 1, 1965	£ 5		£1/5s (£1.25)
Jan. 1, 1968	£ 5	£10	£1/5s (£1.25)
Jan. 1, 1969	£ 6	£11	£1/5s (£1.25)
July 1, 1971	£ 7	£12	—
Apr. 1, 1975	£ 8	£18	—
Jul. 29, 1977	£ 9	£21	—
Nov. 25, 1978	£10	£25	—
Nov. 24, 1979	£12	£34	—
Dec. 1, 1981	£15	£46	—

These inflationary pressures not only add to the politics of TV finance but also operate against a background tendency for both sources of revenue – the BBC's licence fees and ITV's advertising – to get out of phase with costs and with each other. While programme costs escalate broadly in line with inflation, BBC revenues operate on one roller-coaster – a high point after each licence fee increase and a low point before the next; independent television revenues ride another roller-coaster, the highly variable nature of advertising expenditure, plus the equally variable combination of IBA rental, Treasury levy on profits, and since 1981 the compulsory 'subscription' (i.e. subsidy) to the Fourth Channel. One year the headlines proclaim ITV affluence and BBC poverty, but next year the headlines may say the reverse.

1955: Independent Television arrives, and after

Commercial television arrived in Britain in 1955 and fierce controversies surrounded its conception, birth and infancy. Its conception certainly occurred somewhere within the Conservative party which had won the 1951 election. H. H. Wilson's book, *Pressure Group* (1961),[8] sees the campaign as a commercial conspiracy by certain self-seeking businessmen within the Conservative party, who were aided by American advertising interests and opposed by the British establishment. He also claims the public did not want it, although in fact the general trend of opinion poll data was – as often – ambiguous.

A more recent account, while not discounting some profit-motivation, emphasises that many Conservatives saw the issue much more in terms of *competition* and freedom of choice in the face of BBC monopoly. The successful pressure groups also deliberately chose to attack only the BBC's *television* monopoly since they perceived its radio monopoly to be more strongly established and entrenched.[9]

There is much speculation as to whether commercial television might never have happened at all had John Reith not been hostile to Winston Churchill in the 1930s, had not Attlee's partisan antagonism united the Conservatives behind ITV, had the BBC pressed for a second TV channel in the early 1950s or had the BBC listened to the advice of their TV enfant terrible, Norman Collins, rather than driving him – through frustration – to set up the commercial TV lobby.

But more important than such speculations and more significant than the detail of the contemporary controversies is the fact that commercial television was conceived and launched in an atmosphere of high controversy, indeed of root and branch political conflict. ITV also was launched in a great hurry because the Conservative government elected in 1951 had taken three years of intra-party debate, White Papers, and Parliamentary debate in order to legislate commercial TV, and the Labour party was threatening to reverse the decision.

ITV was launched with excessive speed and with grossly inadequate planning and finance. For 12 long months – autumn 1955 to 1956 – it fought desperately for audiences, for advertising and for survival. In the winter of 1956–57 signs of its survival were increasingly apparent; by 1958 the profits were coming in, and by 1959 it was a 'licence to print money' (in Roy Thomson's immortal – and costly – phrase).

Commercial television was doomed to massive early losses because the reckless, politically based lack of planning and investment meant that initially the audience was very small, and the advertising revenue was at a token experimental level only. In September, 1955, when commercial television began, it was limited to the London region and only some 3% of British households could actually receive the signal. But in order to acquire audiences the ITV companies had to put on attractive programming. Faced by this yawning gap between high production cost and low audiences (and hence advertising revenue) commercial television had imprinted on its tribal memory two indelible lessons: first, commercial television is a volatile rags-to-riches (to rags again?) business. Secondly, formulae for attracting and keeping big audiences are paramount.

In February, 1956 the Midlands operation began, and in May, 1956 it was joined by the North-west of England. At the same time increasing proportions of those with television sets were converting them for ITV reception. Research was already showing that among these increasing proportions of the population who could receive both channels, people were switching in epidemic proportions from BBC to ITV. Amongst those who could receive both channels – according to ITV data – the ITV peak of audience share was reached in July – September 1957 with an ITV75 : BBC25 ratio. Even three years later in 1960 it was ITV65 : BBC35.

It was those regional companies (like Roy Thomson's Scottish Television) which escaped the first catastrophic year, and only came on stage during the affluent second act, which made the most spectacular success.

But by this time much of the later pattern of ITV had been established. The companies in London, Birmingham and Manchester were to be dominant; the Independent Television (later Broadcasting) Authority quickly learnt that it must sink or swim with the companies. The companies' most seering experience having been near infant starvation, through lack of advertising revenue, all decided to use their profits of 1959 onwards to diversify into other things.

Paradoxically the companies – despite the political birth of ITV – largely ignored politics and the Pilkington Committee set up by a Conservative government in 1960. The big companies were too busy feuding with each other, diversifying their investments and playing tycoon. They did not even bother to submit collective evidence to Pilkington about the future of television.

The Pilkington Committee – with its ferocious denunciation of commercial television in 1962 – was to imprint the third lesson on ITV's tribal memory: Broadcasting Committees and politicians decide the fate of British television, and, since they do so to a large extent on the basis of ideology and imagery, political public relations and lobbying are important. The BBC, which had learnt this lesson the hard way in the early 1950s, courted the Pilkington Committee and the Conservative government with great finesse. The BBC's prize was the third television channel.

1964–82: BBC2 and three channel competition

The BBC's second national television channel began transmission in April 1964, and it also had severe early difficulties, including the familiar combination of high cost against a very low total audience.

The BBC's courtship had been so ardent and the Pilkington Committee's response so uncritically enthusiastic ('The BBC knows good broadcasting')[10] that neither had thought out too clearly what should happen to the third channel. Both were agreed primarily on the basic point that it should not be another commercial channel.

The BBC's problem was that BBC2 cost a lot of extra money but produced no extra licence fee, or other revenue. The BBC had also (as in 1936) been given the task of technological pioneering on three fronts: BBC2 was in the UHF band (not VHF); it was on 625 lines (instead of 405 lines); and also was the first British TV channel to be in colour (1967). This involved not only vast capital expenditure but also held back audience size, since the new technology followed the now traditional pattern of London first, followed by the more, then less, populated regions. For example after two years (late 1966) BBC2 was technically available to half the population, but within this half was in practice only available to those who had bought the new roof antenna. These factors all held back the BBC2 audience level; moreover initially it was only on the air about four hours per evening and its opening strategy of devoting each night of the week to a different theme clearly indicated an initial lack of any realistic plan for programming.

Nevertheless BBC2 powerfully contributed to what by the 1970s seems – at least in retrospect – to have been a rather stable form of three-handed competition, with the percentage of total audience divided in the ratio of ITV – 50%, BBC1 – 40% and BBC2 – 10%. This provided a more or less stable compromise; the advertisers got a mass audience on the single commercial channel. But with BBC1 programmed as a head-on-competitive channel for the bulk of peak evening time, the BBC was left with more than adequate resources to maintain a total of 50% of the audience, to ensure that virtually all viewers sometimes watched BBC1 and at least occasionally also BBC2 and hence that the licence fee retained political legitimacy.

Although in retrospect this seems a stable pattern of competition, it was nevertheless even in the 1970s marked by frequent panics as the single ITV channel either strayed above 50% (thus frightening the BBC) or strayed below 50% (thus attracting denunciations from the advertising world). This fluctuating pattern continued right up to the end of three-channel competition in 1982. In anticipation of the second commercial channel, BBC2 was programmed more competitively and (with snooker as its new secret weapon) in some weeks went well over 10% of the audience. This was, as usual, successfully answered by ITV in its last months as the lone commercial channel.

The 1970s may well come to be seen as a golden age of successful compromise and stable competition. But if this decade was one of stability, it also took the BBC more than a full decade after 1955 to evolve a successful formula for retaining 50% of the audience. For several years after 1955 the BBC produced very little response at all – partly perhaps relying on the lag in ITV availability outside London and partly simply unwilling to reply in kind to the ITV offering. For the first four years of ITV, the BBC won almost nothing back at all in those households capable of receiving both channels; it was only after four full years of ITV – late 1959 – that the BBC did better than 30:70 against ITV, amongst viewers who had the choice.

Throughout these years the BBC's Director of Television was Gerald Beadle, a man of mainly regional radio experience, who was put in charge of television at the age of 57 and stayed there until 1961.[11]

The ITV network
What came to be known as the ITV system consists of 14 regions (as shown in Map 1); with two companies in London, this makes 15 licensed contractors which in turn fall neatly into three sizes.

- The *outer five*, all in the more remote and less populated areas. They make only about one hour per day of their own

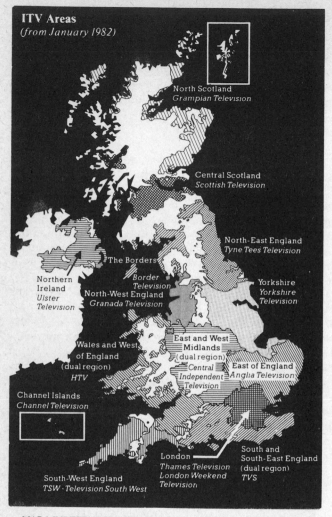

ITV Areas
(from January 1982)

North Scotland
Grampian Television

Central Scotland
Scottish Television

North-East England
Tyne Tees Television

The Borders
*Border
Television*

Northern
Ireland
*Ulster
Television*

North-West England
Granada Television

Yorkshire
*Yorkshire
Television*

East and West
Midlands
(dual region)
*Central
Independent
Television*

East of England
Anglia Television

Wales and West
of England
(dual region)
HTV

Channel Islands
Channel Television

London
*Thames Television
London Weekend
Television*

South and
South-East England
(dual region)
TVS

South-West England
TSW - Television South West

MAP 1: INDEPENDENT TELEVISION'S 14 REGIONS, 1982 ONWARDS

(showing UHF 625-line principal coverage)

programming. These also are the least profitable companies
(they are Ulster, Grampian, Border, Channel and South West).
– The *middle five*, or 'major minors' are similar to the first five but
have bigger populations, much bigger revenues and they each
make about two hours of programming per day mostly for showing in their own region; only a little of this gets on to the ITV
network. These companies are primarily outlets for the net-

worked offerings of their big brothers. (They are TV South, Harlech, Scottish, Anglia, Tyne-Tees.)
- The *five network* companies (based in London, Birmingham, Manchester, Leeds) occupy the four inner and most populated areas. Each of the five is a major centre of television production with its main effort typically spread across a wide range of variety, drama, documentary and current affairs for the national network. (They are Thames, London Weekend, Central, Granada, Yorkshire.)

In 1954–55 the new Independent Television Authority was faced with the horrendous task of planning in some 15 months a new system, which despite years of debate was almost totally undescribed in the 1954 Act. The key strategy was the inner ring of initially three networking centres – London, Birmingham, Manchester – divided into weekday and weekend contracts in order to foster some element of competition.

From 1955 to 1962 the ITA was rather quiescent, leaving the leadership of the system to the tycoons of the major companies with their freshly won experience and commercial battle honours.

1962 and its denunciation by the Pilkington Committee led to a new and much more interventionist phase. Using the stick of its contract renewal power, the ITA now bullied the companies into putting on more serious programming. In 1968 it conducted a sweeping reform of its own system with a radical re-allocation of licences – including the creation of a new networking company and centre (Yorkshire Television in Leeds) and the abolition of the weekday/weekend split except in London. The growing importance of the Authority was marked by its renaming in 1972 as the Independent *Broadcasting* Authority with new powers over commercial radio.

TABLE 5

SOURCES OF PROGRAMMING TRANSMITTED BY A
TYPICAL ITV COMPANY IN 1979–80

5 major network companies	50%
10 regional companies	8%
ITN	7%
Company's own local output	8%
Advertisements	10%
Foreign (films, series, serials)	15%
Other	2%
TOTAL	100

Source: IBA Annual Report 1979–80, p. 34.

There was a further major expansion of the IBA's significance in 1980–82, when the ITV franchises were re-allocated and some other changes were made. In addition two completely new services were launched in late 1982 and early 1983: *The Fourth Channel* is opened by a company which is itself a wholly owned subsidiary of the IBA. The Fourth Channel is intended to provide minority and other programming complementary to the large audience ITV channel. Channel Four does not make its own programming but commissions it from independent sources, from ITN, from film and Hollywood suppliers, and from the 15 regional ITV companies. The 15 ITV companies have the following relationships with the Fourth Channel:

1. Fourth Channel programming is transmitted nationally in all ITV regions,
2. The ITV companies act as programme suppliers to the Fourth Channel,
3. The ITV companies sell advertising for the Fourth Channel in their own regions,
4. The Fourth Channel was launched with the help of large subscriptions (subsidies) from the ITV companies paid via the IBA.

Breakfast television, starting in 1983 was the other innovation. This is networked on ITV and produced entirely by a separate franchised company, *TV-am*.

These extensions to the IBA system are further discussed in Chapter 14.

CHAPTER FIVE

Network radio, recorded music

The most important innovation in post-1945 British radio was Pirate
Radio, which flourished from 1964 to 1967 on ships moored off the
British coast. Although the pirates lost the battle, what they represented – American style Top Forty radio with commercials – won
the war. The pirates came ashore – into BBC local radio stations,
and also into newly organised BBC network radio. Commercial
local radio itself followed. The record industry ceased to have a
sheltered market. American companies moved into Britain, seeing
it not only as a lucrative market but perhaps even more as a talent
source.

The Pirate Radio era was crucially linked to two other powerful
trends of the early 1960s. First *television* had by 1960 unambiguously
taken over as the major medium; but radio took a long time to find
its place as a secondary medium. In 1964 – ten years after the
legislation for commercial television – radio still had not fully
discovered the youth market.

Secondly, *popular music* itself was going through its own revolution in the early 1960s. Tommy Steele and Cliff Richard heralded
the new era of the Beatles and Rolling Stones in which British
record sales doubled – in real terms – every four years. But neither
the record industry nor radio initially recognized rock music as
anything other than the latest passing fad. The Pirate Radio stations
played this new music and achieved an enormous audience response.

The popular radio and music audience was a mystery then; it has
remained something of a mystery since. For example take the basic
point that radio is a *secondary* medium. BBC audience research
indicated in the 1960s that television was the main medium and
dominated the evening hours. People with television mostly only
listened to radio while they were doing something else – eating
breakfast, doing housework, driving; radio also occupied much less
of their time than television. BBC data have long shown that the
peak radio audience is at breakfast, half of all radio listening is
before 11.00 a.m. and only about one-tenth of the day's radio
listening is done in the evening after 7.00 p.m. BBC data have long
indicated also that the typical British adult spends about twice as
much time watching television (around 2½ hours a day) as radio
listening (about 1¼ hours a day). The BBC operated a fairly

demanding definition for radio listening, which in practice aimed to
distinguish between the fact that in many households radios are left
on for many hours and the separate fact of people actively 'listening'
to radio. Thus from 1975 commercial radio data started to indicate
in its research that British adults might be radio 'listening' for not
1¼ hours but for *three* full hours per day. In contrast to the BBC
data the commercial broadcasting research suggests that British
adults 'watch' television for about three hours a day and also 'listen'
to radio for three hours a day.

According to ILR data 8.15 a.m. was the radio peak with 10
million listening: a similar number of British adults listen to a car
radio 'most days' of the week.[1] The 1970s also saw a big surge in the
sheer number of radios, which by 1980 had almost reached one
radio for each person – adult and child – in a household.

The BBC Radio tradition, 1922–70

In retrospect some people may see the second golden age of radio as
in the 1970s (the first was the 1930s). Certainly breakfast television
already makes radio's life more difficult – as will the expansion of
other television channels and video media. The 1970s saw Britain
with four BBC networked radio channels, and the significant development of both BBC and ILR local radio. But although this
pattern was established in the period 1967–73, the triumph of
television occurred a decade – some would say two decades –
earlier.

Radio, more perhaps than any other medium – apart from
newspapers – is an ancient-and-modern medium. Its *secondary*
status means that radio is always finding new places it can reach
which television cannot. Direct broadcast satellites alone will find
many new avenues for radio. But radio is also an *ancient* medium.
At the arrival of ITV in 1955, BBC radio was already 33 years old,
with its finest hours already a decade behind it. Radio carried all the
BBC's traditions. Around 1955 BBC radio was suddenly pushed
from its prime position, to having to play third fiddle behind both
Independent and BBC television. For some years it simply grew
more ancient until, around 1967, the Pirates finally led to radio
innovation within the BBC.

Whereas by the late 1950s television had become brash in terms of
commerce and entertainment – and increasingly also in news and
politics – BBC radio was the inheritor of the BBC's earlier traditions
of decorum and deference. The BBC – BBC radio – had between
1922 and 1939 learnt the habit of deference to four key veto groups –
the major Parliamentary political parties, the press, engineers and
the London cultural establishment.

In view of its Parliament-conferred monopoly and source of

TABLE 6

THE BRITISH RADIO AUDIENCE, SPRING 1982
(in areas of ILR availability)

	Share of audience			
	Weekly hours *(millions)*	%	Weekly reach %	Average hours
Independent local radio	232	33·0	52	13·5
BBC Radio 1	170	24·0	45	11·5
BBC Radio 2	148	21 1	39	11·5
BBC Radio 3	10	1·4	8	3·7
BBC Radio 4	83	11·8	24	10·5
BBC local radio	44	6·3	18	7·6
Radio Luxembourg	5	0·7	4	3·3
Other stations	10	1·4		
Any radio station	702	100	92	23·3

Note: Based on a sample of 16,000 persons (aged 15 and over) conducted for the Joint Industry Committee for Radio Audience Research (JICRAR) by Research Surveys of Great Britain (RSGB).

The study was conducted in the main audience areas of existing ILR radio stations which then contained 75% of the UK population.

'Weekly reach': proportion of the population listening at least once in the last week.

'Average hours': average hours spent listening to that station by each person who listened to that station in the last week.

Source: *The Audience for ILR*, 1982. London: IBA Radio Division. From Independent Local Network Survey (JICRAR) Spring 1982.

finance, the BBC in its early years had to defer to the wishes of Parliament. The established political parties seem to have seen the BBC as a semi-independent extension of the civil service machine – not surprisingly, since it was dependent on a then government department, the Post Office. The Labour party also welcomed the BBC as an early example of public sector enterprise. The first major test of this deference to Parliament came in 1926 with the General Strike. The BBC attempted to stay as neutral as possible but, when it was forced to choose, supported the Government against the strikers. Although this long remained a grievance with Labour, the Labour party had nowhere else to go. Meanwhile the BBC, by leaning towards the government in 1926, gained the favour of the Conservative party which was in power for most of the BBC's early years.

The BBC doctrine effectively was that all major political parties were equal but the party in government was more equal than others.

Closely linked to its deference towards Parliament and government was the BBC's deference to the press. The press collectively had two major interests – it did not want competition either from radio advertising or from radio news. In the case of advertising, the BBC deliberately did not use its existing legal permission to add advertising revenue to licence fee. In the field of radio news, the BBC provided only a minimal amount; it drew this from agency services owned by the newspapers and for many years deferred to the anxieties of the London evening newspapers by transmitting even this agency news only after 7.00 p.m.

The BBC also established a radio policy (later applied to television) of giving engineering and telecommunications considerations marked prominence. In terms of technical standards the BBC insisted on high quality and saw itself as an innovator. In the politics of engineering the BBC was always conservative. Early ideas of vigorous regional radio stations with their own output were soon cut back. Britain – being located in a northern Europe which has many small countries and much population – was inevitably rationed, through international agreements, to limited numbers of wavelengths. Soon this constraint began to be used as a rationalisation for more central control – and regional areas for radio broadcasting were defined around engineering convenience.

Centralization in London also both reflected and cemented all of the interests. The BBC was oriented towards the British establishment which itself was London-based; it was deferential to the London-based Parliament and to the *national* press. Monopoly public service radio was also primarily London radio although one of the two networks carried some regional material and in engineering terms radio radiated out from London as did the railway tracks.

It was this BBC radio tradition, which Radio Caroline – a ship based off the Essex coast and within range of London – was to shatter. Caroline and other pirate stations were funded by advertisers and advertising agencies; as with similar pirate operations off other European coasts they simply adopted the American radio format, and hence broke all the local rules. They paid no royalties for records; they had no licence to operate; they cultivated audience response; and when the Labour Government eventually came to the BBC's rescue – by making illegal the placing of advertising with the pirates – the pirates made no further pretence of political neutrality. Radio Caroline was one of several pirate stations which in their dying days began to broadcast denunciations of Prime Minister Harold Wilson once an hour, on the hour.

In autumn 1967 BBC radio at last entered a new age. BBC Radio One was launched and the 1, 2, 3, 4 format established for the four radio networks. The first BBC local radio 'experiment' also began.

Two years later in 1969 the BBC published *Broadcasting in the Seventies*, heralding – amidst unprecedented anguish in the letters columns of *The Times* – a policy which had in practice been in existence for two years.[2]

Rock and record industry

The relationships between rock music, the record industry, radio – and youth – are analysed in detail by Simon Frith in the *Sociology of Rock* and *Sound Effects*. Frith locates rock music within the British pattern of leisure and the national class system. He comments on the Art School background of many British musicians of the 1960s. He points out that the rock music career was a way of escaping not only a working class, but also a middle class, background. Here the main intention is to discuss the popular music industry in the context of radio, and despite this area's notorious complexity and volatility to venture a few generalizations.

First, the popular music industry is ruled by the charts, to a quite extraordinary degree. It is, of course, the very volatility of the business which leads to the need for some agreed barometer. Until 1982 the charts were constructed by British Market Research Bureau (BRMB) based on a weekly sample of 450 record shops spread across the UK. In 1983 a new electronic Gallup system was introduced based on small electronic keyboards beside the cash tills in 250 sample shops.

Popular radio and the record industry operate in a state of massive dependence upon each other and on the charts. Radio play is usually vital to record sales. On the other hand, the BBC's Radio One plays records from an established playlist which is constructed – with the help of an announced formula – around the sales charts. Radio Two, the BBC's equivalent of an American Middle-of-the-Road (MOR) station, plays music for housewives over age 35, and independent local radio does a mixture of the two. Popular music sales are thus, if not determined, then heavily shaped, by the formula: Radio play sells records, and top sellers get radio play. Attempting to break into this circular formula are two sets of salesmen – those who plug records to producers or disc jockeys, and those who visit record shops, attempting in particular to hype sales in the sampled shops.

Another fact of life is that if radio play is vital, television play is even better. While a BBC Radio One Sunday evening programme once called *Top of the Pops* (later *Top 40*) has long pulled BBC radio's largest audiences, a television *Top of the Pops* – launched in 1964 – has played a key role in British popular music. A more specifically rock show was the *Old Grey Whistle Test*. Until the arrival of the fourth TV channel in 1982 these two shows were the only exceptions to the strange denial by television of the visual aspects of popular music. Until this time also, *Top of the Pops* had been the only major outlet for promotional videos. An important video innovation was pioneered in Britain by K-Tel, which in the mid 1970s began to sell albums of re-issued hit songs with the aid of massive television commercial promotion.

A further aspect of the British music scene in the 1970s – illustrated by K-Tel – was the opening of the British market to foreign competition. From 1955 to 1964 just two British companies – EMI and Decca – had around 75% of the UK record market. With

TABLE 7

BRITISH ALBUM RECORD SALES

	1971	1976	1981
EMI	24·9	21·2	15·9
CBS	13·4	10·6	15·8
Warner	9·3	10·0	11·2
Polydor*	12·2	7·1	7·7
Phonogram*	6·6	7·9	5·6
RCA	6·8	6·4	5·1
Virgin	—	1·4	4·7
K-Tel	—	2·5	4·0
A and M	3·6	3·1	3·8
Chrysalis	—	—	3·2
Ariola/Arista	—	—	3·8
Decca*	11·3	7·7	2·9

* = All part of Polygram group
Source: *Music and Video Week* 13th February 1982, based on data from British Market Research Bureau.

Pye added, three British companies had well over 80%. In the early days of the American rock boom this altered little because the American recording stars were licensed to the British companies. The middle and late Sixties saw massive changes, as the major American companies moved directly into the British market. A European stake had long existed via Philips, and the Philips-Siemens Polygram interests were by 1981 the leading company in Britain with 16% of album sales (Table 7). The American giants – CBS, Warner and RCA – had together 8% of the UK market in 1965, but 28% in 1971 and in 1981 (with K-Tel), 36%. Thus in 1981 these four American companies plus Polygram together had 52% of the UK market.

EMI had had increasing difficulties in its home market – both against the big foreign battalions and against new British companies like Virgin. The record industry has ceased to be 'sheltered' and has become almost as subject to international competition as the film industry. Although records and music have become in some respects *the* mass medium, and the music stars *the* superstars, Britain has no policy of any kind in this field. There are not even the rather minimal protective elements which exist for films. Records are subject to Value Added Tax.

In the absence of anyone other than the BBC and IBA making policy in this field, the stars and the Musicians' Union have a big say. The dominance of the stars, and the financial terms some are able to acquire, are legendary. But equally significant are the policies of the Musicians' Union which ration the amount of recorded music allowed on radio. The details of this are complex but one broad generalisation is that British radio uses up most of its 'needle time' during the higher daytime listening hours and thus plays little recorded music in the evening. This leaves the low audience evening free for talk, phone-ins, minority programming of various kinds, and of course *live* music.

Recorded popular music clearly remains a powerful interest for many young people – but especially for white-collar young men aged around 18; students and young manual workers are also in this core audience. These are the people – with males outnumbering females by two or three to one – who watch the television rock programmes, listen to Radio One, who attend live rock concerts, buy records, and read the music press.[4]

The music press has for some years drawn about 70% of its readership from people under age 24. These publications are the male equivalents of the teenage girls' magazines. Of the five leading music magazines in 1982 four were the same as in the mid-1970s – *Melody Maker* (launched 1926), *New Musical Express* (1952), *Record Mirror* (1953) and *Sounds* (1970); the core audience member for all four was an 18-year-old male in white collar or skilled manual work. The only exception was *Smash Hits* (launched 1979) which had taken over from *FAB 208* and other such publications with a still younger (about age 16) core audience, mainly girls.[5]

BBC network radio in the 1970s

Before 1939 the BBC had two radio channels, one containing partly regional material. The basic scheduling philosophy was to mix up highbrow and lowbrow, music and talk, all on a single channel – with the ultimate Reithian purpose of enticing reluctant listeners towards higher things.

From 1946 to 1967 the BBC attempted to pursue the same purpose by the somewhat different strategy of three national channels, one highbrow (the Third Programme), one middlebrow (Home), and one lowbrow (Light); the two 'lower' channels were intended to contain within them a little material from the next brow level upwards, which would – through some mysterious process – entice Light listeners to try the middlebrow Home, and Home Listeners to sample the true cultural delights of the Third. This strategy, of course, never worked; although the Third Programme in the late 1940s did surprisingly well, the general overwhelming preference for entertainment and popular music (plus some news) was powerfully evident. Long before ITV's quiz and game shows, the most popular radio programme of the post-1945 period was Wilfred Pickles' *Have A Go*.

TABLE 8

BBC RADIO NETWORKS 1981–82

	Radio 1	Radio 2	Radio 3	Radio 4	Total
Music	87%	80%	69%	4%	59%
Current affairs, features, documentaries	6	3	6	45	16
News	2	5	3	15	6
Drama	—	—	2	10	3
Sport	—	7	6	1	4
Other	4	5	14	24	12
TOTAL	100	100	100	100	100

Source: *BBC Annual Report and Handbook 1983* p. 118

In 1967 BBC radio put on its new clothes, but in reality it was only a bit more modern and not a great deal less ancient. *Radio One* was rock music and disc jockeys come ashore from the pirate stations. The second most popular network was *Radio Two*, the old Light Programme in new clothes. *Radio Three* was, of course, a new version of the Third Programme – still largely devoted to serious music.

The biggest innovation was *Radio Four* a mixture of the old Home Service with elements of the American all-news and all-talk formulae. Radio Four included a big expansion of news comment programming. It also became a major stage for drama – carrying 790 hours of drama in 1981–82. Besides some familiar radio serials this includes a large amount of original drama and classics. Radio Four drama can certainly claim to rival in importance the entire range of fringe theatre and theatre-in-a-pub.

Local radio

Although the BBC had a history of expressed interest in local radio, when BBC local radio began in 1967 it was part of a rapidly compacted response to the radio pirates. Initially the BBC hoped for finance from local bodies, including local government. This hope quickly faded.

For the BBC, local radio poses one of its basic dilemmas in a particularly acute form. Extra programming makes for extra cost, but not extra revenue. In this case there is the further problem that since the BBC network channels have the bulk of the radio audience, BBC local stations are costing the BBC a lot of extra money while simply taking audiences from BBC national radio output. BBC local radio also has difficulty devising a programming formula which differs from Radios 1, 2 and 4. A heavily local version of Radio 4 – a network of local all-talk stations – would be extremely expensive.

Commercial Radio – ILR – has no such problems – it is a compromise between BBC Radios 1, 2 and 4 and an American Top Forty station. It taps a new source of advertising – heavily *local* initially. In fact in its early days, in 1973–74, ILR did have some severe problems – yet another major British broadcasting innovation which had a disastrous birth. The IBA – itself inexperienced in radio – must take much of the blame. London was split into two – the news-and-talk London Broadcasting Company and the pop-music-oriented Capital Radio. Both nearly sank in the early days and both were saved from drowning by Canadian interests.

The first station, London Broadcasting (LBC) won its contract in spring 1973 and had its contract renewed in 1982. Ten years after the date of the first contract there were 43 ILR stations covering some 80% of the population; but ILR was a commercial success mainly in the big cities with Capital radio in London and stations in Manchester, Glasgow, Liverpool and Birmingham obtaining the bulk of the advertising revenue. BBC local radio does much less well in the big cities but performs more strongly in some smaller, more middle class locations.

CHAPTER SIX

Film: long time a-dying

The British film industry is an extreme example of the rapid decline which hit many other national film industries in the age of television. At the peak of the cinema's popularity in 1946, the average Briton went over 30 times a year. By 1976 this was down to twice a year, and by 1982 only once a year.

This story has three major villains – of which television is a comparative latecomer. The two other villains are Hollywood and British government policy or non-policy.

Certainly television has taken away the audience; certainly ever since about 1913 – before the American industry even went west to California – the British film industry has suffered from an endlessly successful American invasion. Certainly British government policy has been not only too little and too late, it has also been fragmented, *ad hoc*, inconsistent, and badly informed.

A perennial question asks whether film is an art form or an industry. British governments and the British people have been reluctant to adopt any of the main possible answers to this question. Britain has not followed the United States in defining film as primarily an entertainment industry, nor Sweden in seeing domestic film-making as a cultural artistic enterprise, nor France, Italy and Japan in regarding film as part industry and part art form.

Perpetual indecision has accompanied a seventy year-long decline which about once every decade is relieved by a small revival – in commercial success and film-makers' optimism – before the decline continues. Judged simply by the numbers of people who visit cinemas, the British film business is almost too small to merit further discussion. However, it has a wider significance – partly because the decline of film also tells us something more broadly about other mass media and about public and government attitudes to the media in Britain; but also because the next phase of decline and revival will see film as a key ingredient in the general intermingling of 'old' and 'new' media.

Film as an unBritish business?
Film as a mass medium has certain peculiarities: it has developed into an extreme example of the economies of scale, and film-makers have come to see their 'natural' market as the entire world. With a very high investment involved in the first copy and negligible pro-

duction cost involved in reaching further audiences, one national industry was always likely to dominate the world film market. This industry has been, and is, Hollywood. Ever since 1913 British audiences have seen more American than British films. Hollywood imagery, values and myths have for over sixty years been part of the imaginative and fantasy furniture of British minds. These Hollywood-induced fantasies have existed in the minds not only of the British public but also in the minds of British film-makers and film policy-makers, who have never succeeded in adequately analysing and confronting the reality of the Hollywood challenge.

Film also differs from other mass media in not having filtered down from an élite of educated readers or affluent set-buyers; film filtered up out of the gutter – from fair-ground sideshows, as a music hall 'filler' item, from sleazy halls and converted shops. In the first years of the century, while the Northcliffe newspaper revolution was only reaching the white-collar workers and some of the skilled manual workers, film was establishing itself as the first mass medium, reaching the entire working class, including the destitute and illiterate.

The *production* of films is the traditional forum for star-marketing publicity. The *exhibition* of films in cinemas both involves the main fixed investment and defines film as a medium. But the middle-manning function – *distribution* – has always been the real core. Because they control access to the cinema markets the distributors can determine which films are seen; because they also dominate the finance of production, the distributors determine what films shall be made. Hollywood power is distributor power. In Britain the focus has always been on production (trying to make more British films) and exhibition (the cinema chain issue) – whether one considers the public debate, official policy or (perhaps crucially) the concerns of the trade unions.

Publicity is vital to reaping scale economies; and the whole film business – including the star system – was built around publicity. The film business is the home of 'hype' (hyperbole) and, even more than the rest of the media, is inclined to believe its own myths. Some of these myths concern competition. It is indeed a competitive business; but a strong trend to monopoly has been endemic in all the world's film industries since about 1910.

For this monopoly reason, and because film has always been regarded as the 'bread and circuses' of the poor and young, the film industry has been a target for censorship and other legislation. This legislation has been enormously important in shaping the film business, often into unintended shapes. The Hollywood exporters – confronted with the legislation of over a hundred importing nations – have become connoisseurs of film legislation and have become expert at circumventing all but a few such determined people as Hitler and Stalin.

British governments certainly – in terms of accurate analysis and sophistication of strategy – have been no match for Hollywood.

Britain has turned out many excellent films, directors, producers, technicians and, above all, film actors. What it has never had for any length of time is a *film industry* – an industry in the sense of a stable structure making a steady stream of commercially or artistically successful films. Short phases of such stability always came abruptly to an end – the 1930s' successes were severely cut back in 1939; the late 1940s' boom quickly burst with falling cinema attendances and television; the American-financed revival of the 1960s ended when the Americans ceased their 'swinging London' hype and re-discovered laid back southern California.

The film business, if it is to become an established industry, needs acting, creative management, film technicians, screen-writing, finance, and political lobbying amongst other ingredients, and these skills need to be developed over a period of time by an industry which can provide at least a successful core in each occupation with more or less permanent employment.

The British film industry has never done this. London has produced a flow of virtuoso film actors, but it has provided few with continuity of film employment; creative film-makers – directors and producers – have had to spend too much energy raising money, not enough on making films, at least in Britain. Finance has always been a weak link. Nor has Britain developed a tradition of original film-writing; the novel, and plays (stage, radio and television) have had stronger attractions for writers, and film scripts have tended to be adaptations from these other forms.

The British establishment and film
It has often been said that the British establishment has never really accepted film. But the opposite may be more true. The London establishment accepted the film all too eagerly. Royal family pat-ronage was well established in the 1920s. The mass working-class audience was largely left to Hollywood, while the British film industry provided middlebrow entertainment to the middle class.

The West End Theatre was especially eager and its embrace has always tended towards suffocation. The history of British films could be written in terms of just two influences – the West End Theatre and television. Each in turn has provided actors and acting styles, scripts, and audience-tested themes. British films were first a side-show of the theatre, then a sideshow of television. Both were and are industries in a way that British films never have been.

Few other national film industries have been based in a single city alongside two quite such strong dramatic rivals. Either the West End stage, or BBC/ITV television would have been a serious rival to any film industry.

The theatre may partly explain why – even after the British film industry largely lost its own domestic mass audience in 1914–18 – no avant-garde film industry developed in Britain. Indeed British film intellectuals throughout the 1920s and 1930s seem to have spent much of their energy not in emulating the artistic triumphs of the German, French and Soviet cinemas, but merely in setting up film clubs within which these countries' avant-garde films could be seen.

The pull of the BBC also began long before television. In 1929 Val Gielgud – brother of the famous actor, John – was made head of BBC drama and variety, and the BBC became a major patron of actors, writers, directors and drama. This tradition was later inherited by BBC television and in the 1960s it was already being said that the best plays were to be found on television. Television drama/film quickly achieved the scale and continuity of an established industry – using some of the same west London studios in which the British film has been less successful. Relatively protected from foreign competition, TV drama quickly produced all the different 'levels' of output which the film industry had only aimed at – high-brow single plays by avant-garde writers; glossy costume series partly aimed at the export market; action/adventure imitations of Hollywood; comedies; classics; and authentic domestic soap operas heavily slanted at the working-class audience.

Censorship and other public policy

One major aspect of film policy was censorship. Britain was exceedingly restrictive – aimed at protecting the established order both at home and in the Empire. In the 1930s it was also deferential to most foreign governments including the German.[1] These arrangements alone seem to have ensured that until about 1960 British films lacked not only explicit sex and violence, but much of the colour, feel, conflict and language of everyday life. Many were West End plays presented in filmed versions with the few naughty and irreverent bits removed. It was partly for this reason that the British films of the 1960s – following *Room at the Top* (1958) had such a fresh quality; more relaxed censorship allowed them to move from censored versions of stage plays to liberated versions of television plays.

The other type of public policy directed at films has of course been broadly financial. This has had several elements. A *quota* system dating from 1927, ensuring that a minimum quantity of 'British' films are shown; secondly a *levy* ('Eady') on all films (made statutory in 1957) which is returned in the form of a *subsidy* to films which qualify as 'British made'; a system of *capital funding* – the National Film Finance Corporation – which starting in 1949 provided a minority slice of finance for films which got their major slice of finance from commercial distributors. Additional measures have included favourable tax decisions, and the existence of British Lion in the 1960s as a state-supported 'third force' in production. These policies had some success, especially quotas in the 1930s, but they largely failed for two reasons. During its most continuously success-ful period – the 1940s and 1950s – the British film industry was subjected to massive entertainments tax – about 36% of cinema's gross takings; when this tax finally ended in 1960, the industry itself was less than one third of its peak size.

Unrealistic responses: British film industry and government confront Hollywood and television

An unrealistic attitude towards Hollywood was shown in several aspects of thinking of the British film industry. The chain owner-ships which from the 1930s dominated British cinemas[2] were con-structed explicitly in order to challenge the power of the American distributors; but when these same cinema chains expanded vertically into production and distribution they acquired split person-alities – on the one hand they wanted a strong British film industry, but on the other hand their own cinemas were heavily dependent on Hollywood for a steady supply of the main diet of the British film public.

However it was in their ever-optimistic belief that they could export successfully into the American market that British film executives were most glaringly unrealistic. Hollywood in its classic phase was a cartel and thus Alexander Korda's occasional export successes in the 1930s were misleading. After the Hollywood cartel was broken up in the 1950s, experienced British film men continued to think they could seize some of Hollywood's home market; but since the Hollywood majors continued their dominance, via distri-bution, the odds were stacked against more than brief independent success. Both EMI and Lord Grade in the 1970s established them-selves as major independent producers; they went the common way of 'indy majors' in Hollywood – initial investment, some limited successes, and then costly disaster.

The failure to develop a coherent government strategy is illus-trated by the plethora of narrowly focused official investigations, and narrowly directed pieces of legislation which have dogged the British film industry for fifty years. Enquiries tend to be about only one aspect of the industry – such as only exhibition or only produc-tion employment. Legislation is similarly bitty. The legislation in recent years not only fails to confront the Hollywood film industry, but fails to confront the fact that Hollywood since the 1950s includes *TV production* and since about 1970 also *music production*.

Television is the other great rival which the film industry has failed to confront with adequate realism. Here, of course, it failed alongside many other film industries. There were two reasons why the film industry eventually caved in and allowed feature films on to television screens: First television was evidently doing pretty well even without feature films. Secondly the divisions within the film industry both within Britain and between Britain and Hollywood were such that British television managed (by 1964) to secure Hollywood films in quantity and also the back output of major British independents such as Ealing.

Government film policy has been unrealistic in the face of television – in that it has consistently regarded film and television as separate industries, which since the 1950s has become less and less true.

1930–55: a golden period
The period from the arrival of sound (around 1930) in film until the arrival of ITV in 1955 was the British film industry's nearest thing to a golden age. New legislation required a domestic 'quota' and boosted British productions from only 5% of all films exhibited in Britain in the mid 1920s to around 30% in the mid 1930s.

Audiences were still high until 1955 – and it was in the late 1950s that the most devasting audience drop occurred. But even in the golden age between 1930 and 1955 over two-thirds of all British exhibited films were American made and distributed. The British production sector was, however, moderately prosperous in the 1930–55 period. During this period Britain developed several characteristic types of film: off-beat comedies, horror films, suspense melodramas, and documentaries (which had a new lease of life in the Second World War).

But these successes carried with them numerous signs that total disaster might not be far away. Hollywood had captured the bulk of the British audience in general and the working-class audience in particular.[3] The seeds of all this went back much earlier and even before 1913 Britain was a happy hunting-ground for film exporters – then mainly from France and Scandinavia. But in 1913, American film exports increasingly deluged Britain. The lead which American films gained before the First World War was consolidated during it. American films have dominated British cinema screens in every single year since 1915; and the people who have watched these films have mainly been working-class Britons.

The English language has obviously played some part, but before the late 1920s the silent movies gave United States products few special advantages in the British market. Britain was uniquely attractive to the Hollywood distributors because it was the most affluent European market. Some Hollywood films made 50% of their entire foreign earnings in Britain in 1925, compared with 4% in 1980.

British cinema owners and businessmen were relatively ineffective at resisting such harsh selling tactics as block booking and blind buying (contracting for a year's supply in advance). But most of all, the British working-class audience loved American films; British films not only cost cinema owners more to show, but they were less popular with British audiences. With a few low budget exceptions (such as George Formby and Gracie Fields films in the 1930s and the 'Carry On' romps of the Sixties and Seventies) British film-makers largely gave up trying to woo back the British working class. Like John Reith at the BBC they focused on middle-brow inoffensive material aimed at the new middle-class suburbs.

With the contraction of the total audience and the targeting of the US and European film production industry at young adults, the audience has grown steadily more confined in age terms. In 1960 it took an age bracket of 14 years (16–29) to account for half the audience; by 1980 half the audience was aged 18–24, a span of only seven years. But in 1980 even the 18–24 age band on average went to a cinema only once every six weeks, while they watched TV about 15 hours a week – meaning that even this peak cinema group saw about 90 hours of television for each cinema visit. The data for other forms of 'going out' are not directly comparable, but film-going – even among unmarried young adults – has clearly failed to keep up in competition especially with 'going out' for food, drink and music, or staying in for music and television. The fact that British film interests were also involved in TV and music may have encouraged them to ignore films.

1955–70: Decline and 'revival'

After 1955 the British film industry experienced box office disaster (Figure 2) and a spiral of declining audiences, closing cinemas, cut-backs in domestic production, and further audience losses. The 1960s gave some indications of a respite from decline. Hollywood distributors began to finance a revival in British film production. *Saturday Night and Sunday Morning* (1960) was one of several examples of an American-financed film which was about, and appealed to, British working-class people.

It was at this slightly optimistic time that the Monopolies Commission investigated the dominance of two British companies, Rank and ABC, in the ownership of cinemas. The Rank and ABC cinema

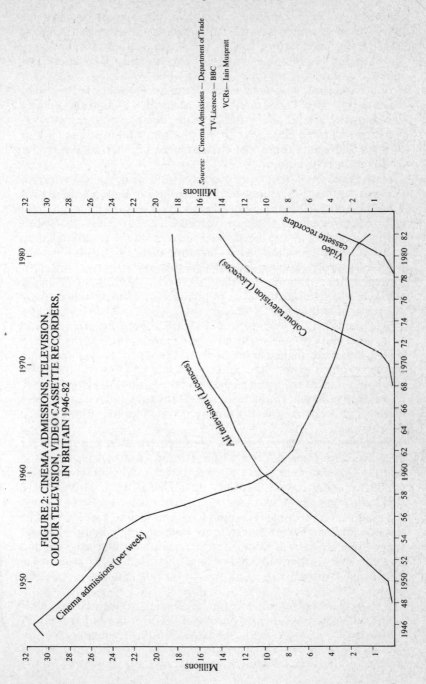

FIGURE 2: CINEMA ADMISSIONS, TELEVISION, COLOUR TELEVISION, VIDEO CASSETTE RECORDERS, IN BRITAIN 1946-82

Sources: Cinema Admissions — Department of Trade
TV-Licences — BBC
VCRs — Iain Muspratt

chains did indeed dominate – in 1965 together they owned over two-fifths of all cinema seats in Britain; as the industry had declined their relative dominance had greatly increased. And of the very large cinemas – 2,000 seats and over – Rank and ABC had in 1964 four-fifths of the British total.[4]

Some ninety of these very large cinemas were the key to the whole 'release pattern'. The Commission concluded that while getting your film on to the Rank or ABC circuit did not guarantee success, not getting it on to either circuit did guarantee failure. The bulk of the films shown on these two circuits were supplied by the Hollywood major distributors.

Both Rank and ABC also produced and distributed their own films and gave these films preferential treatment on their own exhibition circuits. In the early 1960s ABC and Rank between them averaged fifteen feature films produced each year. The total British output of feature films officially registered with the Board of Trade averaged 74 in the same years. The four-fifths of British films not wholly financed by Rank and ABC involved a variety of different arrangements, including partial ABC or Rank financing. But the majority of these four-fifths were financed directly or indirectly by American distributors.[5]

The American distributors in Britain offered two things: first access to a market – especially a foreign market, often in the United States. Secondly finance to produce the film or support in obtaining finance from a bank. The bulk was usually 70% of the total estimated cost, called 'front money'; on the basis of this front money a freelance producer could normally get the remainder – called 'end money' – elsewhere, most often from the National Film Finance Corporation.

The latter was part of the government created apparatus for encouraging film production within Britain. Another part was the famous 'Eady money', a levy operated by the British Film Fund on exhibition and paid back as a subsidy to *British made* films at a rate related to the film's earnings in British cinemas. Bowing to a definition of 'British made' which gave primacy to employment of trade union members rather than to some uniquely British cultural vision, the regulations allowed a film with an American star and director, plus American finance and distribution, to qualify for subsidy as 'British made', if all the supporting cast and technicians were British.

The freelance producer was the key figure, frequently an American resident temporarily or permanently in or around Britain. A film project would start with a freelance producer showing a screenplay idea to a Hollywood distributor. Inevitably with an American distributor providing the bulk of the finance, the screenplay would be written and re-written with heavy emphasis on likely acceptability in the American domestic market. The 1960s revival of the British cinema involved films largely made for American and world audiences; the consequent exaggeration of North of England squalor or the contrived glitter of 'swinging London' could be seen as at last getting British films into the serious film business of myth-making. Another view was that American finance and stars, American vetted scripts, and the whole prepacking-for-the-market strategy produced mid-Atlantic phoneyness. The Monopolies Commission said:

> One producer told us for example that if a film is being made for an American company, even though all or most of the creative people connected with it are British, 'inevitably they dance to the American tune of the people who put up the American money and I think undoubtedly the character of films is changed by this factor.'[6]

Another anxiety was that one day the Americans might pick up their marbles and go home. But the Commission could see no solution to this. With minor exceptions it endorsed the existing pattern – cinemas dominated by two British circuits showing Hollywood products plus some Hollywood-financed 'made in Britain' films.

A few years later, in 1969–70, yet another crisis hit Hollywood. European film-making was getting too expensive; the Beatles excitement was over. The Americans were drawn home, and the Hollywood publicists departed announcing, as they left, that London was swinging no more. After the 'revival' of the 1960, decline returned in the 1970s.

1947–48 and the Great British Film Policy Disaster
The failure of any systematic policy towards the British film industry was characteristic of the 1945–55 period in general and of 1947–48 in particular.

On August 6th 1947 began perhaps the most catastrophic and ludicrous episode in the entire history of British governmental media policy. In the context of the dollar crisis and the fact that Hollywood films accounted for 4% of all dollar imports, the Chancellor of the Exchequer (Hugh Dalton) imposed a 75% duty on imported films; this duty, moreover, was to be paid in advance. The Hollywood trade association declared an immediate and total boycott. After pressure from British exhibitors (starved of their main source of films) and negotiations with the Hollywood interests, an Anglo-American Film Agreement was reached on March 11th 1948. This agreement, which specified that imports would resume, while the bulk of Hollywood earnings would be 'blocked' in Britain, had several consequences unanticipated by the British government:

- The 'blocked' earnings defined the British industry as a dollar-saver, but also encouraged Hollywood to make films in Britain, thus further increasing its dominance.
- Imports of Made-In-Hollywood films resumed in 1948; the seven-month boycott ensured that both the American supply and the British demand were stronger than ever.
- The quota of films which had to be British made was raised in 1948 to 45% although in the Second World War the quota had been around 15%. In fact in none of the next few years did British production reach as high as 25% of all films registered for exhibition.
- Nevertheless the British film producers, especially J. Arthur Rank, despite not having been consulted in the original decision, agreed radically to increase their production in order to meet the 45% British quota. Rank did indeed greatly increase production; his expanded output did badly againt the increased Hollywood challenge and by 1949 Rank was reporting gigantic losses.[7]

The Economist, commenting on Mr Rank's problems, pointed out the grossly false optimism of government policy:

The reports, and the statement by Mr J. Arthur Rank which accompanies them, explode beyond question certain of the assumptions on which Government policy for the film industry has been based. The first of these rosy and (it is now apparent) indefensible assumptions is that the modest scale of the industry's production in recent years had been a quite temporary manifestation, in some way the result of the war. The shortage of bank finance and of risk capital for film-making is also (it has been assumed) temporary. Once the Treasury has primed the pump, the argument runs, and once the industry has made an effort to restore a sound relationship between costs and returns, British films can be produced in growing volume on a basis of financial independence. Thereafter they can enjoy a high and constantly growing proportion of screen time in British cinemas, together with a growing export trade.[8]

Realisation that something was profoundly wrong with British film policy thus clearly existed at the time. This has a wider significance, because had a more rational film policy been evolved in this period – when the British film industry was still relatively strong – it would have needed to encompass also television; had a combined film and television policy been established, British media policy and the British media industry might now look quite different. So here – with benefit of hindsight – is a list of points which could have made for the development of a coherent British film policy in the years 1945–55:

1. Realistic analysis was first required of what was already known. In 1927 the British film industry had virtually been re-created by the original Quota Act and this experience offered many lessons. Also by 1949 several recent official reports on the film industry were available – including Palache (1944) on Monopoly, Gater (1949) on Film Production Costs, and Plant (1949) on Distribution and Exhibition. In 1950 the first Annual Report of the National Film Finance Corporation was published. All of these documents reflected the fragmented nature of policy-making, but taken together – as they were in the PEP *Report on the British Film Industry* (1952) – it was quite possible to assemble a realistic analysis.

2. Any nation's national film policy needs to be a Hollywood policy. Probably at least half the films to be exhibited in Britain would need to come from Hollywood. But it might have been possible around 1950 to get near to a break-even situation with most of the cost of Hollywood imports balanced by British exports to the world. Such a policy needed to consider all aspects of Hollywood, including Hollywood films made in Britain and the westward drain of British talent. In addition to a Hollywood policy, a European policy was needed – perhaps co-production with the French and Italian industries.

   British weaknesses and strengths needed realistic evaluation. Britain was until the late 1960s Hollywood's most valuable single market and in 1950 – with much of the Empire still intact – the British government had significant potential bargaining power in any negotiations with Hollywood.

   The key requirement for a viable export presence was access to, or control of, a major international distributor. J. Arthur Rank was well aware of this and was in New York looking at distribution possibilities when the original 1947 announcement was made. He had already bought a 'showcase' cinema in New York City and owned cinema chains in Canada and Australia.

3. A stable and positive continuing policy of quota/subsidy/taxation was also necessary. Instead British policy in these

areas was unstable, unpredictable and punitive. The domestic quota was raised – unrealistically – from 15% to 45% in three years, despite pre-war experience which pointed to the need for continuity and a slow build-up. Subsidy needs to encompass all sections of the industry – for example to include modernising cinemas – whereas the British subsidy (Eady money) was simply a flat-rate payment proportional to box-office gross; this also ruled out the possibility of discriminating in favour of films of artistic or other merit (as most European film subsidies do). Finally there was the punitive level of Entertainment Tax, which was only reduced and eventually abolished after the audience had departed.

4. The British film industry suffered from a bad case of Whitehall policy fragmentation. Instead of a single department giving a strong lead there was the Treasury (whence came Eady), the Board of Trade (concerned with boosting film exports while discouraging monopoly), and the Home Office (concerned with censorship). There was no policy connection with the BBC or its then Whitehall godfather, the Post Office.

5. Monopoly concerns played a central part in film policy; in 1943–44 the Palache committee was considering film monopoly. Such anxieties in war-time were something of a luxury, not least because the monopoly (or duopoly) tendencies in Britain were linked to cartel tendencies in Los Angeles. Probably the 'third force' (in addition to Rank and ABPC) was realistic. But the attitude of the Labour government to Rank was hopelessly ambivalent. They tended to see him as an ogre monopolist; he was indeed the dominant force in all branches of British films in the 1940s but his was also the only organization which could realistically have become a world film force – including distribution. The Labour government failed to consult him on key decisions and then persuaded him to expand too fast in 1947–8. The Labour politicians preferred the blandishments and charm of the much less effectual Alexander Korda – yet another example of image being preferred to substance.

6. Film policy was confronted with the radically opposed interests of exhibitors, producers and trade unions. Very little effort was put into trying to hammer out an agreed compromise[9] – expressed in a realistic quota and other related measures.

7. Bi-partisanship is needed to establish policy continuity over a long period. But instead quite different visions of the film industry were pursued before and after 1951. Labour favoured the Unions and was suspicious of monopoly; the Conserva-

tives favoured competition and were suspicious of any strong
government policy.
8. Finally to be effective a national film policy needed to take
   account of television.[10] Many simple connections were
   ignored; Hollywood by 1952 made both films and TV – but was
   a strong seller of films to cinemas, while a weak seller to
   television (the BBC – and later ITV – being a strong buyer).
   Co-ordination could also have occurred in the matter of films
   on television. Tax and/or TV levy incentives could have been
   used. And ITV offered many film-cum-TV opportunities.

In fact, of course, none of this policy co-ordination occurred. And
when ITV appeared on the horizon, the British film industry – still in
1955 with 72% of its peak audience – became deeply involved. Both
British film majors were involved – ABC as an initial ITV network
company and Rank in Southern; Granada was also a networker.
Nor were the Unions left behind in the rush. The technicians union,
ACT, which had experienced unemployment, became – as ACTT –
one of the main beneficiaries of, and powers within, television.
   In this way the film industry – already with divided loyalties –
acquired yet other loyalties.

The cinema is dead. Long live the film.
In 1982, as in almost every single year since 1946 the British film
audience reduced in size once again – but, also as usual, better
things were said to be around the corner. This time the drop in
audiences was larger than usual, but so also was the hope – the new
fourth television channel was to commission feature films.
   As Figure 2 shows one of the new media – the market for
pre-recorded video cassettes already had a substantially higher
retail gross in 1982 than did the British cinema.[11] In 1982 the
ever-shrinking British cinema audience represented one visit to the
cinema per Briton per year. In fact the audience was more than ever
slanted to teenagers and young adults; the remaining audience was
also by now somewhat up-market in social class terms. Instead of
the huge picture palaces of old, if you ventured into a British cinema
you were likely to share the experience with less than 100 other
people. British film exhibition was dominated each year by a few
large grossing Hollywood distributed films, typically heavily promoted on television; while a few films still grossed in the millions of
pounds, many feature films grossed under £50,000 throughout
Britain.
   The flood of films on television which began in 1964 still continued. In 1981 three British TV channels showed 951 feature films –
some of the most popular material on TV at some of the lowest

prices to acquire. Prices paid for TV showings of the few very popular films were moving up, but there were still large supplies of American, European and Asian super-cheap feature films – which Channel Four duly started to show, raising the total in 1983 to some 25 feature films per week on British television. These films of course receive national promotion on television, something which the distributors of most cinema films cannot afford.

Some cinema films manage to acquire free publicity on television programmes of new film excerpts. And more Britons see such programmes than go to the cinema; for example, in the winter of 1979–80 the main BBC film programme was seen by about 3.5 million each week,[12] whereas only some 2 million people were visiting the cinema each week.[13]

Despite the now nearly non-existent home market, and the near total retreat of the former British majors from production, a British film industry continues. To simplify only a little, Britain makes three kinds of films: First, London acts as one of the main out-of-town production centres for Hollywood, specializing in multi-million dollar budget fantasy, science fiction, and special effects – the Superman, James Bond,[14] and Star Wars series for example – although these often do location work in two or three other countries as well. Second, there are the 'little pictures' with budgets on the scale of TV drama, greatly boosted since 1982 by patronage from Channel Four. Thirdly there is an uneasy middle range of British films – some aspiring to join the multi-million dollar major Hollywood distributor ranks, others closer to the 'little picture' model.

1983, the seventieth anniversary of American dominance in British cinemas, was marked by the appearance of another Monopolies and Mergers Commission report on *Films*. Even more pessimistic and fatalistic than in its 1966 report, the Commission confirmed that, yes, two exhibition chains and two closely allied (and Hollywood dominated) distributor groups had strengthened their combined monopoly position. However, no, nothing much could be done about it. Indeed the Commission foresaw the home video market as likely to close yet more cinemas.

As usual, other industry observers were more optimistic. British films won the Best Film Oscar in both 1982 and 1983, which some saw as indicating the imminence of revival. Also in 1983 an optimistic government White Paper on Cable stressed both the centrality of feature films as the prime attraction of Cable and also the export prospects for British industry.

CHAPTER SEVEN

Newspapers: slow fade

Television has transformed the press and may kill it entirely. Thus goes one familiar argument. Almost equally familiar, however, is the reverse: the press is disgustingly alive and well, living more wickedly and profitably than ever.

Both lines of argument are enabled to persist for several reasons: Even without television, or without commerical television, there would have been some kind of electronic 'press revolution'. The press in many ways has retained roughly its previous share of the action; or to change the metaphor, television is the icing on the cake but the cake itself remains the press. Much of the difference of opinion, perhaps especially in Britain, concerns the future. Will those two Toronto sages, Roy Thomson and Marshall McLuhan, eventually be proved correct – by a mass slaughter of newspapers and the migration of classified advertising into video-land?

As an introduction we can list some ways in which the British press has been significantly altered in the age of (if not by) television:

1. *Sales decline*: In the 25 years after the arrival of commercial television the total daily sale of newspapers in Britain dropped from around 30 million to about 23 million (Figure 3) – a decline of over a quarter in sales against population. The biggest drop was in London evening sales; there were huge drops in Sunday sales, provincial dailies, in weekly papers and in magazines. But – a major exception – national morning dailies have remained at around 15 million throughout the post-war period. A huge contraction in middle-brow daily sales has been compensated by increases in the tabloid 'naughties' led by *The Sun* and in the weighty haughties, led by the *Daily Telegraph*. (Figures 4, 5)
2. *Share of advertising*. The press has been remarkably successful in holding on to about two-thirds of all British advertising expenditure (Table 9) since around 1960. But, of course, before 1955 the press had almost all media advertising and a new phase of slow decline against TV and radio began in 1973–74.
3. *Pattern of ownership*. Television has played its part in a change in ownership pattern. Press companies were allowed to buy

FIGURE 3: BRITISH NEWSPAPER CIRCULATIONS, 1920-82

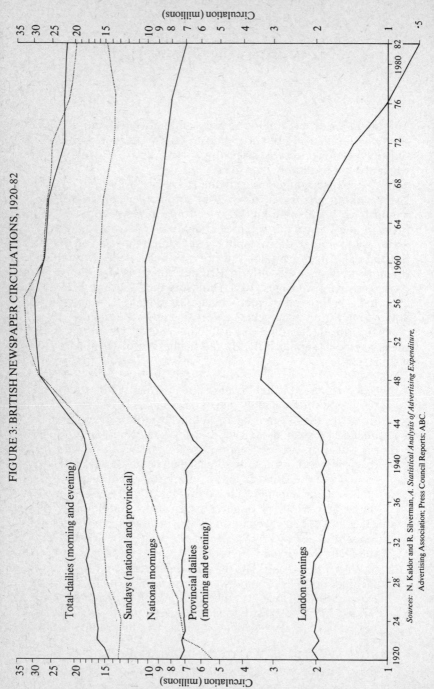

Total-dailies (morning and evening)

Sundays (national and provincial)

National mornings

Provincial dailies (morning and evening)

London evenings

Sources: N. Kaldor and R. Silverman. *A. Statistical Analysis of Advertising Expenditure,* Advertising Association; Press Council Reports; ABC.

FIGURE 4: POPULAR NATIONAL DAILY NEWSPAPER CIRCULATIONS

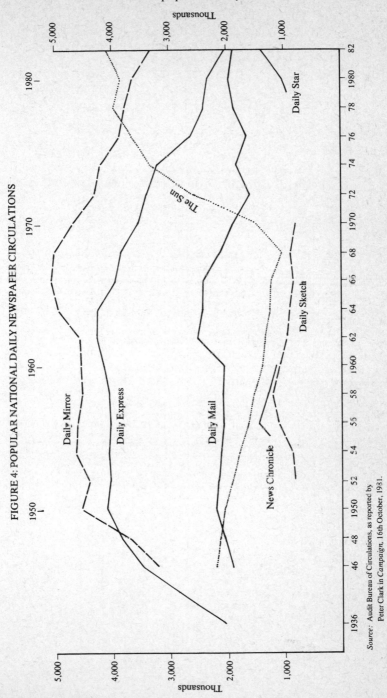

Source: Audit Bureau of Circulations, as reported by
Peter Clark in *Campaign*, 16th October, 1931.

TABLE 9

BRITISH ADVERTISING EXPENDITURE: PERCENTAGES BY MEDIA

Year	1954	55	56	57	58	59	1960	61	62	63	64	65	66	1967
						Percentages of totals								
National newspapers	17·2	18·8	19·8	19·4	18·9	20·1	19·8	18·9	19·8	20·2	20·7	21·3	20·6	18·3
Regional newspapers	31·2	31·8	29·4	26·6	24·1	23·8	23·8	23·7	23·0	22·6	23·6	21·1	20·4	23·6
Magazines & periodicals	18·5	17·6	16·2	14·0	13·3	12·5	12·4	11·8	11·2	11·9	11·1	11·6	11·7	10·0
Trade & technical press	13·4	11·9	11·2	10·8	10·0	9·2	9·6	9·5	9·5	9·2	8·9	9·4	10·1	9·4
Directories	1·3	1·1	1·0	0·9	1·2	0·7	0·6	0·6	0·6	0·8	0·7	1·0	1·2	1·5
Press production costs	6·4	6·3	6·6	5·9	5·2	5·1	4·6	4·4	4·6	4·6	4·3	4·4	4·4	4·4
Total press	88·0	87·5	84·2	77·6	72·7	71·4	70·9	68·9	68·7	69·3	69·3	68·8	68·4	67·2
Television	—	1·1	5·6	13·1	19·3	20·9	22·3	24·6	25·0	24·5	24·5	25·7	25·5	27·1
Poster & transport	8·9	8·6	7·6	6·8	6·0	5·9	5·0	4·7	4·6	4·6	4·3	3·6	4·0	3·9
Cinema	2·5	2·2	2·0	2·3	1·6	1·5	1·5	1·5	1·4	1·3	1·4	1·5	1·4	1·3
Radio	0·7	0·7	0·6	0·5	0·4	0·4	0·3	0·3	0·3	0·3	0·5	0·5	0·7	0·4
TOTAL ALL MEDIA	100·0	100·0	100·0	100·0	100·0	100·0	100·0	100·0	100·0	100·0	100·0	100·0	100·0	100·0

Year	1968	69	70	71	72	73	74	1975	76	77	78	79	1980	1981	1982
					percentages of totals										
National newspapers	19·7	20·4	19·5	18·3	18·4	18·3	17·8	16·8	16·6	16·7	16·1	16·3	16·7	16·6	16·5
Regional newspapers	24·1	24·8	25·8	25·7	26·5	29·3	30·4	29·3	27·9	26·4	26·3	27·9	25·0	24·3	23·6
Magazines & periodicals	9·9	9·7	9·2	9·1	8·5	8·2	7·9	8·2	7·7	7·7	7·8	8·5	7·5	7·1	6·7
Trade & technical press	9·1	9·2	9·6	8·8	8·6	8·4	8·9	8·9	8·7	8·9	9·2	9·5	8·4	7·9	7·9
Directories	1·6	1·7	2·0	2·2	2·1	1·9	1·8	2·1	2·6	2·9	2·7	2·5	3·2	3·4	4·0
Press productions costs	4·6	5·3	6·1	6·6	6·2	5·3	5·3	5·1	4·9	4·9	5·2	5·6	5·1	5·2	4·9
Total press	69·0	71·1	72·2	70·7	70·3	71·4	72·1	70·2	68·4	67·5	67·4	70·3	65·9	64·5	63·5
Television	25·6	23·7	22·6	24·2	24·9	24·0	22·6	24·4	25·8	26·6	26·3	22·1	27·1	28·7	29·7
Poster & transport	4·0	3·9	4·0	3·9	3·7	3·5	3·8	3·6	3·6	3·6	3·7	4·4	4·2	4·1	4·0
Cinema	1·2	1·1	1·1	1·0	1·0	0·8	0·9	0·7	0·7	0·6	0·7	0·8	0·7	0·6	0·6
Radio	0·2	0·2	0·2	0·2	0·1	0·2	0·7	0·1	1·5	1·7	1·9	2·4	2·1	2·1	2·2
TOTAL ALL MEDIA	100·0	100·0	100·0	100·0	100·0	100·0	100·0	100·0	100·0	100·0	100·0	100·0	100·0	100·0	100·0

Source: Advertising Association data reported in: M. J. Waterson, 'Satellites, cable and wild, wild women', *Admap*, October 1982.

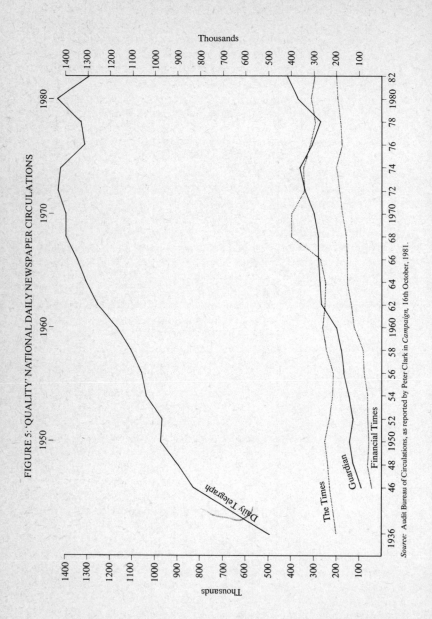

FIGURE 5: 'QUALITY' NATIONAL DAILY NEWSPAPER CIRCULATIONS

Thousands

Daily Telegraph

The Times

Guardian

Financial Times

Source: Audit Bureau of Circulations, as reported by Peter Clark in *Campaign*, 16th October, 1981.

into commercial television – a vital first step in the transfer of the ownership of the press to conglomerates whose prime interest was in other industries and/or other countries. In the 1950s typical press owners had been eccentric individuals – some had inherited from founding fathers. Their goals were an unpredictable mixture of profit, politics and family tradition. The further the British media moved into the new era of television and multi-media conglomerates, the more such old-fashioned eccentric motivation weakened. Family con- trollers of several national newspapers and many provincial and magazine companies simply ran out of motivation. Some modestly profitable newspapers were sold for 20 or 30 times their annual profits to corporate managers confident of their ability to extract higher profit levels. But some conglomerates bought (mainly national) papers as prestige tax losses.

4. *Content of the press* changed significantly. Television became the great entertainer and provider (with radio) of vivid news summaries. Serious newspapers boomed; the populars be- came tabloid supplements to television, with the television schedules and related features increasingly the core of the newspaper.

5. *Audience time and money* spent on the press declined slowly but steadily. The predominant newspaper form – the tabloid – was designed in recognition of these facts.

6. *Press competition increased* in the television age. In the past the British press had experienced alternating decades of in- creasing and decreasing competition. The 1930s saw increas- ing competition, the 1940s – with newsprint rationing – a decrease. The 1950s saw increasing, and the 1960s decreasing, competition. However the increasingly competitive 1970s have been followed by further increases in competition in the 1980s.

The Press reflects British history, and caricatures social divisions
Britain's history of gradual change, and its lack of recent revolutions and invasions, is reflected in its press. One of the commonest birth dates for surviving provincial newspapers is 1870. Some newspapers are older – most of the most prestigious ones are; the commonest birth period for popular national papers is around 1900. In most comparable countries some kind of war or revolution has scythed down many of the old titles. But in contrast to Paris, Berlin or New York, only mild versions of such shocks have been experienced in Britain; management and labour reflect this tradition as does the survival until the 1980s of the British national press among narrow crowded streets in the heart of western Europe's largest city.

Apart from television, the nearest thing to revolution experienced by the British press in recent decades has been Rupert Murdoch. But his first British title was the Sunday *News of the World*, which was launched in 1843, and already had over a century's experience of crime news, populism, titillation and sport. His national daily, *The Sun*, was a relative newcomer (born 1912) but had – before Murdoch's extravagant TV promotion – in the 1930s (as the *Daily Herald*) been in the forefront of buying circulation with free insurance, saucepans, and the collected works of Charles Dickens.

In addition to its age and its connoisseur's collection of exotic labour practices, the British press in its own industrial and marketing structure unintentionally caricatures Britain in other ways. It further exaggerates the very considerable polarisation between London and 'the provinces', between the middle class and working class, and between the well and less well educated.

That Fleet Street dominates in sales is often regarded as something which dates back to the founding of *The Times* in 1785. In fact Fleet Street national morning sales only passed those of the combined provincial dailies in 1923 (Figure 3), when the 'Northcliffe Revolution' of halfpenny morning papers was being consolidated by the printing of satellite editions in Manchester. Between 1920 and 1938 sales of Fleet Street national morning dailies increased from 5 to 10 million; by 1948 sales reached 15 million. This rapid trend towards London dominance paralleled similar developments in industry and politics. But the sales dominance of Fleet Street went further, with the construction of chains of provincial newspapers – many of them local monopolies. In the years 1929–34 26 competing provincial dailies were closed leaving in 1934 only 125 remaining. This led to a division of labour by which provincial papers made money (and in some cases delivered votes) while Fleet Street papers pursued prestige and in some cases charged for it with losses. This division was also reflected by time of publication; the national dailies were all morning papers (containing the serious news of politics, finance and sport) while the provincials were primarily *evening* papers, carrying little national news.

Other real British distinctions which are exaggerated by the structure of the press include those of social class and education. The 1947–49 Royal Commission referred to 'quality' and 'popular' national newspapers. Other nations have had similar distinctions – in France the *Grand* and *Petit* press – but in Britain this tradition is peculiarly long; it dates back to *The Times* and its radical rivals of the 1830s. To some extent the distinction between the large size prestige papers of the 1980s and the popular tabloids reflects real differences in education, reader interest and income. These real

FIGURE 6: NATIONAL NEWSPAPER READERS:
SOCIAL CLASS AND AGE, 1981

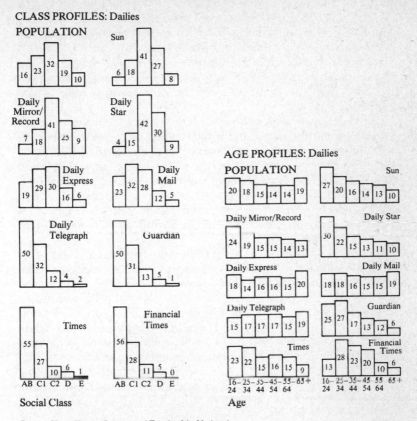

Source: Harry Henry, 'Patterns and Trends of the National
Newspaper Press', *Admap*, September 1982, pp. 501-16.

differences have become exaggerated because the two types of
paper have not only, since the 1970s, acquired different physical
sizes, but they rely on different prime sources of revenue. The
'prestige' papers operate primarily from an *advertising* revenue
base; this forces them 'up market' more than a sales revenue base
would require – because advertisers are willing to pay several times
as much to reach readers who are several times as wealthy.

The popular tabloids take advertising but the low prices charged
per thousand readers means that they spend most of the resulting
revenue on the paper, production, ink and wage costs of putting
these advertisements into the paper; they operate from a primary
sales revenue base, which forces them to try to maximise sales. This

tendency has probably existed at least since 1930 when the *Daily Herald* began to recruit large numbers of working-class people who had previously not read a daily (Figure 7). The tabloids also sell a much larger proportion of copies at newsagents (and less than the prestige papers in home delivery) which also encourages what critics regard as 'lowest common denominator' visual appeal.

In terms of education and income, therefore, nearly all the national papers appeal either well below or well above what might be regarded as the 'real' level of the large central bulk of the population.

A further way in which the British press may seem to caricature British national characteristics is the struggle between strong printing trade unions and multi-millionaire owners. There are elements of an Ealing comedy in this because both sides know that trade union featherbedding, although real, certainly costs the industry overall less than it obtains in government *de facto* subsidy through Value Added Tax zero-rating. In effect the combined power of newspaper owners and trade unions results in the government subsidizing overmanning.

Nevertheless the British press as an industry lacks a vision of its own goals and priorities. It lacks an effective trade association – like for example the American Newspaper Publishers' Association (ANPA) which has vigorously pursued a coherent collective industry policy of political lobbying, commercial and technical research, innovation in technology, and aggressive opposition to trade unions. The British press, both in its own industrial behaviour and its front page news presentation, exaggerates the real national obsession with industrial relations. It also tends, in handling its own problems, towards unrealistic enthusiasm for the currently fashionable solution; in the 1960s this was 'realistic cover prices', and in the 1970s 'new technology'.

Much confusion derives from misunderstandings of American practice and its relevance to Britain. But also the British press industry's currently favoured solutions vary from decade to decade, because competitive conditions themselves have a habit of going into reverse about every ten years.

1930s' competition, 1940s' deepfreeze, 1950s' competition

In 1930 and 1937 five national dailies each had sales of over a million. But competition was less fierce than this suggests. The supposedly big clash of the Conservative press was between Lord Beaverbrook's rising *Daily Express* and Lord Rothermere's sinking *Daily Mail*; but their political co-operation (Empire free trade) also extended into the commercial sphere – until 1934 Rothermere's group owned 49% of Beaverbrook's *Evening Standard*.

FIGURE 7: PENETRATION OF NATIONAL
    MORNING NEWSPAPERS BY INCOME GROUPS, 1935

(Percentage of families in various income groups taking
 each National Daily in 1935
 Depth of block proportional to number of families in group)

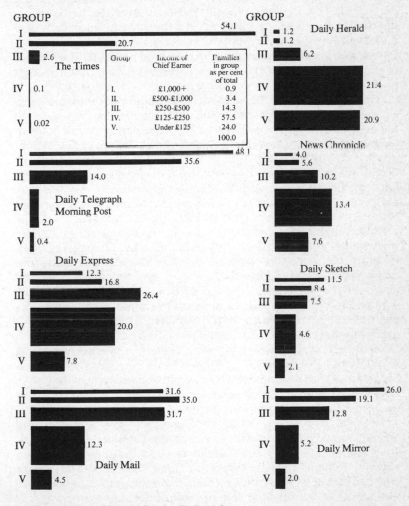

Group	Income of Chief Earner	Families in group as per cent of total
I.	£1,000+	0.9
II.	£500-£1,000	3.4
III.	£250-£500	14.3
IV.	£125-£250	57.5
V.	Under £125	24.0
		100.0

Source: Political and Economic Planning, *The British Press,*
    London: PEP, 1938.

Rothermere's family also in 1930 owned the *Daily Mirror* and by 1935 the *Mirror* under new ownership was still an up-market second newspaper (Figure 7). The *News Chronicle* (a 1930 merger of the *Daily News* and *Daily Chronicle*) was owned by the Cadbury chocolate family in the Liberal interest and – as usually with this mould of paper – it was losing market share steadily in the 1930s.

The sales promotion wars around 1930 were largely instigated by a single newspaper, the *Daily Herald*, which was pursuing Labour party goals with capitalist fervour. However even the *Herald* was a less than overwhelming challenge to the others, because it was building its big sale heavily out of genuinely working-class people, a fair proportion of whom even by 1935 still did not read a daily paper (Figure 7). Its sales fervour was creating the daily habit in new readers.

Although far from being a decade of all-out national press competition, the 1930s were extremely competitive compared with the 1940s. When the war came in 1939 circulations were pegged. Newsprint was very severely rationed and in 1945 paper consumption was down to only a quarter of 1939 levels; with dollar problems, this rationing continued. In 1947 the national dailies were still only between a quarter and a third of their pre-war size.

But in several other respects newsprint rationing was the answer to a newspaper owner's prayers. While pages were cut back, the sale price stayed the same and there was a surplus of advertising; selling a newspaper of one-third size but at the full retail price was extremely profitable. For a short period sales were allowed to expand – and the *Daily Mirror*'s sale boomed – but in 1947 the dollar crisis and devaluation brought back severe restrictions.

Fleet Street managers liked newsprint rationing and were reluctant to see it go. Beaverbrook in 1946 claimed that the government had given the press four new freedoms – freedom from competition, advertising revenue, newsprint and freedom from enterprise. *The Times* became increasingly restless with the harsh restriction on pages. In 1955 as the ending of these controls approached, only *The Times* was enthusiastic. The others actually wanted the government to dismantle the controls more slowly.[1]

This was with good reason, because the 1950s were already turning out to be a very competitive decade. Commercial television arrived in 1955 and in 1958 already passed the total advertising revenue of the national newspapers (Table 9). This coincided with both the ending of newsprint rationing and the unfreezing of other forces of change artificially held in check since 1939.

FIGURE 8: THE BERMUDA TRIANGLE AND
THE DEATH OF NATIONAL NEWSPAPERS

('the last reported position of those national
newspapers that have sunk since 1955, as well as the
current (1977) plots of the survivors'. Michael
Mander)

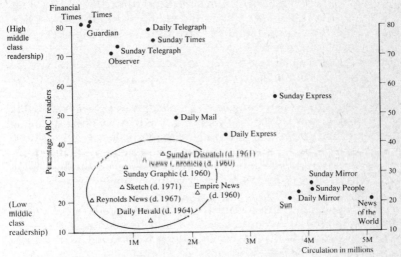

Note:
The seven national newspapers which died between 1960 and 1971 – four of them in
1960-61 – are shown in the circle of lowish circulation and low percentage of ABC1
readers. The survivors were all higher on circulation and/or ABC1 percentage.

Source:
Michael Mander, 'The Integration of advertising and circulation sales policies', in Harry Henry (ed.),
Behind the Headlines, 1978, p.79.

1960s: the golden age of limited competition

Around 1960 the British press was seen to be in a state of crisis, and
there was another widely acknowledged crisis around 1970. But in
between lay the 1960s which was – especially for newspaper managers now looking back in retrospect – an entire decade of muted
competition, a golden age of high standards and high profits.

Just as 1970 marked the transition back to competition, so 1960
had marked the transition from 'excessive' competition in the late
1950s to the mature and tranquil 1960s – a decade presided over by
Lord Roy Thomson and Cecil King.

In 1960 occurred some spectacular newspaper closures. In October 1960 the national morning *News Chronicle* and *The Star* (a
London evening) were closed by the Cadbury family – an overnight

combined loss of some 1.9 million daily sales. This led to the setting
up of the Shawcross Royal Commission on the Press in March, 1961.
However the newspaper deaths around this time had three other
aspects:

1. Three national Sunday papers – *the Empire News* (actually
    Manchester published), *Sunday Dispatch* and *Sunday Graphic*
    – all closed between October 1960 and June 1961. With lowish
    sales (average: 1·5 million) and mainly working-class reader-
    ships these three fatalities – like others – all belonged to the
    Bermuda Triangle (Figure 8).
2. Five provincial *mornings* – in Nottingham, Brighton, Man-
    chester, Birmingham and Glasgow – all closed between 1948
    and 1961.
3. The provincial evening field saw a major wave of closures; the
    peak year was 1963 (the year after the Royal Commission had
    finished its labours) – evenings with total sales of some 650,000
    copies closed in Birmingham, Nottingham, Manchester,
    Leicester, Leeds and Edinburgh, leaving all of these large
    cities with one remaining monopoly evening.[2]

All of these deaths were doubtless unfortunate, but the more benign
face of the 1960s was represented by Thomson and by Cecil King at
IPC – two mammoth new organisations both aided by the early
commercial television dividends and both fuelled by monopoly
profits, but both dedicated to enlightened journalism, business
efficiency, and muted partisanship.

It was in July 1959 that Roy Thomson bought control of the
Sunday Times and the Kemsley chain from Lord Kemsley. Thomson's cash reserves and credit rating stood high from his majority
holding in Scottish Television. Thomson was regarded as unusual
because of his lack of partisanship; the core of his empire was the
regional papers – renamed Thomson Regional Newspapers – to
which he applied advertising sales techniques previously used in
Wolverhampton but not widely known in Britain. Thomson was
disarmingly modest in public and his commercial tactics although
aggressive, lacked any quality of bruising sales competition. The
Sunday Times set the prestige newspaper pace, and the regional
papers helped to establish political neutrality as the acceptable face
of local press monopoly.

The other pace-setting organisation was the International Publishing Corporation which also made press concentration respectable and helped to banish fierce competition. IPC was the result of a
series of mergers, the last of which involved the *Daily Mirror* group
in acquiring Odham's. This gave IPC some 200 magazines, and

much printing capacity. It united the *Daily Mirror*, already the national circulation leader, with the sinking *Daily Herald*, thus putting both pro-Labour national dailies – and in 1961 a 6 million daily combined sale – under one management. IPC and Cecil King were willing to accept the burden of the *Daily Herald* and re-launched it as *The Sun* in 1964; the latter was known as 'King's Cross', and it continued the long sales slide.

But IPC was widely regarded as a good thing. The existence of two popular pro-Labour dailies calmed anxieties on all sides of national politics. The *Daily Mirror* was the daily popular leader throughout the 1960s, reaching its sales peak of 5·28 million in late 1967. It did this without increased sensationalism; in retrospect we can see that the *Mirror* did so well because the down-market competition was so feeble – *The Sun* (with which it had a big readership overlap) and the *Daily Sketch* (the *Daily Mail*'s anaemic stable companion).

The *Daily Mirror* in the 1960s was much admired, as it made gallant efforts to include small doses of enlightenment. It and *The Sun*'s partisanship were right-wing Labour; Cecil King as the IPC Chairman fitted the role of the eccentric press lord – he delighted in treating the world in general and Prime Ministers in particular in a truly Kingly manner.

Thomson and King, while quite different personalities and not on especially friendly terms, had much in common. Both were 'characters', basically decent men, getting on in years; both had been extremely lucky, both were buoyed up by press monopoly and television profits, both could afford to adopt all the most acceptable and least competitive public positions. They believed that 'responsibility' and profit could be combined. They were against cheap sensationalism, and the support of Thomson and IPC was central to a consensus against crude journalism which gave the Press Council some weight. Foreign correspondents were numerous, new fields of journalism were pioneered.

The prestige papers also did well, with the *Sunday Times* setting the pace. *The Guardian*, which had started its London print in 1960 established itself as another serious national daily. The *Financial Times* also had its great period of expansion; the *Daily Telegraph* continued its sales advance with the *Sunday Telegraph* launched in 1961.

The 1960s were a golden age indeed.

The 1970s: return of press competition

The year 1969–70 marks a distinct change in the competitive atmosphere. The single event which symbolises this change was the sale of *The Sun* by IPC to young Rupert Murdoch in November,

1969. *The Sun* quickly became the pacesetter in a return to old-fashioned bruising competition.

Behind the transformation of *The Sun* lay two broader sets of factors: first the break-up of the IPC–Thomson consensus on muted press competition; secondly, there were major economic forces affecting the British economy in general, varying from sterling devaluation in 1967 to the world oil price rise in 1973, which profoundly affected the press.

Even before 1969–70 there were signs that competition was hotting up. The prestige national daily field was at this time the most competitive; *The Guardian* was in difficulties for much of the 1960s and *The Times* was sold by the Astor family to Thomson in 1967. And 1968 saw a take-over battle for the *News of the World*, won by Rupert Murdoch in January, 1969.

But perhaps more significant than Murdoch's arrival was the decline and fall of IPC. The International Publishing Corporation, with its typically grandiose title, had acquired excessive numbers of failing magazines and old printing presses, an excess of liberal wishful thinking and a lack of strategic managerial insight. The declining profit performance of IPC led to the sacking of Cecil King as Chairman in 1968 and the take-over by Reed in 1970. During the intervening period, under Hugh Cudlipp's Chairmanship, IPC made several disastrous decisions. The *Daily Mirror* – IPC's one enormously profitable publication – was losing touch with both its readers and with financial reality. 'Mirrorscope' – launched in January, 1968 – was a twice-a-week semi-educational four-page feature which epitomized IPC's right-wing Labour belief in enlightenment for the masses. Lack of financial realism was typified by the launch of a weekly colour magazine for the *Daily Mirror* in October, 1969. This lost money on an epic scale, and the advertising was so priced that the more pages were sold the more money would be lost.[3] Next month and with money gushing out of the front door, Cudlipp and IPC compounded their errors by selling *The Sun* to Murdoch. *The Sun* was sold on give-away terms in order to avoid redundancy payments; the *Daily Mirror* magazine was launched to use up spare printing capacity at Odham's in Watford. In 1970 one of Reed's first decisions on taking over IPC was to close the *Mirror* magazine. Murdoch not only printed *The Sun* on the *News of the World*'s presses but set out to produce a daily version of that naughty Sunday. No 'Mirrorscope' enlightenment for him, but nude females and bruising competition instead.

At its take-over, *The Sun* was selling about one million copies. This was doubled in less than two years and by late 1973 *The Sun* had reached 3 million. *The Sun* set out in pursuit of the *Daily Mirror* which it eventually passed in 1978. But more importantly *The Sun*'s arrival signalled the rapid transformation of the popular newspaper scene from a fairly decorous contest, led by King's tabloid *Daily Mirror* and the large size *Daily Express*, into an all-tabloid endless circulation war.

Associated Newspapers closed its sinking *Daily Sketch* in 1971 and re-launched its also sinking *Daily Mail* as a tabloid in both size and character. The popular daily revolution was completed by the *Daily Express* going tabloid in 1977, and then – as its sales continued to slide – launching another tabloid, the *Daily Star*, initially to keep busy its Manchester presses. Britain now had five national daily tabloids. Their perpetual sales war was characterised by even more expensive promotion. Murdoch initiated massive television advertising – spending £2 million on TV promotion of *The Sun* in 1971. The *Daily Star* initiated Bingo in 1981, using large cash prizes – and TV promotion – to entice new readers.

The transformation of competition in the 1970s also involved a change of approach by Thomson. Roy Thomson – nervous of too much dependence on advertising revenue – diversified into non-media activities, such as travel, and then into oil exploration in the North Sea. His investment in *The Times* was paid for by the profits of the *Sunday Times* but it distracted public attention from two other major facets of Thomson activity. One was the concentration on Thomson Regional Newspapers as the provider of monopoly profits and positive cash flow (at cost of future competitive dangers); secondly the cash flow went increasingly into North Sea oil where it was ultimately so profitable as to transform Thomson into an oil-based conglomerate. This in turn was a major step towards the conglomeratization of the entire British press.

More broadly the conglomeratization of the press – with its implications for maintaining an overcrowded level of competition – which occurred in the 1970s, derived from the general state of the British and world economics. The British press in the 1970s found itself experiencing an exaggerated version of the standard trade cycle – with years of crisis and years of huge profits alternating rapidly. Many costs rose dizzily. Newsprint nearly doubled in price within a single year in 1973–74 thus accelerating the tabloid trend. Revenue also shot up and down. 1973 was a spectacularly good year for press advertising – with many newspapers having to turn away advertisers (some of whom went into freesheets). 1974 and 1975 saw the reverse, an excess of press capacity and an advertising famine. Inflation also led to frequent cover-price increases, which, some newspapers then found, led to permanent circulation losses.

The 1970s woes of Fleet Street were epitomised by the *Daily Express*; when its owner, Lord Beaverbrook, died in 1964 the *Express* was still selling 4·2 million copies a day. Between 1970 and early 1983 the *Daily Express* had seven editors, its cover price rose in eleven jumps and by 1,440%, it shrank to tabloid size, and had three separate ownerships (in 1967 it was bought by Trafalgar House, and in 1982 demerged into Fleet Holdings). By late 1982 its circulation was below 2 million copies, less than half its 1964 sale.

The 1980s: the competitive pace quickens again
The new decade of the 1980s opened with a series of events, each an ominous warning to the press of increased competitive pressures. The 1980s were going to be the second consecutive decade in which competition quickened. The most financially rewarding press areas – such as women's weekly magazines (next chapter) and provincial evening newspapers – were in the late 1970s already experiencing fresh competition.

The events around 1980 included the year long closedown of Times Newspapers (November 1978 to November 1979); the passing of the Broadcasting Act in 1980 and the setting up of a fourth television channel; the first Bingo promotional war of 1981–2. Beyond the media, the economic depression had its own severe consequences; most notably the huge growth in unemployment led to a massive contraction from 1980 in job advertising – the great mainstay of the provincial evening press and of the prestige national press.

As the British press enters the new age of multi-channel electronic media a number of previously existing dilemmas are exacerbated, and some may remain acute for the remainder of the 1980s. The excessive number of Fleet Street titles is not only a cause of frenetic competition, it is also an effect of such competition. For example, the decline of the *Daily Express* played a part in the launching of two new national dailies, the *Daily Star* (launched in 1979 to help the *Daily Express*) and the *Mail on Sunday* (launched in 1982 and intended to kill the *Sunday Express*) which itself was involved in a new trend towards glossy colour magazines and sections given away with Fleet Street populars.

A related dilemma is posed by the subsidization of Fleet Street titles by conglomerates. How can Fleet Street achieve more realistic and efficient proportions when corporate godfathers insist on subsidizing excess – excess manning, excess capacity, excessive sensationalism, and excessive numbers of titles?

Another dilemma concerns the struggle between the national press and the provincial press. In the 1960s and 1970s each survived by going its own way. The national press had about two-thirds of sales, all the prestige, and all the problems, including too little advertising. The provincial dailies in the 1970s had about one-third of sales, little prestige, little competition and the lion's share of newspaper advertising. In 1973–6 the regional newspapers had nearly twice as much advertising as the nationals (Table 9). But while they prided themselves on efficient management, the provincial press managers failed to realise that their success was insecurely based. The previous golden financial decade for the provincial press, the 1940s, resulted from the accidents of newsprint rationing, which pushed advertising out of Fleet Street into the provincials. The golden 1970s were built on a virtual monopoly of local advertising. But around 1980 all of this was changing; in particular the provincial dailies were losing advertising and sales in a rapid spiral of decline – with the rampaging growth of freesheets and the steady growth of local radio. While 42% of UK adults read a provincial evening in 1970, only 32% did so in 1981/82.

Whereas the national press is increasingly challenged by television, the national and provincial dailies seem determined to fight each other to the death. Yet the Fleet Street nationals can never seize the provincials' advertising; and the provincial dailies – being mainly in the evening – are fighting against the overwhelming international trend towards daily newspapers as a primarily *morning* medium. While television eats into the (provincial) evenings' audience, it also eats into the national mornings' display advertising.

The extraordinarily rapid growth of freesheets dates largely from the late 1970s although Murdoch and others dabbled in the area from 1969 on. The freesheets threaten mainly the paid-for local weeklies, which have always been a strong part of the provincial press scene in Britain. But they could become the dominant provincial press medium – especially if the provincial evenings continue to wither before the combined assaults of national morning tabloids and national television. With some four fifths of national morning newspaper sales already consisting of tabloids, further major incursions of local freesheets could lead to a tarnished tabloid-cum-giveaway image for all newspapers, except the remaining national prestige papers – themselves supported by corporate godfathers.

The Times encapsulates the dilemmas of the prestige press. It was controlled by Colonel Astor and family until 1967, by Thomson until 1981, and then by Murdoch. *The Observer* was owned by David Astor and family until 1976, by Atlantic Richfield (oil-based conglomerate) of Los Angeles until 1981, and then by Mr 'Tiny' Rowland and Lonrho (another highly controversial conglomerate). The *Financial Times* is already owned by a bank-based conglomerate. *The Guardian* is always achieving new triumphs but its source of subsidy, the *Manchester Evening News*, suffered severe sales and advertising losses from the late 1970s. The *Sunday Telegraph* has been in trouble since its birth and the *Daily Telegraph* may be the leading sick man among the haughties in the 1980s. It is all very sad. But the name of the disease is excessive competition; the dilemma is acute, because nobody wants to believe this unpalatable fact. Resuscitation by corporate godfathers cannot cure the disease, but it can keep the paper – and the dilemma – alive, perhaps for a long time.

A popular line in diagnosis points towards trade union malpractice, for which the already fashionable cure – further popularized by the McGregor Royal Commission on the Press (1974–77) – has been 'new technology'. Electronic printing, computer storage, and direct keyboarding of copy by journalists is an American prescription suited to American local press monopoly conditions. In Britain it may achieve some considerable savings, but basically it is not the solution because the initial diagnosis is mistaken. Union malpractice is only a symptom; the disease is excessive competition (nationally) and *was* also excessive monopoly (regionally).

'New technology' has an important part to play, but in addition to real benefits it is a prescription with some side effects. In order to get it installed, management has to make special payments (often regarded as a major aspect of the union disease). New technology leads to considerably earlier deadlines which is not the most obvious way for the press to compete with burgeoning non-stop electronic news.

Moreover in practice 'new technology' in Britain has often exacerbated the classic problem of surplus printing capacity. Many provincial newspapers in the heady 1970s re-equipped with modern plant of much bigger capacity than previously, just as they were about to enter a period of lower sales, lower advertising, lower pagination. Fleet Street cheerfully followed. Excess printing capacity has been behind many dubious decisions in the British press and the 1980s may well continue this tradition.

CHAPTER EIGHT

Magazines

Magazines are volatile things. Readerships age, editors lose their sure touch, and new cohorts of magazines come forward. Successful magazines – like films – produce a flock of imitators; some attack the success head on, some try to remove a particular slice of its market. Major magazine companies typically 'kill' or merge 10% of their titles each year, while launching a similar proportion of new titles – some of which themselves may be killed after only a few weeks.

In any country the magazine industry is shaped in part by the newspaper and radio/television industry. Nations with mainly local newspapers (USA) or with restricted television advertising (West Germany) tend to have a strong magazine sector. In Britain magazines are weak, mainly because national newspapers and television dominate the national audience and get the cream of national advertising. Magazines – badly hit by commercial television – attracted 32% of advertising in 1954, but only 22% of advertising revenue in 1960, and 15% in 1982 (Table 9). Perhaps the largest single example is the women's weekly magazines – with titles like *Woman* and *Woman's Own* – which in the 1950s reached proportions of the female public on a scale achieved in no other country by women's *weeklies* (as opposed to women's monthlies). This phenomenon coincided with the early years of television, and as commercial television grew, women's weeklies declined. Their peak circulation of 12·21 million in 1958 fell by almost half to 6·26 million in 1982 (Table 10). But the story of women's weeklies also parallels that of the popular Sunday newspapers, which reached a peak in circulation around the same time. The highest sale for any woman's weekly magazine in Britain was *Woman*'s 3·49 million circulation in early 1957. The *News of the World* peaked a little earlier in 1950 with sales of over 8 million per Sunday maintained from 1949 to 1954.

The British-style Sunday newspaper – traditionally separate from a daily paper – was really a *news* paper only in name. If the Sunday papers are regarded as magazines then their sales plateau in the 1950s is literally the same story as the women's weekly magazines. The point is also made by the subsequent blossoming of glossy colour supplements in the Sunday newspapers.

The rapid rise of the women's weeklies in the 1940s and their

TABLE 10

ADULT WOMEN'S WEEKLY MAGAZINE CIRCULATIONS, 1938–82
(Circulation in thousands January – June each year)

	1938	1950	1960	1970	1980	1982
Woman	750	2,067	3,103	2,148	1,456	1,339
Woman's Own	357	1,605	2,317	1,779	1,551	1,403
Woman's Realm	—	—	1,273	1,069	747	636
Woman's Weekly	498	1,582	1,460	1,735	1,483	1,486
My Weekly	—	197	—	800*	832	750
People's Friend	—	—	—	500	690*	650*
Woman's Mirror	—	—	1,082	—	—	—
Woman's Day	—	—	930	—	—	—
Woman's Illustrated	148	510	705	—	—	—
Woman's World	—	403	—	—	—	—
Woman's Companion	176	226	190	—	—	—
Home Notes	151	346	—	—	—	—
Home Chat	127	321	—	—	—	—
TOTAL	2,207	7,257	11,060	8,031	6,759	6,264

* Estimates for 1980 by Harry Henry; for 1970 and 1982 by the author.
Sources: Cynthia White, *Women's Magazines 1693–1968;* Harry Henry, 'The circulations and readerships of the weekly magazines', *Admap* October 1982; Audit Bureau of circulations (January – June 1982).

decline in the 1960s is but one example of the tendency of *categories* of publications to rise and fall. But within categories there is also an often rapid turnover of titles. The very definitions of categories are also always changing; for example 'Women's' magazines are heavily read by children, and 'young women's' magazines are read by the elderly, by children, and by men of all ages.

Both volatility and stability may also be increased by the presence in Britain of one dominant company – the International Publishing Corporation; in a multiple merger in 1958–61 the Mirror newspaper group acquired four[1] previously separate magazine companies. IPC since then has dominated the big league of women's magazines and many of the most lucrative specialized trade and technical areas. IPC's masters have themselves always been anxious about the dangers of ossification amongst their 200 magazines and have adopted a ruthless corporate attitude towards sinking titles and encroaching opposition. Their preference has been for the massive launch of a new title with promotional heavy artillery – directed against any promising new magazine title on the horizon.

IPC's main competitors are some dozen much smaller companies – but often with 20 or 30 magazine titles – which are typically run in an equally aggressive manner. Amongst these are two important American magazine companies, National Magazine Company (*Good Housekeeping*, *Cosmopolitan*) and Condé Nast (*Vogue*); it is characteristic of British magazine management that the latest American magazine successes are quickly considered for their prospects in Britain, and American research soothsayers are frequently consulted on problems of female life styles, corporate structure, and marketing gimmickry. But while the magazine industry's head is a-whirl with new ideas and new competition, its feet are firmly planted in some very old-fashioned printing arrangements.

Magazines can be small enterprises. But in Britain the magazine scene is dominated by the big boys. First, there is IPC – a big brother indeed with an effective monopoly in key fields which it is highly anxious to protect. The magazine business is also very closely integrated with the *newspaper* business in the case of IPC, and of other major magazine publishers such as D. C. Thomson (of Dundee and comic fame) as well as the other Thomson (of Toronto and oil fame). Moreover the two biggest magazines by far in Britain are *Radio Times* and *TV Times*, the official programme guides of the BBC and the ITV companies.

Polarization: mass general sale v. segmented targets
Table 11 illustrates a general theme of the magazine market in the television age. Of the 25 publications attracting the most display advertising in 1982 thirteen were wholly or partly magazines. But five of these were magazines incorporated into Sunday newspapers. Of the eight straight magazines, the two most highly placed were *TV Times* and *Radio Times*. Five of the publications are women's magazines, and there is *The Economist*, a weekly which actually beat two prestige national dailies. But perhaps the most remarkable performer is *Good Housekeeping* – the only *monthly* publication.

The eight magazines in the list illustrate the fact that magazines overall attract only about half as much total revenue as newspapers. The eight strong magazines in this table also emphasize that while many new magazines are launched, the large advertising revenues usually belong to older publications. Only two of these eight affluent magazines were launched after 1939, and their average date of birth was 1923 (the birth date in fact of *Radio Times*).

Table 11 also shows the extent to which Sunday newspaper magazines dominate Sunday newspaper advertising – in two cases giving the Sunday paper overall more display revenue than its daily stable mate. Of all British consumer magazine advertising about three-tenths goes into Sunday newspaper magazines and about four-tenths into women's magazines. Thus a very few magazines

TABLE 11

LEADERS IN PRESS DISPLAY ADVERTISING REVENUE, 1982

	Title	1982 Display advertising revenue (£ *millions*)
1	Daily Mirror	56·5
2	The Sun	53·8
3	Sunday Express (+ magazine)	53·6
4	Sunday Times (+ magazine)	47·4
5	Daily Mail	45·8
6	Daily Express	44·3
7	News of the World (+ magazine)	42·7
8	Financial Times	41·1
9	Daily Telegraph	38·8
10	TV Times	30·0
11	The Observer (+ magazine)	28·1
12	Radio Times	23·4
13	Sunday Telegraph (+ magazine)	20·5
14	Sunday Mirror	18·1
15	Woman's Own	16·6
16	Sunday People	15·5
17	Daily Star	15·5
18	Woman	15·0
19	The Standard	14·5
20	The Economist	14·3
21	The Guardian	12·3
22	The Times	11·8
23	Woman's Weekly	8·4
24	Good Housekeeping	7·4
25	Woman's Realm	6·8

*The figures are taken from MEAL and are based on card-rates; they relate to *display* only, not classified advertising (which latter accounts for about a quarter of national newspaper and a tenth of consumer magazine advertising).
Source: Admap Feb. 1983, p. 83.

have cornered the mass market, even though most magazines have had to seek out specialized and segmented markets.

Apart from the national newspapers and associated supplements, it is the 'mass' sale magazines which have suffered since 1950, while 'targeted' magazines have prospered. General women's magazines have sunk, while more specialized *monthly* publications aimed at women and teenagers have prospered.

The newspaper magazines are one example of a trend towards

free publications, entirely financed by advertising. This is also true of much of the trade and technical magazine area – a heavily targeted magazine can 'deliver' an entire occupation or industry free of any sales charge to its readers. All of this leads to more dependence on advertising and thus further emphasises the need to deliver either a mass audience, or a carefully defined audience of special interest to advertisers.

These trends towards free material and heavier advertising dependence to some extent derive from American examples. And magazines are – on the whole – more open to international influences than are newspapers. *Good Housekeeping*, in some respects Britain's senior woman's magazine, was launched in 1922 by a Hearst subsidiary. *Cosmopolitan*, the 'new' woman's magazine launched in London fifty years later is in fact a British version of an American magazine, itself a re-launch of another much earlier American magazine named by Hearst after the Hollywood film company he ran for Marion Davies. Magazine trade, however, goes in two directions – *The Economist*'s American sales playing a major part in its affluence.

Mass sale magazines

The big development in women's weekly magazines had scarcely started in 1938. The massive growth occurred after the Second World War, with sales in 1958 more than four times those of 1947 and six times those of 1938.[2]

There was one huge surge in sales in the late 1940s, as newsprint restrictions were lifted for magazines more quickly than for newspapers. Magazine sales boomed again between 1952 and 1958 – as advertisers with goods to sell, magazine publishers with plentiful paper, and housewives tasting unfamiliar affluence, all participated in a great consumer boom. W. D. McClelland has also pointed out that in the late 1950s many young housewives had little experience of choosing non-rationed goods and eagerly sought out the advice offered by the magazines and their advertisers.[3]

Three major new women's weeklies were launched to satisfy the demands of women, some of whom were eager to read several magazines per week. *Woman's Mirror* (1956), *Woman's Realm* (1958) and *Woman's Day* (1958) each quickly reached sales of over one million, but they also overcrowded the market at the very time when commercial television was competing both for advertisers and audiences.

Consequently the women's weekly magazine market plunged from growth and expansion straight into contraction. *Woman's Day* and *Woman's Mirror* were closed in 1961 and 1966 respectively, each with a sale of over 800,000. Since then the sales have continued to fall steadily; the six remaining women's weeklies' collective sale in the early 1980s was about half the total of 1958 and was still falling. The four IPC titles – *Woman*, *Woman's Own*, *Woman's Realm*, and *Woman's Weekly* – lost a quarter of their women's readership in the twelve years 1970–82. But two women's weeklies owned by D. C. Thomson (*My Weekly* and *People's Friend*) have revived into successful long life. With the 1950s high plateau not far behind, it appears that the successful women's weeklies were those launched earliest. *My Weekly* was launched in 1910 and *Women's Weekly* dates from 1911. These dates closely match popular national newspapers.

There have been unsuccessful attempts to launch new women's weeklies. One such attempt was *Candida* expensively launched by IPC in October 1972 and closed after seven issues because it failed to reach its initial 300,000 circulation target. It is sometimes wrongly assumed that such an episode indicates the unprofitable nature of this field. On the contrary such expensive launches are a dreadful warning to competitors not to trespass; meanwhile the still sizeable women's weekly market (shared between IPC and D. C. Thomson on a roughly 3:1 basis) remains profitable. Both the prohibitive cost of the necessary promotional entry fee and the profitability of the established titles is emphasised by IPC Magazines' promotional expenditure – £5·2 million in 1981, much of it for *Woman* and *Woman's Own* and mainly spent on television.

The sales history of the women's weeklies – steep rise in the late 1940s and 1950s, quick decline after 1958 – parallels that of the Sunday newspapers and the *Radio Times* and *TV Times*. But it is also paralleled by popular general 'magazines' – in both magazine and newspaper format.

It is sometimes claimed that *Picture Post* – the highly successful and admired picture magazine of the 1940s – died in May 1957 of wounds inflicted by television. This was not the view of its owner Sir Edward Hulton, nor of Tom Hopkinson who edited the paper in its most successful phase (1940–1950).[4] Hopkinson's own explanation focuses on Edward Hulton, who disliked the leftward slant of *Picture Post* after 1945. *Picture Post* had accidentally been born and achieved rapid success at the perfect moment – shortly before newsprint rationing was introduced at the start of the war in late 1939. Another 'accident' was the early picture editing skills of Stefan Lorant who was also involved in the birth of *Life* magazine. The newsprint rationing favoured *Picture Post* because its sudden success in picture journalism was 'frozen' by the rationing system; in the early and mid 1940s picture magazines were competing primarily with six-page newspapers containing few pictures. *John Bull*, *Everybody's*, *Illustrated*, and *Picture Post* made the 1940s a decade of popular general picture magazines. But by 1950 these 'general' magazines were competing with much larger daily newspapers and with television – both more obvious media for news pictures – as well as *Radio Times*, the women's weeklies and the Sundays. All of these media were setting records and 'general' magazines felt the full blast. Not only *Picture Post*, but the three other major general picture magazines folded.

Somewhat more successful were other general 'magazines' in newspaper format – such as *Weekend*, *Weekly News*, *Titbits*, and *Reveille*. All four of these were published by newspaper companies, could fill spare printing press time, and resembled popular Sunday newspapers without any pretence of carrying news. Three of these publications sank steadily after 1960, with *Reveille* closing in 1979; this left the Scottish orientated *Weekly News* and the American monthly *Reader's Digest* as the only still strong contenders. It was not that the British people did not want any general weekly magazines; merely that they had more than a dozen already – in the form of women's weeklies, Sunday newspapers, and programme guides.

The Sundays: magazines in newspaper format

Sunday newspapers can be regarded simply as magazines in newspaper format. True the British Sundays do traditionally contain some news from Saturday – primarily sport. The sports news is heavily editionised – Scottish and Welsh football in the early editions, London football in the last edition – but national Sundays have unusually early deadlines and have trouble accommodating late finishing sports such as cricket. This in turn stems from a century-old tradition of a separate distribution system for Sundays, dating from Victorian reluctance by sabbath-observing distributors such as W. H. Smith to handle *Sunday* newspapers.

One other major kind of 'late' news are Saturday political speeches made by politicians out in the constituencies (but the texts of these are often available under embargo on Friday).

The great bulk of Sunday newspaper content is what is known in newspapers as 'features', but is also the kind of material handled in other countries by news magazines. The prestige Sunday newspapers have much in common with news magazines, although since Roy Thomson added a colour magazine to the *Sunday Times* in 1961 the three heavy Sundays are a double package – news magazine outside, consumer magazine inside. The colour magazines sell themselves to advertisers with the argument that they are the best medium for advertising in colour to 'up market' men *and* women. In other words they are similar to those up market semi-luxury magazines for serious women which also have a lot of men readers.

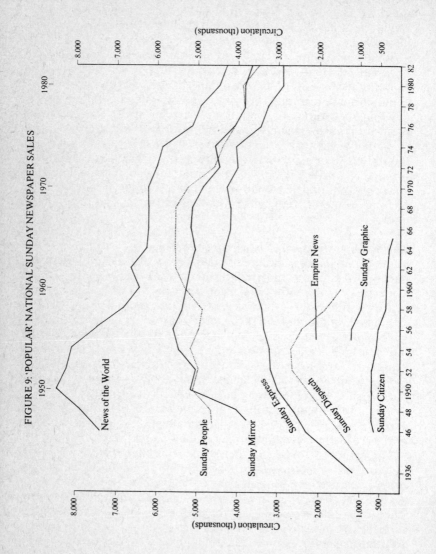

FIGURE 9: 'POPULAR' NATIONAL SUNDAY NEWSPAPER SALES

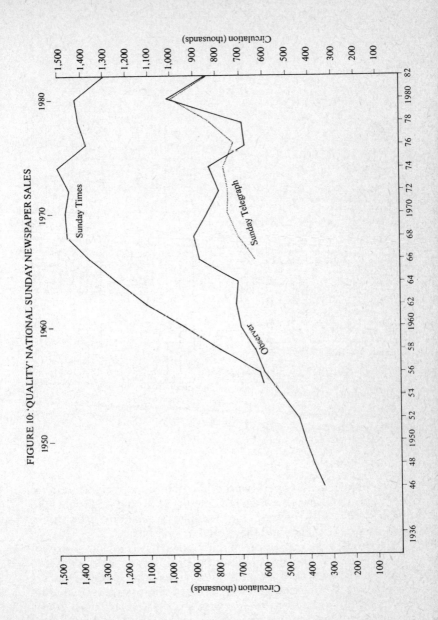

FIGURE 10: 'QUALITY' NATIONAL SUNDAY NEWSPAPER SALES

FIGURE 11: SUNDAY NATIONAL
            NEWSPAPER READERSHIP,
            BY SOCIAL CLASS AND AGE, 1981-82

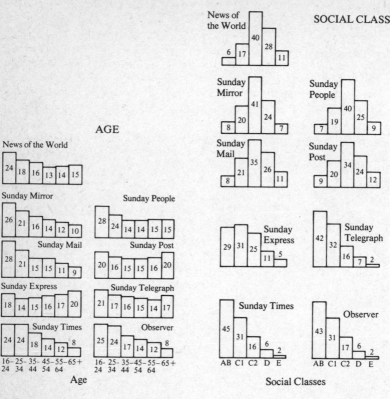

Source: Harry Henry, 'Patterns and Trends of the
           National Newspaper Press', *Admap*,
           September, 1982.

The Sunday newspapers were, like the women's and general magazines, a primarily *national* medium. Compared with the national daily newspapers, the Sunday circulations grew more rapidly than the dailies and then fell more rapidly.

The Sundays did not outreach daily sales, if one includes provincials as well. At the peak of newspaper sales around 1955–56, Sunday and daily sales were quite similar. But whereas on weekdays most adults were reading two or three daily papers including national mornings and *regional* evenings, on Sundays most adults were also reading two or three newspapers – but in this case all national ones.

In recent years the Sunday papers – like the general and women's magazines – have fallen well behind the combined daily effort of nationals and provincials. On Sunday the largest sellers have lost sales the most, whereas the more serious publications have greatly expanded both sales and advertising. This puts the Sunday newspapers broadly in line with general trends – decline of all mass publications (except national dailies) matched by an increase in more targetted up-market media, which also have the advantage of youngish readerships (Figure 11).

With the development of colour magazines in the heavy Sundays from 1962 on, and in the popular Sundays (*Sunday Express*, *News of the World*, and *Mail-on-Sunday*) in 1981–2, the magazine character of the Sunday newspaper becomes more evident. A separate development however brings Sundays closer to daily newspapers. In 1937 and even in 1947 the normal pattern was of a Sunday newspaper with an identity and personnel quite separate from any daily paper. Although they tended to be printed on daily newspaper's presses, some Sundays were entirely separate animals – the *News of the World* and *Sunday Dispatch*, like the *Sunday Times* and the *Observer* were indeed separate Sundays. In some cases there was a closer connection – the *Daily Mirror* already in 1937 had a stable companion, although its name then was still *Sunday Pictorial*. The only full identification was in the *Express* stable. Even here the *Sunday Express* had a different character and history; launched by Beaverbrook in 1918, the *Sunday Express* was for many years the weak partner but in 1962 it passed the *Daily Express* in sales and subsequently its profits, and more affluent readership, subsidized the daily.

The separate Sundays – with their many anomalies – have richly contributed to the variety and complexity both of Fleet Street's editorial output and of its exotic labour practices. But the King/Thomson and the Murdoch eras did much to bring Sundays and dailies together. The marriage of *The Times* and the *Sunday Times* in 1967 (after a century and a half of separate existence) proved to be a stormy marriage indeed – as is likely to be the case when one partner can earn much more money on Sunday than the other partner can on six days a week (see Table 11).

Radio Times and TV Times

The *Radio Times*, at first alone and then with the *TV Times* (and other early ITV guides) has dominated British magazine sales since 1945. Something similar has happened in several comparable countries, and the dominance of programme guides in the magazine field is yet another reminder to the entire magazine industry that it is living in the age of television.

The peak in sales of the combined guides was in 1960 – with 11·7 million weekly copies. This makes quite a sharp peak, with a steep rise in the 1940s and a very steep fall to 1971 – a loss of nearly half the total sales in a decade. This sales graph, of course, roughly parallels that of the women's magazines and Sunday newspapers.

What damaged the programme guides? For once television could hardly be the villain, since the big sales decline took place against a background of increasing television hours and viewing and the arrival of BBC2. It was the newspapers – mainly the *daily* newspapers – which damaged the guides. The daily newspapers began around 1960 to give rapidly increasing amounts of space to the evening TV schedule. Both the *Daily Mail* and *The Times* at least trebled their TV schedule space between 1959 and 1966 (and these schedules are very heavily consulted according to many research studies). It was also suggested that newspapers with share-holdings in ITV had a financial interest in advertising its schedules.[5]

After the steep sales drop of the 1960s each guide has held on to a three million sale. *Radio Times* has the more up-market readership clearly weighted with listeners to talk on Radio 4 and serious music on Radio 3. *TV Times* has a readership evenly spread by social class/income. But there is a very high duplicated readership; three-quarters of the readers of one guide also read the other.

Both programme magazines are important to the broadcasters as flagships and as publicists which also make a very healthy profit. Both magazines have a strong appeal to advertisers – they offer a week-long continuing readership as well as special attention at a particular time of the week. *TV Times* can be used in conjunction with TV advertising campaigns. Critics complain that the two guides have two monopolistic advantages. First, they have a monopoly of advance information on the schedules. Secondly, both guides receive massive quantities of free advertising on their respective channels – which would cost any other magazine literally millions of pounds a year. Critics claim that both magazines use these advantages to plug entertainment stars and programmes and to attract advertisers – not to inform the public.

The *Radio Times*' artwork – especially its covers – has been notable since its launch in 1923. *TV Times* has been admired for its efficiency in delivering information through the week and through its numerous ITV regional editions. In 1981 its long-time editor Peter Jackson (previously editor of an Automobile Association magazine) moved to the *News of the World* to launch its *Sun Day* colour magazine, and then on to the *Sunday Times* magazine. This career established Jackson as London's most successful magazine editor. All four magazines were part of something else.

TABLE 12   101

WOMEN'S MONTHLY MAGAZINES, 1971–81

	Circulation (*thousands*)			Women readers 1981		
	1971	1976	1981	Readers per copy	% aged 16–34	% ABC1
(ALL ADULT WOMEN)					(36)	(40)
1 HOME SERVICE Good Housekeeping, Ideal Home, Homes & Gardens, House & Garden	592	737	845	7·8	37	62
2 SUPERMARKET Family Circle, Living, Home & Freezer, Food Magazine	1,767	1,792	1,494	3·5	43	51
3 HIGH FASHION Vogue, Harpers & Queen	136	151	184	13·2	50	62
4 GENERAL Woman & Home, She, Woman's Journal, Annabel, Nova, Flair, Vanity Fair	1,501	1,231	1,350	5·0	38	56
5 YOUNG WOMEN'S Cosmopolitan, Woman's World, Over 21, Company, Honey, 19, Look Now	323	1,023	1,492	4·3	74	54
6 ROMANTIC FICTION True Romances, True Story, True Magazine, Hers/New Love, Woman's Story	1,020	763	505	7·2	59	22
7 MISCELLANEOUS Pins & Needles, Womancraft, Parents, Mother	253	256	288	6·2	53	40
TOTAL	5,002	5,953	6,158	5·3	50	52

Source: Harry Henry, 'The Women's Monthly Magazines', *Admap* June 1982, pp. 344, 346.

Consumer magazines in the television age

Compared with trade and technical magazines the consumer magazine field has a much smaller number of larger sale titles. Trade and
technical magazines with a sale of over 100,000 are unusual; but in
1980 there were some 72 consumer magazines in Britain with sales
over this figure.

In the television age the trend has indeed been towards less
mammoth consumer magazine sales and more magazines appealing
to more specialized – although in some cases still quite large –
segments of the public. Apart from women's magazines – the
biggest sales tend to be in relatively few fields: popular music (e.g.
New Musical Express), puzzles (*Puzzler*); motorcycles and cars
(e.g. *Motor Cycle News*), *Do It Yourself* and similar titles, and
gardening (e.g. *Garden News*). A major leisure interest which
appeals to millions may support perhaps two magazines each with a
sale of 100,000 and some smaller circulations as well. The biggest
fields for special interest consumer magazines in 1981 were Teenage
and Pop Music, Motoring, Men's (Sex) magazines, Hi-Fi and
Radio, Gardening, Photography, Angling, Boating, Camping, and
Do-It-Yourself.[6]

The biggest single field for consumer magazines – apart from
women's weeklies – is women's *monthly* magazines. One estimate is
that 27 women's monthlies died between 1970 and 1982. The
women's monthlies shade off into teenage magazines; the market is
segmented by several major variables – social class and income; age;
attitudes ('new' woman, or traditional housewife); and main content concerns – food, fiction, fashion, sex life, family and children,
house and home. Women's *monthlies* gained sales in the 1970s
mainly due to the success of the young women's magazines (Table
12). Specialized magazines of this sort are highly volatile and to be
commercially successful need to get several things into focus.

According to one argument, successful women's monthlies all
specialize in either 'Body' or 'Home' advertising, although the
weeklies can do both (Figure 12).

Certainly any magazine needs to appeal to both readers and
advertisers; in terms of content and personnel it needs to strike
some balance between editorial and advertising. Even if it succeeds
in all this, it is another matter to maintain these delicate balances
over time.

Magazines for the 'new' woman are notoriously difficult. Some
like *Nova* (1965–74) were ahead of their time, it seems. Others,
through their very success fall behind or acquire 'ageing' readerships; an internal battle often ensues between those who wish to
adjust the content to match the now older readership and those who
want to seek a new younger readership in order to retain the original

FIGURE 12: 'BODY' VERSUS 'HOME' WOMEN'S MAGAZINES: 1981-82
ADVERTISING CONTENT

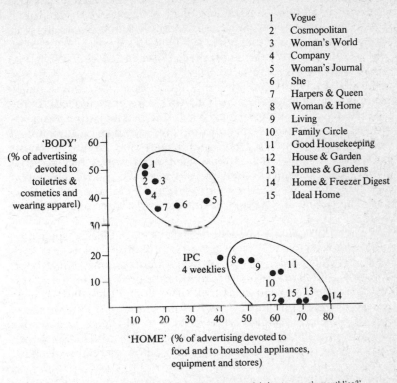

1 Vogue
2 Cosmopolitan
3 Woman's World
4 Company
5 Woman's Journal
6 She
7 Harpers & Queen
8 Woman & Home
9 Living
10 Family Circle
11 Good Housekeeping
12 House & Garden
13 Homes & Gardens
14 Home & Freezer Digest
15 Ideal Home

Source: Michael Bird, 'What's so special about women's monthlies?',
Admap, June 1982. p. 361

youthful readership profile of the magazine. Those who want to re-juvenate the magazine will advocate 're-positioning' it in the market with a younger profile; those who disagree claim that no magazine has ever been successfully re-launched or re-positioned. Very often there is a personality aspect to such discussions – for example a successful newish magazine is often identified with a particular editor; an example is the association of Audrey Slaughter in the 1960s and 1970s with a succession of young women's publications – *Honey*, *Petticoat* and *Over 21*.

Other major consumer magazine fields are volatile in other ways. Take for example the consumer car magazines. One advertising analysis[7] considered some 40 separate car magazines in 1982. This is obviously a field of much reader interest and much product advertising. However for these very reasons the field is somewhat over-

crowded with magazines. Of 40 magazines only 4 were weekly;
moreover the magazines only attract a very small share of new car
advertising – most of which goes into newspapers and television. In
this field a generalization seems valid that applies across consumer
magazines – the younger the magazine itself and the younger its
readers, the more the magazine will have to rely on sales revenue.
Old established titles like *Autocar* (b. 1895) and *Motor* (b. 1903) do
much better at attracting advertising.

A completely different kind of publication – not really a 'magazine' – is the *part-publication*. Partworks are encyclopaedias published in a finite number of 'parts' and sold in a magazine format by
newsagents. The part-work concept comes from Italy. In Britain it
saw its peak in the late 1960s; major television promotion boosts
sales of the first few issues, after which the partwork typically settles
down to a regular sale for perhaps 100 weeks. The size of this regular
sale determines whether the partwork makes a big profit or a big
loss. The potential for profit lies in the fairly high retail price per
week.

Marshall Cavendish, the leading partwork publisher, spent £8·6
million in 1981 on television advertising with partworks on such
topics as knitting, '*Doctor's Answers*', photography, and Robert
Carrier Cooking. Partworks are an interesting example of a 'magazine' field which has had to face television competition but has been
able to benefit from massive television promotion. Partworks are
also an extreme example of how success rapidly leads to excessive
competition, which produced many loss-makers in 1970. Since then
partworks have been – like neighbouring fields – in relative decline.

Trade and technical magazines

Trade and technical magazines are more numerous, but with smaller circulations than consumer magazines. Only eight British trade
and technical magazines have sales of over 100,000. Just over thirty
have sales of 50,000 or more and these are mainly in a few large
occupational/industrial areas such as the civil service, accountancy,
medicine and nursing, professional engineering, farming, office
equipment, electronics and computing.[8] In these areas the leading
publication – such as *Farmer's Weekly* – is an editorially potent
magazine, packed with very profitable advertising. The leading
magazine company, IPC, is in a strong position in several of these
major fields – the Royal Commission noted that in 1974 IPC had a
60% share or more of sales in agricultural, catering, electrical, radio
and electrical goods and transport magazines.[9]

However, the great majority of trade and technical magazines
have much smaller sales – 10,000 copies a month for example. At
the bottom end there are many hundreds of publications with sales

of a few thousand or even a few hundred. Facts about these are
unreliable. Of the 700 with ABC-audited circulations about two-
fifths are 'controlled circulation', mailed free, and financed entirely
by advertising. Others go to subscribing members of associations;
only a quarter are simply 'paid for'. Some 2,500 'House' magazines
are produced by managements for their employees, and another
massive array of trade union publications. If all of these publications are included, the total number of British trade and technical 'magazines' – many in newspaper format – must be over
10,000.

But, while there are no real equivalents to the few massive
consumer magazines, the trade and technical field is still dominated
by perhaps a hundred titles, with IPC and some dozen other
companies in a leading position. The entire grocery and supermarket business, for example, has one dominant weekly publication,
The Grocer (founded 1861), two lesser weeklies and two major
monthlies. The comparatively new field of computers had in 1982 at
least 28 weekly and monthly magazines; but only four of these were
weeklies and just two of these weeklies – *Computing* and *Computer
Weekly* – had a dominant position among senior people in data
processing. Of the four weeklies, two were owned by IPC and two
by one other major publisher (VNU).[10]

Journals of opinion: A fragmentation of egg-heads
It is a well established part of the conventional wisdom that Britain's
weekly 'journals of opinion' have – with the exception of *The
Economist* – been in decline at least since the 1960s, mainly as a
result of expanded political, arts and 'magazine' coverage in the
heavier Sunday newspapers.

There is something in this. The *New Statesman*, for example, hit
its sales peak of 94,000 in 1960, and – familiar story – after a plateau
in the 1960s, fell steeply until by 1982 its sale of 34,000 was only 36%
of the peak level; between 1970 and 1982 it had five editors (Paul
Johnson, Richard Crossman, Anthony Howard, Bruce Page, Hugh
Stephenson). The *New Statesman*'s traditional offerings of political
opinion and cultural reviews became an uncompetitive buy, compared with the fuller and cheaper offerings of the advertising-rich
Sunday newspapers.

This common view of decline was repeated by the McGregor
Royal Commission on the Press in 1977, which published a table
showing huge sales losses between 1961 and 1976 – with *The
Economist* as the main exception. However this account of decline
is a gross over-simplification. Nor has *The Economist* in fact much
increased its British sale; the great bulk of that increase has been in
export sales.

True, the Sunday newspapers have had a big impact on the *New Statesman* and *The Spectator*. The daily papers like *The Guardian* and *Financial Times* have probably contributed also. But much of the 'decline' argument depends upon a dated definition of 'journal of opinion' originally adopted by the 1947–49 Ross Royal Commission on the Press with backward glances to the 1930s. Their list was *The Economist*, *New Statesman*, *Spectator*, *Time and Tide*, *Tribune* and *Truth*. They did also mention another 80 political periodicals listed in the directories, and a much larger number of local constituency publications.

Problems of definition and the lack of audited circulations for many publications suggest caution. Nevertheless especially if one sticks to the term 'journal of opinion' then there does appear to have been a very big increase in the total number and total circulation of such publications. The *New Statesman*'s loss of sale has been enormously outweighed by a vast new army of weekly and monthly publications on the political left. And in addition to *The Economist* several other established titles are still doing well, such as *Punch*, *Country Life* and *Illustrated London News*. 'Journals of opinion' have followed the pattern of women's *monthly* magazines; while a few major titles may have declined there has been a major increase in new, smaller, titles and a fragmentation of the field of 'opinion' into many smaller sub-areas. These include:

- *Educational and science* publications appealing to broad segments of the now greatly increased number of graduates. The *Times Educational Supplement*, *New Scientist*, *New Society* and the *Times Higher Education Supplement* with a combined 1982 sale of 223,000 per week represent the emergence of a 'mass' public with higher education.
- *Left politics* and politics generally have fragmented into many small publications, some like *The Leveller* and *New Socialist* with a strong general appeal.
- The *popular music magazines* (combined 1982 circulation: 772,000) carry plenty of opinion and values and perhaps replace in part such middle-brow literary publications as *John O'London's Weekly*.
- *Literary publications* themselves have grown more serious and numerous, but also more opinionated in both politics and the arts. *The Times Literary Supplement* has a number of competitors, and the combined 1982 circulation of this category was about 75,000.[11]
- *Underground publications* of various kinds have emerged, with the fortnightly *Private Eye* showing remarkable circulation strength.

- Listings magazines such as *Time Out* and *City Limits* (combined 1982 sale of 75,000) have boomed and not only in London.
- *Feminist politics and Gay Rights* publications have blossomed – for example *Spare Rib* and *Gay News* (19,000) and these carry a lot of more general politics and opinion.
- *The American news magazines* – mainly *Time* and *Newsweek* – have slowly built up a significant British sale.
- *'Pressure' and 'Lobby'* publications have greatly expanded; for example a whole new range of 'environmental' publications which also deal with mainstream politics.

Magazines in a multi-media future

The many new sorts of 'journal of opinion', like the many new sorts of 'women's', hobby, and trade and technical publications, are all indications of the vigour and volatility of 'magazines'. The competition from other magazines and from other media will probably continue to increase. The planners of the fourth television channel, not surprisingly, set their sights in 1982 on magazines; they were trying to take away into television further slices of the larger and lusher magazine advertising areas. Successful magazines are also an obvious way of identifying booming hobby and interest areas, as well as established journalists and experts – ready-made also for transfer to television.

Virtually all of the burgeoning on-screen and video developments will compete with magazines. It also seems inevitable that newspapers will continue to adopt and incorporate more and more 'magazine' sections and approaches. Magazines are likely to be an area of still higher risks and rewards, of ever higher birth and death rates.

Media audiences, media bias

CHAPTER NINE

Audiences and content

Most popular media products offer direct and powerful human involvement. Table 13 shows some findings from a 1958 piece of BBC research. All categories of the public put 'plays' as their top or second preference. Heavy ITV viewers favoured plays and quizzes; heavy BBC viewers plays and news; people in their twenties favoured plays, feature films, news and crime series, those in their sixties preferred plays, news and quizzes; men favoured sports, plays and news; while women liked plays, news and quizzes. None of this has changed much since – with the possible exception of a slow decline of interest in news. None of it was very new in 1958.

Indeed a 1938 BBC study of radio preferences had found much the same things. The categories used were different but the most popular fare of 1938 was 'Variety', followed by cinema organs, military bands, dance music and radio plays.[1]

The least popular offering of 1938 radio was 'chamber music'. The least popular categories on 1958 television were 'serious music' and opera.

The 1940s were an exception – a decade during which popular taste apparently became markedly more serious and elevated. The Reithian goals of self-improvement via radio seemed capable of achievement; popular newspapers became not only thinner, but more meaty. All this was, however, connected with the war, and the 1950s were to reveal that popular taste had, after all, returned to its previous concerns.

Only weeks into the war in December, 1939, the BBC radio news was getting massive audiences. BBC radio news was regularly heard for nearly six years by about 25% (8 a.m.), 40% (6 p.m.) and 50% (9 p.m.) of the population. The legendary audience appeal of Winston Churchill's broadcasts had a factual basis – three times in 1941–42 he reached over 70% of the population. The evening news on D-Day (June, 1944) was heard by 80%. In war-time people feel exceptionally involved in the news, but this sinks away quickly with peace.

War conditions also produced misleading evidence of public taste for serious newspapers. Under severe paper rationing, the newspapers largely dispensed with the lighter kinds of news and devoted most of their six- and eight-page papers to serious (war) news. The thinner papers retained the pre-war sales price, and advertising

TABLE 13

BRITISH PUBLIC'S TELEVISION PREFERENCES, 1958

Scale	Those who viewed		Age		Men	Women	Scale
	Nearly all ITV (N=214)	Nearly all BBC (N=74)	20–29 yrs (133)	60–69 yrs (163)	viewers (560)	viewers (684)	
+64							+63
						Plays	
+60		Plays					+59
					Sports		
+56	Plays						+55
				Plays			
+52		News	Plays				+51
+48		Travel					+47
				News	Plays, News		
+44	Quizzes	Animals and birds					+43
						News	
+40	Sports, westerns, variety						+39
				Quizzes sports, animals and birds, travel			

	News	Documentaries	Feature films, news	Variety	Travel Variety	Quizzes	
+36							+35
	Crime series Feature films	Current affairs Sports	Crime series Variety	Current affairs	Animals and birds Current affairs Documentaries Westerns Feature films	Travel	
+32						Variety Animals and birds Feature films	+31
			Sports				
+28	Travel	Variety	Westerns, travel	Religious services Documentaries	Documentaries	Documentaries, Current A.	+27
				Light music	Crime series		
+24	Comedy film series	Light music, songs	Quizzes Comedy film series			Religious services	+23
	Animals and birds		Light music				
+20	Current affairs	Religious services			Light music, songs Comedy film series	Comedy film series	+19

TABLE 13

BRITISH PUBLIC'S TELEVISION PREFERENCES, 1958

Scale	Those who viewed		Age		Men	Women	Scale
	Nearly all ITV (N=214)	Nearly all BBC (N=74)	20–29 yrs (133)	60–69 yrs (163)	viewers (560)	viewers (684)	
+16		Feature films	Animals and birds, Documentaries	Comedy film series, Feature films	Science	Crime series	+15
+12	Documentaries, Light music, song, Religious services	Science, Quizzes		Crime series	Religious services	Sports, Westerns	+11
+8			Current affairs				
			Science	Westerns		Westerns	+7
+4		Serious music					

Comedy film series	Religious services			Science	+3
Crime series					0
Westerns					
	Science			Serious music	−3
Opera					
		Serious music			−7
	Serious music		Serious music		−11
				Opera	−15
		Opera	Opera		−19
Serious music	Opera				−23
Opera					−27

0	
−4	Science
−8	Opera
−12	
−16	
−20	Serious music
−24	Opera

Note: 1 = 'particularly like'; ½ = like; 0 = indifferent; −½ = dislike; −1 = 'particularly dislike'.
Source: BBC, The Public and the Programmes, 1959.

rates for the small space available were steeply raised. The news-papers were in a sellers' market, which continued into the late 1940s. Similarly, with the BBC monopoly still intact, the public – with only limited choice – continued even in the late 1940s to show what were widely taken to be signs of 'improved' taste. But BBC television, the *News Chronicle* and *Picture Post* were soon to discover that taste had 'improved' very little.

Sure signs of this existed even during the war. After the news and Churchill, the biggest audiences went to variety and comedy shows. By the late 1940s Churchill was no longer the biggest audience puller – instead there was a new star in the land who by early 1948 was attracting an unprecedented, and never since repeated (on radio or TV), average weekly audience of 54% of the population. The name of this all-time superstar of British broadcasting was Wilfred Pickles.[2] His show *Have a Go* used a quiz-comedy format; quizzes had previously been frowned on by Reith and the successful *Brains Trust*, although fitting the quiz-comedy format, had deliberately featured intellectuals. Pickles' show broke new ground in comedy – in contrast to the slick Hollywood radio comedies and their equally slick, professionally written and performed British rivals – *Have A Go* was deliberately folksy. Working-class people talked about themselves and, however they answered the quiz questions, they always won the very small prizes. 'The money' was dispensed by Mabel ('at the table'), who was indeed Mrs Pickles – giving the show a powerful family ingredient. Finally Pickles, himself, with his homely North-Country style and accent was in fact a highly experienced and talented radio professional, who continued to perform everywhere – on the stage, television, in the newspapers and in books.

The appeal of the comedy-quiz, which Pickles demonstrated on late 1940s radio, was to be seen again on late 1950s commercial television. But formats other than the comedy-quiz also offer human involvement. The two major categories of action melodrama and comedy allow the audience the opportunity to fantasize with the cops and robbers and to laugh with the studio audience. Televised sport, radio phone-ins, beauty competitions, and animal shows all offer human involvement.

The most popular radio show after *Have a Go* was *The Archers*: a village-based soap opera; overtly dedicated to agricultural propaganda, it performed the slightly different function of riveting its audience with the sense of belonging to an authentic rural community. Two of the most long-time popular television shows have been *Coronation Street* and *Crossroads* – each of them soap operas with a strong *family* theme. Perhaps the most remarkable success of all is *This is Your Life*, a long-lived format borrowed from 1950s Amer-

TABLE 14

25 LARGEST BRITISH TELEVISION AUDIENCES OF 1977

	(millions)
Morecambe And Wise Christmas Show (BBC-1) (Christmas Day)	28·7
Mike Yarwood Christmas Show (BBC-1) (Christmas Day)	26·1
Bruce Forsyth And The Generation Game (BBC-1) (Christmas Day)	24·6
Miss World (BBC-1) (17 November)	24·5
You Only Live Twice, film (ITV) (20 November)	24·5
The Silver Jubilee Royal Variety Gala (ITV) (4 December)	24·5
The Royal Windsor Big Top (BBC-1) (29 May)	22·8
The Queen's Speech (All channels) (Christmas Day)	22·7
Jesus Of Nazareth (ITV) (10 April)	22·3
Silver Jubilee Fires Of Friendship (BBC-1) (6 June)	22·0
Silver Jubilee Day Of Celebration (BBC-1) (7 June)	22·0
Jesus Of Nazareth (ITV) (3 April)	21·9
Starsky And Hutch (BBC-1) (4 February)	21·4
Eurovision Song Contest (BBC-1) (7 May)	21·0
The Dirty Dozen, film (BBC-1) (Boxing Day)	20·8
Bruce Forsyth And The Generation Game (BBC-1) (3 December)	20·5
The Two Ronnies (BBC-1) (10 December)	20·5
European Cup Final (BBC-1) (25 May)	20·5
England v Italy – World Cup (ITV) (16 November)	20·5
Bruce Forsyth And The Generation Game (BBC-1) (26 November)	20·2
Bruce Forsyth And The Generation Game (BBC-1) (10 December)	20·1
Planet Of The Apes, film (ITV) (24 March)	20·0
The Two Ronnies (BBC-1) (Boxing Day)	20·0
Starsky And Hutch (BBC-1) (15 January)	20·0
Thunderball, film (ITV) (26 February)	20·0

Source: BBC Audience Research, reported in *Broadcast*, 23rd January 1978.

ican television and embarrassingly high on human involvement often with strong family overtones.

There are many different ways of counting up the most popular programmes – especially in British television which is so devoted to the mini-series. Lists of top audiences of the week, month, year and channel all reveal (and conceal) slightly different details – but the popular themes change little from week to week or year to year.

Consider first (Table 14) the 25 most popular shows of 1977, a year which contained a greater than usual number of Royal top shows. No less than 5 of the 25 are Royal events – due to 1977 being the Silver Jubilee of Queen Elizabeth's accession. Amongst the remainder there are four comedy-quiz shows (*Bruce Forsyth and the Generation Game*); four comedy shows; four feature films stressing Hollywood violence and fantasy; two episodes each of *Jesus* and *Starsky*; two international football cup contests; and finally two other international contests – *Miss World* and the *Eurovision Song Contest* each of which is carefully structured to combine human involvement with a truly enormous audience.

Next consider the average audience sizes for different categories of programme over the entire year of 1980 (Figure 13). The Figure is based on 25 weeks in London and 23 weeks in other regions, with a diary panel of 500 viewers in each case. Action-Adventure and Soap Opera get the largest audiences – any programme of this type at any time of the day, week or year averages around 20% of the total potential audience (or around 10 million viewers). News and sport fall in the middle range, with all the more demanding types of programming (except plays and films) averaging 2–6% (1 to 3 million).

'Human interest' is a term of American origin which the British press has made truly its own. James Curran, in an excellent historical account of readership and content research in British newspapers, shows that since the 1920s – with the exception of the 1940s, that atypical decade of newsprint-rationed high-mindedness – the British national press has been carrying steadily greater proportions of 'human interest' and lower proportions of political and other serious news. The trend towards more human interest became strong in the late 1930s because readership research revealed readers' preferences for light material. A 1934 survey of readers of six national popular daily newspapers showed that above average reader interest focused upon accidents, court and divorce news, personal gossip and letters. The same study (conducted for the *News Chronicle*) also showed that among readers of national 'quality' dailies in 1934, the highest readership figures were achieved by court and divorce news; in contrast, foreign politics and industry and commerce scored lowest.

Between 1936 and 1946 (when newsprint rationing was still operating at nearly full force) the national newspapers roughly doubled the proportion of their strictly limited space devoted to public affairs. The *Daily Express*, *Daily Mail*, *Daily Mirror*, *Daily Telegraph* and *Sunday Express* more than doubled their proportions and even *The Observer* raised its serious content from 26% to 47% of a much smaller editorial space. But after 1947, as the papers expanded in size, they gave over most of the new space to advertising and light material:

FIGURE 13: TELEVISION AUDIENCE SIZE AND PROGRAMME TYPE, 1980

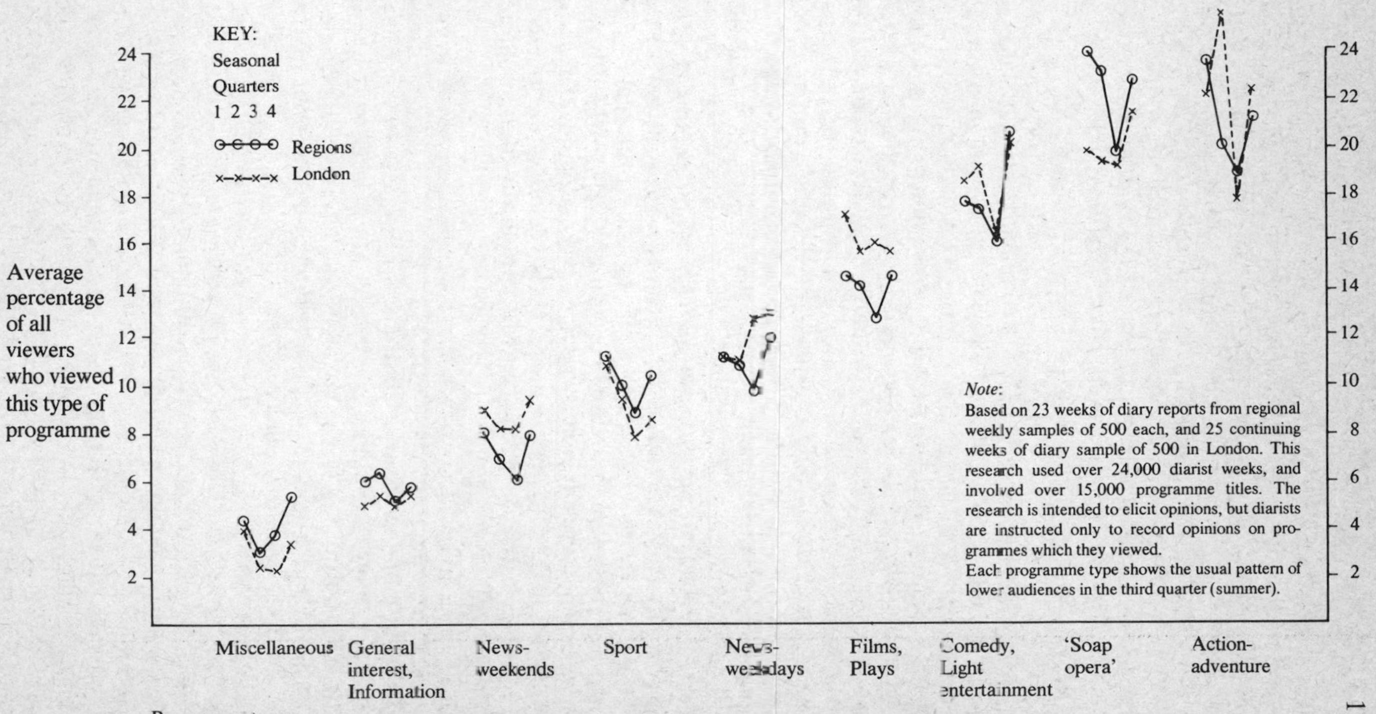

KEY:

Seasonal
Quarters
1 2 3 4

o–o–o–o Regions
x–x–x–x London

Note:
Based on 23 weeks of diary reports from regional
weekly samples of 500 each, and 25 continuing
weeks of diary sample of 500 in London. This
research used over 24,000 diarist weeks, and
involved over 15,000 programme titles. The
research is intended to elicit opinions, but diarists
are instructed only to record opinions on programmes which they viewed.
Each programme type shows the usual pattern of
lower audiences in the third quarter (summer).

Source: 'A Box for All Seasons', IBA Audience Research Department, p. 10.

Average
percentage
of all
viewers
who viewed
this type of
programme

24 · 22 · 20 · 18 · 16 · 14 · 12 · 10 · 8 · 6 · 4 · 2

Programme types

Miscellaneous   General   News-   Sport   News-   Films,   Comedy,   'Soap   Action-
                 interest, weekends   weekdays Plays   Light   opera'   adventure
                 Information   Entertainment

Between 1946 and 1976, the proportion of editorial space devoted to current affairs declined by at least half in all sample papers, and in the case of three papers (the *Daily Herald/Sun*, the *Sunday Pictorial/Sunday Mirror* and the *People/Sunday People*) by two-thirds. Public-affairs content in all the sample popular papers in 1976 was dwarfed by human-interest material and indeed occupied less space than sports did in all seven papers . . . public affairs, including both news and features, shrank to less than 15% in four papers.[3]

Curran provides powerful evidence that readers of both the popular and more serious newspapers had a high involvement with light human interest material.

Since the 1920s there have been two major shifts away from public affairs press coverage – led, says Curran, by the *Daily Mirror* in the late 1930s and *The Sun* in the early 1970s. But as early as 1963 readers of four popular national dailies favoured 'tragic human-interest stories concerning ordinary people' and 'human-interest stories concerning celebrities', followed by cartoons, letters, 'light' human interest stories about ordinary people, 'sex, love, romance stories concerning ordinary people', horoscopes and crime and court stories concerning ordinary people. A similar pattern was to be found among the greatly increased readerships of the 'serious' Sunday newspapers. Giving men's and women's preferences equal weight, the most popular items – according to a 1969–71 study were firstly 'human interest (ordinary people)', secondly the main review article (only in the *Sunday Times* and *Observer* and often devoted to the confessions of artistic celebrities), and thirdly 'human interest (celebrities)'.

Popularity: drama, humour, music
Drama, humour and music are perhaps the three major ingredients of media popularity. But these categories are so large as to include most of the output of the electronic media; and much of the more popular press media at least aim for drama and humour. Within each broad category there is a very wide range in many aspects, not least popularity.

Series dramas on television are probably the most consistently popular material to be found within the British media; even amongst super-popular series drama there are several categories – the domestic British soap-operas (like *Coronation Street*) which are true serials with a continuing plot; the popular *series* which in Britain may appear in short bursts over a period of years; *mini-series* – typically novels dramatized into a few episodes.

Each category has its typical audience and attractions. The

soap-operas have the famous problem that the actors' patience or the actors themselves may not survive as long as the audience appeal; not only actors die, but waves of novice producers, directors and writers are always trying literally to put new life into the old serial, sometimes by killing off characters. The problems of the *mini-series* are quite different; whereas the soap opera's leading actors become stars, the mini-series needs to cast stars into the leading parts to attract an audience – and successful mini-series typically attract an increasing audience size towards the last episode.

But some of the least popular media material is also drama. The BBC puts on some 900 hours a year of radio drama (mostly on radio 4) – and much of it – at least in national broadcasting terms – reaches small audiences, numbered at most in hundreds of thousands.

Why do some dramas get audiences of 100,000 or less and others 10 million or more? Any drama has an anticipated audience level, and to him who seems most likely to be popular shall be given the resources to ensure that he is popular – such material is put on to prime time evening television, and is given hundreds of thousands of pounds to spend on stars, costumes, colour and weeks of time. From him who hath not much chance of popularity these things are taken away – he gets on to radio, at one of even radio's less popular times, he gets unknown actors and few of them, a simple sound studio with minimal technical back up, no costumes or colour, at most a few days' preparation time, and a budget of a few hundred, or at most a few thousand, pounds. Radio drama is not much more than a few people in a sound-proof room talking into a tape-recorder and the fact that it gets even tens or thousands of listeners is perhaps further witness to the riveting attraction of almost any kind of drama.

Much drama falls between these two polar areas. At least three important categories of television drama typically attract middle range audiences, of, say, between two and four million (4% to 8% of the population over the age of 5). These middling popular dramas include the serious single plays, which are intended to win some artistic prestige points; the historical costume dramas, often based on Victorian novels, and intended to recoup some of their high cost through export sales; and the 'docudrama' series – intended to dress up recent historical events (such as *Winston Churchill: The Wilderness Years*) in fictional/documentary clothing and hence to reach a bigger audience.

Within music the wide range is even more obvious; slightly less obvious is that music has often provided the most popular material across the whole range of electronic media. George Formby, as comedian-singer, was probably the most popular British *film* star of the 1930s. Gracie Fields, another singing film star, was on Christmas Day 1939 the first person ever to be heard on radio by two-thirds of the entire British population. Music is still not only the staple of radio, but for many of the years of television a variously titled hit parade show on early Sunday evenings has drawn Britain's biggest radio audience. And the long-running television music show, *Top of the Pops* indicates the shape of many video things to come.

Popularity: crime, conflict, violence

The continuing universal appeal of murder and other violent crimes in all media – films, television, and not least the press – is obvious. Much research has been done about children and media violence, crime TV series, and about the screen and public image of the police; but nobody seems to have bothered to investigate what exactly it is about both fictional and factual murder which is so appealing.

Murderers' true confessions were on sale at English executions before the appearance of regular newspapers; and three hundred years later, in the 1950s, similar material could still be found in some of Fleet Street's popular Sundays. In Britain as in other countries there were few things better for newspaper sales than a *series* of murders. Similarly for sales of detective novels and Hollywood; but the murder series has proved even more suitable for the television series.

A 'problem' in Britain is that murders are relatively scarce, and serial murders even scarcer. When a genuine example occurs, the popular newspapers outdo themselves with energetic pursuit – especially since this is one of the few sorts of 'big' story on which the popular newspapers sense that they can still outdo television. One press advantage is that multiple murderers tend to murder prostitutes, an aspect about which television experiences more inhibitions; such a case was the 'Yorkshire Ripper' finally brought to trial in 1981 and so-called because most of the victims were prostitutes (like those of Jack the Ripper).

Presumably such a story strikes a number of different emotional chords – it offers fear and warnings to potential victims, and fantasised sadism and heroism to covert sadists and heroes; it offers not only hunters, hunted and mystery, but also unintended humour (once again the police play Keystone Cops and lose the trail). Often the court case – with its grizzly facts and unexpected details – sells the most newspapers. In the good old days there was the theatrical ritual of the Judge putting on his black cap for sentencing; then the appeal, and the confessions either before, or immediately after, the execution. Sometimes there was even a sequel – with new evidence, the newspapers suggest the cops may have got the wrong man.

Other crime stories have their similar or lesser appeals – again intensely human. Whether or not media coverage of crime makes people more anxious about the threat of robbery (as some research suggests), the two things surely complement each other. Having watched the TV crime series and also bolted the door, we head for bed, our minds filled with images of crime both fictional and factual. No shortage of human involvement here.

Sport

Sport has been another newspaper staple, for at least a hundred years. Sport is obviously strong in raw drama, and personal identification; sport via the media has a local community aspect of supporting your local team and a nostalgic element of recalling the days when you yourself scored goals or tripped opponents. All of the newspapers, including the more serious like *The Times*, have long carried several pages of sport (see Table 15). Radio and television both followed where the press led. But early audience research also showed two great limitations of sport: first the audience was split up into separate segments each interested in different sports; and secondly sport was mostly of interest to men in general and boys in particular. Because advertisers were mainly interested in women and most women were apparently not interested in sport, ITV for some years after its 1955 birth left sport mainly to the BBC. Early research showed that heavy ITV viewers, especially men, did want to see sport (Table 13) but initially they had to switch over to the BBC to see it.

Sport has, since about 1960, slowly but steadily moved into a more and more central place not only in British television, but also in the press. This change has many aspects. Just previous to its 1967 franchise re-allocations the ITA negotiated with ITV companies arrangements for stronger networked sports coverage;[4] several sports producers moved into high executive positions in British television; *colour* television was probably very important, because sharply defined colour close-ups could imprint the sports stars' features on the public memory, facilitating the key transformation of the star of a particular sport into the super-rich showbiz superstar.

More and more sports – attracted by the appeal of potential fame and fortune via television – began to preen themselves for television presentation. Television money, in building up sports stars, also helped to attract other sponsorship money from sports goods manufacturers, soft drink and insurance companies. This money has been accompanied by increasingly urgent attention to research on the sports audience.

Professional sport has become *internationalised*, leading in some

TABLE 15

ANALYSIS OF TOTAL NEWS SPACE (NOT FEATURES) IN THREE NATIONAL DAILIES, 1927, 37, 47, 75

	The Times				Daily Mail				Daily Mirror			
	1927	1937	1947	1975	1927	1937	1947	1975	1927	1937	1947	1975
HOME NEWS												
Political, social economic	14	12	23	21	10	6	23	18	10	5	21	14
law, police accidents	6	5	3	5	12	9	11	12	15	20	23	11
personalities, court news etc.	7	8	7	4	6	6	4	2	6	8	3	3
sport	18	21	16	14	27	36	33	34	37	36	24	53
other	6	6	2	3	11	9	9	7	13	14	15	8
HOME NEWS, TOTAL	51	52	51	47	66	66	80	73	81	83	86	89
EXTERNAL NEWS	17	11	28	23	18	17	16	16	12	11	14	10
OTHER NEWS												
Financial, commercial, scientific	32	37	21	30	16	17	4	10	7	6	0	1
TOTAL	100	100	100	100	100	100	100	100	100	100	100	100
ALL POLITICAL, SOCIAL, ECONOMIC	27	22	49	38	20	17	36	25	16	8	30	18

Sources: *Royal Commission on the Press 1947–49 Report*, p. 250; Royal Commission on the Press (1977) *Analysis of Newspaper Content*, pp. 17–18.

sports to a circus of international superstars. Association Football has invented innumerable European competitions. And, while women still are less enthusiastic than men, more women have become more interested in sport – via television. In the case of football the bigger the occasion typically, the bigger the proportion of women in the TV audience. For the 1982 World Cup research indicated women reporting a level of appreciation only a little below that expressed by men.[5]

Athletics has a strong television case because it has the strongest combined appeal to men and women (Table 16); it is a major area of women's sports involvement, and all of us remember the school sports day and know the difference between the hurdles and the high jump. Moreover athletics focuses on individuals and thus manufactures stars.

The importance of personal involvement was illustrated by the rise around 1980 of two new sports to television fame – the two traditional British pub 'sports' of snooker (pool) and darts, which were ranked second and fifth in interest among sports by men and sixth equal by women (Table 16). Week long 'International Snooker' contests produced week long ratings records for BBC2.[6]

TABLE 16

SPORTS RANKED IN ORDER OF INTEREST, BY MEN AND WOMEN
(*June 1979 and February 1980*)

Men	Interested	Women	Interested
1. Football	71%	1. Skating	63%
2. Snooker	62	2. { Athletics	53
3. Athletics	61	2. { Show-jumping	53
4. Boxing	51	4. Tennis	51
5. Darts	50	5. Swimming	41
6. Tennis	49	6. { Darts	37
7. Cricket	47	6. { Snooker	37
8. Motor racing	46	8. Football	36
9. Wrestling	41	9. Wrestling	28
10. { Golf	40	10. Golf	27
10. { Rugby Union	40	11. Horse racing	26
N = 887		N = 958	

Source: Eleanor Cowie and Vivien Marles, 'The Public and Sport', *BBC Broadcasting Research Findings* 7, 1980, p. 95.
Note: A separate IBA report indicated that in London in February 1982 the two most popular TV sports for men and women combined were snooker and athletics. The five most popular sports were for men: snooker, athletics, football, tennis and boxing; for London women: ice-skating, gymnastics, tennis, athletics, snooker. See G. Reardon and J. M. Wober, *Interest in Sport on Television*, IBA Audience Research Department, 1982, p. 10.

With the Murdoch tabloid revolution in Fleet Street in the early 1970s the popular newspapers all increased their number of sports pages. The other more subtle change is that sports stars in their new guise as entertainment superstars have increasingly invaded the general news and feature pages; when the *Mail on Sunday* was launched in 1982 it chose as its first audience-grabbing sensational serial, the confessions of a woman tennis player, Billie Jean King. Meanwhile, television has been searching for more and more ways of presenting sports stars as entertainment celebrities – such as mixing them up with stars of other sports in newly contrived contests, or putting them into comedy-quiz formats.

Made in USA

These latter examples are reminders of two other formulae used by the British media at least since late Victorian times: import it from the United States, or, better still, copy it.[7] Since the 1960s several other variants have developed such as: 'Made in Britain' shows which were aimed at the US national TV networks and in fact achieved the lesser glory of national syndication (the Lew Grade approach); the co-production deal (under which the BBC claims total editorial control); another increasingly popular development is the American short take (for example five minutes of some exotically dangerous American sport sandwiched into a British-made programme).

Hollywood feature films, world heavyweight title fights, and space shots have achieved a fair proportion of Britain's very highest television audience figures. More typically American materials are popular but not the most popular. If they were not popular (or prestigious) they would no longer be used; American materials are used to do particular things for the schedules – such as build the early evening audience, or to hold the late evening audience. With schedulers pursuing different strategies on different evenings of the week, the proportion of imports also varies radically. In late 1981 BBC2 had 32% of imported programming on Saturdays, against only 6% on Wednesdays; ITV (London Weekend) had 24% of imports on Saturday, on Sunday only 7%.[8]

Of the two main American television formats the action-melodramas travel a little better than the comedies; perhaps comedies have too many verbal twists and local references, while the action shows, as fantasy, are more universal. Whatever the reason, there is often just one American imported series each season which gets sky high ratings. *Kojak* was a big success in 1974–75; in 1980 *Dallas* had the unusual achievement for an import of the highest audience of the year (27 million).[9] In 1977–8 *Starsky and Hutch* was a great success in Britain. Indeed at the very moment when American youth was beginning to switch off the two bohemian Los Angeles policemen, British children were voting the two actors involved as the two most popular male characters on television; *Charlie's Angels* and *The Bionic Woman* provided the most popular females.[10]

The extreme popularity of certain American shows with British children is a long-running phenomenon, which probably says something about the inadequacies both of British children's programming and of Hollywood adult programming. One of the (unresearched) oddities is that these American series include many local references (to the American school system or politics, or local Californian geography) which very few British children can realistically be expected to understand. Perhaps this adds an exotic quality to the fantasy.

Formally the imports are supposed to be around 14%; in terms of most years' few most popular programmes the figure is higher, but in terms of the week's top twenty the figure is lower. If one adds direct copies – such as the Hollywood game shows typically translated into a slightly gentler British comedy-quiz format – then the proportion of 'American' material is much higher (as is the proportion of 'British' material on US television). But the *popularity* of both the direct and indirect Hollywood imports is so obvious that its full significance may be ignored. American television places an extreme emphasis on competition and – despite the loss of linguistic nuances – the various forms of Hollywood imports have been a key factor in attuning British audiences to more competitive and popular output (overall) than is provided in most other European countries.

Nor is this confined to television. The *Sunday Times* doubled its sales between 1957 and 1967 and established itself as Britain's most successful prestige paper by adopting many American Sunday newspaper practices – such as sectionalization and the colour magazine; also important were serializations of American books, several of them about John F. Kennedy's life and death.[11]

Age, sex, social class, place, time
Age, sex and social class are the variables which traditionally produce the strongest findings from survey research. Age and sex segment media audiences, although pop music listening by young people and the reading of men's sex magazines by men are extreme examples. Social class is important in the media – less so in shaping the television audience, more so in radio and press.

Where you live largely determines whether you read a provincial evening newspaper, since the bulk of evening sales are within a very few urban miles of the production centre. Time (of day, week and year) are also crucial. Children's favourite medium is television and those aged 5–15 are especially heavy viewers. Heaviest viewers of all are boys aged 15 or under – possibly because girls do more household chores. At 16 this changes radically. The 16+ age group are the lightest viewers of television – because they are often outside the home, or certainly the sitting room. They are the heaviest users of radio, records and cinema films. The 16+ age-group are especially irregular *buyers* of papers; but they do read newspapers and buy magazines, often age specific ones.

Somewhere in the early 20s, and typically at the point of marriage, all this changes again. It is only at marriage – or setting up housekeeping – that Britons start both to buy and to read a daily paper; television viewing increases, and cinema attendance virtually ends – especially after the birth of the first child. People in their forties are typically quite heavy users of all the stay-at-home media: television, radio and newspapers.

People around the age of 60 are especially heavy readers of newspapers, but this drops off sharply after 65. Radio listening also declines. Elderly people are very reluctant to listen to Radio 1 and its contemporary sounds; many prefer the talk of Radio 4. Elderly people are also heavy television viewers (especially ITV). This heavy TV diet is a reversion back towards the youth pattern in another sense; while old people dislike youth culture and its music, they like children's television – substantial proportions of whose audience is old people viewing without a child present. Elderly people are great complainers about such things as excessive violence, explicit sex and lack of respect for authority; such attitudes probably partly explain their liking for children's programming.

In terms of the major media of newspapers and television, the proportions of men and women tend to be fairly even, although of course there are differences *within* the medium – sport and politics being preferred by men, women's features and entertainment news preferred by women. National daily newspapers in 1981 had 55 men readers for every 45 women readers; the only main exception was the *Financial Times* with men constituting 74% of the readers. On Sundays however, more women read national newspapers, making the gender balance almost equal. The *Daily Mail* has, as part of its strategy as an up-market tabloid, attempted to lure the affluent female readers beloved by advertisers, but still has more men readers.

Magazines mostly fall neatly into one of three gender categories. Those like the Sunday newspaper magazines, and the broadcast programme magazines, which are balanced equally between men and women; women's magazines read mainly by women; and men's

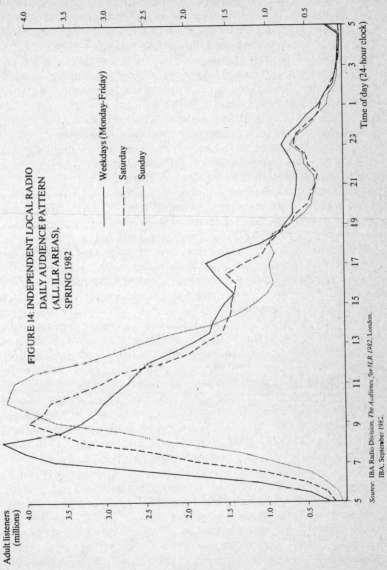

FIGURE 14: INDEPENDENT LOCAL RADIO
DAILY AUDIENCE PATTERN
(ALL ILR AREAS),
SPRING 1982

Weekdays (Monday–Friday)
Saturday
Sunday

Adult listeners
(millions)

Time of day (24-hour clock)

Source: IBA Radio Division, *The Audience for ILR 1982*, London,
IBA, September 1982.

sex magazines and most professional and technical magazines read mainly by men.

Time of day or year greatly influences the kind of audience for radio. On weekdays, breakfast and driving-to-work give radio its peak audiences from 7 a.m. to 8.30 a.m.; the other early morning medium is newspapers. During the day there is a continuing lower level of use of newspapers and radio, both with housewives at home and with men and women at work. The mid-day meal break marks a small new blip in (morning) newspaper reading and in radio; it also marks the start of a significant audience for television. The afternoon sees a continuing decline in the radio audience, as television programming starts to attract audiences initially of housewives and retired people, but then of children returning from school.

In the early evening all the media battle it out together, not only with each other but with other activities such as preparing and eating food. At any time in the early evening fewer men are home, but of people already home a bigger proportion of men devote their prime attention to television. Around 6 p.m. many Britons are eating, the radio is beginning its final descent into an evening of negligible audiences, while the television audience is already large. Around 6 to 7 p.m. evening newspapers get their main readers, but morning newspapers are still being read. The majority of the evening television audience cue their viewing with a newspaper TV schedule. As the evening progresses some young people watch television and increasingly large proportions also give it their main attention. Television hits its peak audience around 9 p.m., and the 'truce' which ends at this hour is realistic in that fairly few children under ten years continue to view. The adult TV audience declines sharply after 10 p.m., and there is a small increase in the radio audience around 11 p.m. as people go to bed.

Quite big differences occur at the weekend; Saturday has (unwisely) been partly handed over by the newspapers to television – morning papers are thin, and many British evening papers publish only a sports edition on Saturday. Daytime television gets its main audience on weekend afternoons. On Sundays many people – survey research confirms – stay in bed for an extra two hours, perhaps reading a Sunday newspaper; the largest Sunday radio audience is at 10 to 11 a.m. Summer is the quietest time for the media. Britons watch about half an hour less television per day (much of it repeats); newspapers get thinner and lose sales; only the cinema does well. The autumn and the winter are the biggest times especially for audiences and advertisers. The Christmas holiday usually records the year's highest television audiences, with Christmas Day traditionally attracting for the BBC the year's largest audiences of all (Table 14).

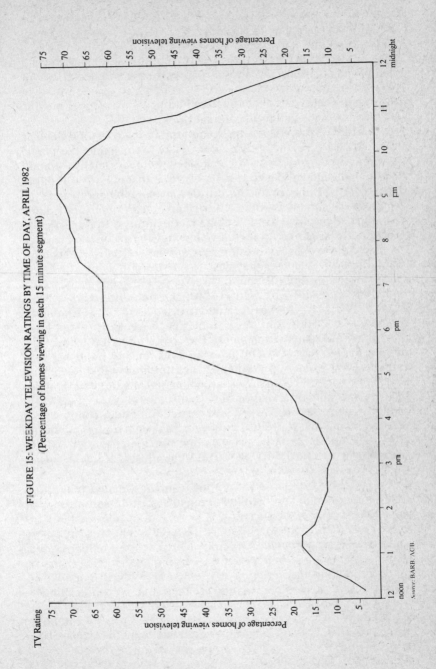

FIGURE 15: WEEKDAY TELEVISION RATINGS BY TIME OF DAY, APRIL 1982
(Percentage of homes viewing in each 15 minute segment)

TV Rating

Percentage of homes viewing television

Source: BARB, ACB.

The numbers: getting and playing
The national mass media audience in Britain is one of the most heavily researched in the world. Compared with the sprawling, fragmented and localised American media, the *national* pattern of mass media in Britain provides a relatively easy and neat focus for survey research. The system is also sufficiently competitive and advertising–focused to need the data badly, and wealthy enough to be able to provide it in prodigal quantities.

Nevertheless there is always something in the assertion that the more data we have, the less we know. Take for example, the simple question: how many hours a week does the average British adult devote to the media? The central problem is that nobody sets out to answer the overall question. Or only leisure researchers do and they are more concerned with the 'constructive' uses of leisure. Media research is typically devoted by one media interest to its particular medium, because even, say, television viewing is complex enough and secondly because interested parties who collect numbers have in mind specific purposes they wish to pursue with them.

The most notorious difference used to be between the television audience figures for BBC and ITV which often differed by at least 10%. The BBC system was designed to discover the size of audience for hundreds of different programmes each week. It used a huge *quota* national sample each day of the year – interviewing nearly a million people in a year. In its early days the ITV audience was estimated by Television Audience Measurement (TAM) and the American Nielsen company by attaching automatic recording devices to a sample of television sets. Subsequently a co-operatively funded system was established and carried out under contract by a research company. It produced different answers from those of the BBC, because the Joint Industry Committee for Television Advertising Research (JICTAR) was interested in just that – primarily in the ads between the programmes.

Eventually in 1981, after prompting from the Annan Committee, the BBC in practice accepted the enemy's system by setting up with the ITV Companies Association (ITCA) a jointly owned Broadcasters' Audience Research Board (BARB). This research now makes available three sorts of information – the number of sets switched on (via the meters); the numbers and characteristics of people watching the sets (via diaries); and a third index which enables audience members to indicate their level of appreciation of the programme. Even so, there are still some doubts both about the proportion of 'viewers' who are devoting their primary attention to the programmes, and many more doubts about how many people move, or turn, away from the screen (or blip their remote control devices) during the commercial breaks.

About radio listening there continues to be confusion; indeed the confusion was greatly increased by the arrival of commercial local radio. ILR quickly started to do research as to its local audiences, and these seemed to contradict BBC data in two major respects. The new research seemed to show ILR beating not only BBC local radio but also the BBC national channels. Secondly the ILR research suggested that typical adults 'listened' to radio for not nine hours but something more like 23 hours per week. Some of this difference resulted from the 'inviting' ILR research method of self-completion diaries split into quarter hour time periods (as opposed to the BBC's use of interviews). But also ILR research conducted by JICRAR (Joint Industry Committee for Radio Audience Research) was keen to demonstrate that – admittedly as a *secondary* activity – many people had the radio on for very long slabs of time.

Press research is different again and the central research has focused on *readership* (as opposed to circulation) and the personal and consumer characteristics of readers of a list of publications. This central research has long been run by JICNARS (Joint Industry Committee for National Readership Research) – with a separate massive national random sample survey every three months (which are added into six monthly and yearly figures). This 'readership' research in fact focuses on just about everything except detailed readership itself; there is other 'reading and noting' research which is primarily designed to discover how many people read how much of each advertisement and of the editorial text adjoining. For its chosen purposes the JICNARS research is probably very accurate, but it is not good at telling us even how long people spend reading national newspapers and magazines.

The press research is also unable to tell us about the total reading time or total reading matter of particular categories of people – national, regional and local newspapers; Sundays; freesheets; women's magazines and technical magazines. This is too much to fit into one study, and problems of defining 'readership' alone would also be prohibitive.

Meanwhile the people for whom the numbers were collected are playing them in various ways. The advertisers run their questions through the computer – for example which of various combinations of peak and off-peak spots will reach the widest proportion of the social class C1C2 under the age of 34 women target for the least cost per thousand? From this point of view the single ITV channel was always a blunt instrument which 'hit' millions of people who were not in the prescribed target audience. The arrival of a smaller second commercial channel has made for a much wider range of possible combinations and choices, but its audiences are again typically not sharply defined.

The television channel schedulers are, of course, playing the numbers in a different way. It has often been stated that the key to the scheduler's art is to stack up big audiences in the early evening which will stay with the channel through the evening. This truism is, however, only half true. Under British television conditions the middle and end of peak time have long had the fixed blocks of the BBC1 main news at 9 p.m. and the ITV/ITN main news at 10 p.m.; this makes for a very inflexible structure, and the main flexibility resides at the front end of peak time – before 9 p.m. – before which time, moreover, well over half of all TV viewing is done (Figure 15). The arguments about grabbing-them-in-early-evening and the 'inheritance' of audiences assume that there is a very high degree of channel loyalty in television. This, however, is not the case; most audience members, even before the fourth channel, sampled at least once a week all the available channels. This is inevitable given a choice from four channels each of which puts on a wide range of both popular and less popular programming. The 'inheritance factor' is not totally imaginary[12] but it seems to work only over very short time spans; the audience may wait briefly to see what the next offering is like, but having seen it, may quickly switch away.

In radio, channel loyalty is a different matter – as one might expect in a system of specialized channels each appealing heavily to its own specific sectors of the population. This system deliberately avoids the old Reithian mixture within a single channel: it plays to particular tastes and thus achieves channel loyalty. Most radio listeners focus heavily on a single channel or two channels, ignoring the others.

In the case of both national and regional daily newspapers 'channel loyalty' has long been high because most copies have been home delivered on order, and even those who buy their copy on the street – especially common among the new 1970s purchasers of *The Sun* – tend to stick to the same paper. In the case of tabloids, news executives try so to use research data as to draw the reader through all the pages; the British tabloid is designed to be read – or at least looked at – in its entirety. Typically about 60% of a tabloid's contents is in fact 'look at' material – pictures, headlines, cartoons and display advertising – and consequently high proportions of readers do 'look at' at least the headlines and pictures on all pages. This 'thin tabloid' concept is radically different from the American sectionalized approach, now favoured by some British Sundays and provincial evenings; once there are separate sections research inevitably shows that some readers fail even to open one or more entire sections.

Primary, secondary and tertiary audience hours: some estimates
It has long been recognized that a distinction needs to be made
between media consumption as 'primary' or as 'secondary' activity.
Radio in the age of television has become mainly a secondary
activity; and television itself – especially earlier in the day – is also
often secondary.[13]

Table 17 shows how adding the secondary activity data – especially the JICRAR/commercial local radio data – approximately
doubles audience time. There are also yet other data summarized
in the third column which includes media consumption as a
'tertiary' activity. 'Tertiary' here has no single definition; but the
television rating system does report household 'viewing' of around
five hours per day – although a particular individual might not be
home, or, if home, not in the relevant room. 'Tertiary' could literally mean that one listens to the sound through the wall, while await-
ing the next item; or tertiary might refer to glancing back and
forth at a newspaper, opened at the TV schedule or the sports
fixtures. Finally 'tertiary' can refer to the possibility of one person
'attending' to three media simultaneously; one might be glancing
at the television with its sound turned down, listening to radio
news-on-the-hour, while inspecting the schedules in the newspaper.

TABLE 17

BRITISH ADULTS: ESTIMATED AVERAGE HOURS SPENT PER WEEK
WITH MAJOR MEDIA, 1982

	Primary activity (narrow definition)	Primary and secondary activity (looser definition)	Primary, secondary and tertiary activity (including set 'switched on', 'looking at' newspaper etc)
Television	18[1]	21[2]	35[2]
Radio	2	23[3]	30
Newspaper and magazines	5	6	10
TOTAL HOURS per week	25	50	75

Sources: Author's estimates based on: 1 BBC, 1980; 2 BARB, 1982; 3 JICRAR, 1982.

1982 may prove to have been the last year in which estimates even of this accuracy could be made. In autumn 1982 there was a drop in the television ratings, at least half of which appeared to be caused by video cassette recording for 'time shift' viewing purposes. The even more rapid spread of remote control devices and of households containing two or more television sets all add to the complexities of estimating audience hours and levels of attention.

Ingredients of unpopularity: politics and art

Two of the most unpopular types of programming on British television are Party Political Broadcasts and serious art. Nevertheless there is a very strong urge to put these things on; one solution is to put them on sparingly and in defiance of public unpopularity. The other solution is to dress them up as something more appealing – investigative documentaries or 'current affairs' in the case of politics, problem drama or magazine programmes in the case of the arts.

Victorian politicians used to speculate as to who, if anyone, read the editorial articles and the long Parliamentary reports of speeches in the newspapers. The latter especially have shrunk in recent decades; as excerpts of the scripts of Debates have shrunk, political coverage has increasingly been dominated by Lobby correspondents – no longer anonymous, and less secretive – who give more drama-critic-cum-personal-investigation and personality-oriented accounts or in-fighting in the Cabinet. But the political parties – seeing the extent to which they have lost control of both press and TV coverage – have clung tenaciously to the Party Political Broadcasts.[14]

The dilemmas surrounding PPBs can be illustrated by the audience figures for the May 1979 General Election. During the election campaign there were several different sorts of television which covered the contest but got low audiences. BBC1 and BBC2 each had late evening *daily* programmes on the election which averaged 1·7 and 0·9 million viewers respectively. Five peak-time evening current affairs programmes featuring interviews with the three main party leaders averaged about 3 million. Nine other networked election programmes each got under one million. Numerous networked radio programmes (Radio 4) all scored under a million, and some as low as 100,000. This amounts to nearly one hundred networked election radio and TV programmes in a three-week period, each averaging an audience of around one million (2·5% of all adults).

There were, however, three main sorts of exceptions to this tale of unpopular politicians. In particular the six programmes on the 6–7 p.m. BBC *Nationwide* popular news magazine slot each had an average audience of 7 million. Secondly, the regular news programmes which of course mixed election and non-election news and got their usual biggish audiences; and thirdly the 13 Party Political Broadcasts (5 each to Labour and Conservative, 3 to Liberal) each of which had an average audience of 10·6 million – mainly of course because each was brief and shown on all three then existing national channels.[15]

In other words, politics – even in a very brief and highly polarised General Election campaign – when labelled as such tends to get low audiences. As a politician the only ways to get respectably sized audiences are to take your chance on popular general programmes which are under someone else's editorial control – the News or *Nationwide* – or to use the rationed semi-compulsion of Party Political Broadcasts shown on all three channels.

Arts programmes do not have similar opportunities. But the nearest equivalent is perhaps the showing of an entire opera, which happens a few times a year. The audiences tend to be above or below half a million, partly depending on the popularity of the opera. This is an operation nearly as controversial as the PPB; some opera lovers believe neither the screen nor the sound system of television to be adequate to the task, and supporters of other arts resent the large slices of arts budgets which are thus spent on a single small opera audience.

One of the obvious 'solutions' – dressing art up into an arts magazine programme – hardly seems to work. The audiences remain small and unappreciative, and music annoyingly remains the most popular arts subject on television.[16] There continues to be one, and only one, reasonably certain way of attracting reasonably big audiences (e.g. 4 million) to reasonably demanding 'artistic' matter – and this is drama. The serious one-shot dramas and current affairs (or documentary) on television have much in common besides their controversial subject matter. Together they constitute the only reliable ways of persuading decent-sized audiences to watch art and politics.

The preferences which the British television audience had expressed in 1958 with two channels (Table 13) differed little from those expressed in the ratings 25 years later when four channels were available (Table 18). In the second week of January 1983 ITV had all ten largest audiences; *Coronation Street* filled the top two slots – with the top ten dominated by drama and comedy series, quizzes, an American TV movie, and three 'factual' items all strong in personality, fantasy and the exotic. The same kinds of programming topped all four channels, including Channel Four in Welsh. The film of Harold Pinter's *The Homecoming* was seen by two million people on Channel Four, but it was an exception; the new channel's still small audiences otherwise preferred light entertainment material – soap operas and comedies old and new, a golden hits item, and films.

TABLE 18: TOP RATED TELEVISION, 1983
(*Week ending 16th January 1983*)

National Top Tens

BBC1	Individuals viewing (*millions*)	ITV	Individuals viewing (*millions*)
1 Hi-De-Hi!	13·40	1 Coronation Street (Wed) (GRA)	16·55
2 Skorpion	11·40		
3 Holiday '83	11·30	2 Coronation Street (Mon) (GRA)	16·35
4 Nanny	11·10		
5 Mastermind	11·05	3 This Is Your Life (THA)	16·05
6 Top Of The Pops	10·75		
7 Emery	10·25	4 That's My Boy (YTV)	14·10
8 The Les Dawson Show	10·20	5 The Guinness Book of Records Special (ITV)	13·85
9 News and Sport	10·10	6 Family Fortunes (CEN)	13·80
10 Wildlife On One	9·95	7 Night Terror (ITV)	13·65
		8 The Gentle Touch (LWT)	13·60
		9 Wish You Were Here (THA)	13·50
		10 Punchlines (LWT)	13·45

BBC2	(*millions*)	CHANNEL 4	(*millions*)
1 Dad's Army	6·90	1 The Irish RM	3·40
2 Pot Black '83 (Mon)	6·05	2 Hotel Paradiso	2·40
3 M*A*S*H	5·00	3 Upstairs, Downstairs	2·30
4 The Belles of St Trinians	4·35	4 The Homecoming	2·15
5 Pot Black '83 (Fri)	3·85	4 The Paul Hogan Show	2·15
6 Invasion Of The Body Snatchers	3·70	6 Brookside (Tue)	2·00
6 The Nolans	3·70	7 The Munsters	1·85
8 Doctors' Dilemmas	3·55	8 Brookside (Wed)	1·75
9 Russell Harty (Tue)		9 The Lady Is A Tramp	1·50
10 Forty Minutes	3·50	10 Unforgettable	1·45
	2·90		

TABLE 18 – *cont.*

Selected Regional Top Tens

LONDON	TVR (*percentage of homes*)	S4C: WELSH CHANNEL 4	Individuals viewing (*thousands*)
1 Coronation Street (Mon 10 Jan) (GRA)	31	*In Welsh*	
2 This Is Your Life (THA)	29	1 Pobl Y Cwm (Serial) (BBC)	192
2 Coronation Street (Wed 12 Jan) (GRA)	29	2 Great Western (Series) (Ind)	148
2 The Guinness Book of Records Special (ITV)	29	3 Rhaglen Hywel Gwynfryn (L Ent) (BBC)	139
5 Night Terror (ITV)	26	4 Cyfeiriad (Series) (HTV)	125
6 Wish You Were Here (THA)	25	5 Minafon (Drama) (Ind)	115
6 Crossroads (Tue 11 Jan) (CEN)	25	*In English*	
6 That's My Boy (YTV)	25	1 The Addams Family	158
		2 Battlestar Galactica	154
6 The Gentle Touch (LWT)	25	3 Hotel Paradiso	152
10 Skorpion (BBC)	24	4 The Lady Is A Tramp	114
10 The Fall Guy (ITV)	24	5 Upstairs, Downstairs	96
10 Punchlines (LWT)	24		
10 Hi-De-Hi! (BBC)	24		
10 Mastermind (BBC)	24		
10 The Professionals (LWT)	24		

CENTRAL SCOTLAND	TVR (*percentage of homes*)	MIDLANDS EAST AND WEST	TVR (*percentage of homes*)
1 Family Fortunes (CEN)	33	1 Coronation Street (Mon 10 Jan) (GRA)	32
2 This Is Your Life (THA)	32	1 Coronation Street (Wed 12 Jan) (GRA)	32
3 Night Terror (ITV)	31	3 This Is Your Life (THA)	31
3 Coronation Street (Wed 12 Jan) (GRA)	31	4 Emmerdale Farm (Tue 11 Jan) (YTV)	29
5 Coronation Street (Mon 10 Jan) (GRA)	29	4 Emmerdale Farm (Thu 13 Jan) (YTV)	29
5 It Takes A Worried Man (THA)	29	4 Hi-De-Hi! (BBC)	29

TABLE 18 – *cont.*

Selected Regional Top Tens

CENTRAL SCOTLAND	TVR (*percentage of homes*)	MIDLANDS EAST AND WEST	Individuals viewing (*thousands*)
5 That's My Boy (YTV)	29	7 Wish You Were Here (THA)	28
8 Benson (ITV)	28	7 Mike Yarwood In Persons (THA)	28
8 Tom Dick and Harriet (THA)	28	9 Central News (Tue 11 Jan) (CEN)	27
8 Falcon Crest (ITV)	28	9 Central News (Wed 12 Jan) (CEN)	27
8 Punchlines (LWT)	28	9 Family Fortunes (CEN)	27
		9 That's My Boy (YTV)	27
		9 Holiday '83 (BBC)	27

Week's hours of viewing, share of audience and average daily reach

	Average viewing per head (*hrs:mins*)	Share of total viewing		Average daily reach (%)
		%		
All TV	22:54	100	Any TV	75·5
BBC1	7:55	35	BBC1	55·2
BBC2	1:48	8	BBC2	23·6
Total BBC	9:43	43	Any BBC	60·3
ITV	12:14	53	ITV	61·1
Channel 4	0:57	4	Channel 4	12·9
Total ITV	13:11	58	Any ITV	63·4

Source: BARB/AGB

CHAPTER TEN

Bias?

This chapter will consider some of the main sorts of 'bias' which critics claim to see in the output of the British media. The most common kind of such criticism, especially since around 1970, has accused the media of conservative bias and has claimed that the media reflect and support the existing pattern of social and economic inequality. Some versions of this critique assert that the media actually *create* further injustice and inequality – by establishing a new, or newly significant type of injustice, namely media injustice.

The media are said to be biased against trade unions and in favour of big business and management; against women and in favour of traditional male chauvinist values; against ethnic minorities; and against certain age categories especially certain sections of both the elderly and the young. This bias, it is said, results in trade unions – not owners and management – being blamed by the media for Britain's economic ills; women are presented on the media largely as seen by men rather than as women see themselves; ethnic minorities are presented in a negative light as the 'immigrant problem', the 'Asian problem' the 'black crime problem'; finally old people are either ignored or seen as the 'old people problem,' while the working-class young are presented in the context of deviance, excess, violence and irrationality.

There are two broad sorts of assumptions behind the selection of media content – *news* values and *cultural* values. News values (see also next chapter) claim to go hand in hand with one type of neutrality – party political neutrality. Newspapers and factual TV/radio claim to be politically neutral as between political parties, news values require that more attention should be paid to the government, because it is more newsworthy, but this attention will be critical because news values not only stress those people who are in power, they also stress conflict, bad news, disasters, negative events.

The *cultural* values behind media selections have some similarities. The Annan Committee favoured the term 'pluralism' – putting on a wide range of material. Clearly the media do indeed put on both politics and quiz shows, both opera and soap opera, both rock music and plays by avant-garde authors. But critics can, and do, ask whether this pluralism does not seek to hide some less attractive basis of selection. Behind cultural pluralism do there not lurk the old forces of the artistic establishment, now buttressed by state subsidies and by additional advertising-related finance? Is not the whole of the BBC's music output a reflection either of regressive taxation and of subsidy to the cultural elite (Radio 3) or a reflection of commercial and advertising related pop culture (Radios 1 and 2)?

'Neutral' news values and 'plural' cultural values clearly have in common certain vaguely liberal, centrist assumptions of muddling through the middle, and of attempting to reflect what exists by adopting a common-sense, reasonable compromise framework of selection. Clearly in both cases there is tension between *accepting* what news or culture is on offer, and *selecting* on the basis of centrist but vague criteria. In both cases there is a big element of accepting and recognising a hierarchy. News values are explicitly hierarchical – people at the top of governments, organizations, trade unions, or football teams are assumed to have more interesting things to say, and thus receive more attention than do mere voters, employees, union members or reserve players. Cultural values are also explicitly hierarchical in that 'pluralism' aims not at giving all musicians – regardless of talent – an equal airing; pluralism seeks the best from a wide variety of types of music (or drama or humour). Cultural pluralism calls for 'good of its kind' – a compromise involving equal tolerance of even the most popular material, balanced with the hierarchical assumption that some quizzes, tabloid newspapers, and imported action dramas are better than others.

The defenders of both news values and cultural values cannot deny that in terms of access to the media these criteria are hierarchical. But the critics also find themselves in difficulties. Some who criticise news values for being too hierarchical (too much access for top people) are the same people who criticize cultural values for not being hierarchical enough (too much commercial junk). Other critics see common forces (conservative – business – the state – advertising) behind the unsavoury hierarchy of both news and cultural values.

Almost everyone recognizes that there must be selection and there must be some kind of hierarchy behind this – not many people want their television screens filled permanently by *amateur* actors, rock singers, journalists, politicians, comedians and footballers. However critics tend to assert that certain categories (e.g. government ministers, management, opera singers) receive unfairly gentle, or extensive, access and treatment. The trade union critique in effect says that while trade unions receive the full aggressive blast of negative news values, these news values are suspended for management which receives 'extra fair' treatment especially on the financial pages of the serious newspapers – treatment which in practice is achieved via special financial advertising.

The best example of 'extra fair' treatment is the coverage of the royal family. Ordinary news values are suspended; no 'other side' of the argument ('and now 20 minutes for the anti-monarchists') is given equal time for reply; scheduling is very favourable – for example the Queen's annual address to the nation just happens to be on Christmas day, the best ratings day of the year. Even this example of the 'extra fair' concept is not without its problems; certain lesser members of the royal family receive more critical coverage. It could also be argued that any politician who had so little opposition and such a high opinion poll rating would earn equally gentle treatment.

Nevertheless 'extra fair' treatment is a viable concept which summarizes some of the major demands on, and critiques of, media coverage. Trade unionists and women are each saying: we are not just some small minority; we are half the population (in the case of women, or *working* population in the case of trade unionists) and we have at least as good a case as the other side (men, management) for extra fair treatment. Ethnic minorities are also saying that it is unfair to operate the usual conflict and negative news values about them; in effect they claim that – at least in media coverage – a little positive discrimination would be justified, rather than the existing *de facto* discrimination via reckless application of general bad news values to issues which are too complex and to people who are too vulnerable to weather such treatment.

Pro-capitalist, anti-working class? Or anti-establishment?

The critique from the political left became noticeably sharper during the 1970s; the Glasgow Media Group's *Bad News* (1976) and other critical research was quoted by several prominent Labour politicians and by national leaders of some of the largest trade unions.

A very brief summary of the critique would be as follows:

All General Elections since February 1974 have shown the national press to be quite openly and explicitly biased towards the Conservative party; the popular tabloid nationals – led by Rupert Murdoch's gutter press *Sun* newspaper – have waged an increasingly virulent campaign against the Labour party and the trade unions. What *The Sun* and *Daily Mail* do so shamelessly, the rest of the press does a little less blatantly; the press is owned by big business and serves its interests. While the broadcasting organizations are less biased, they also lean towards the Conservative party, big business, the state and the advertising industry. Although some journalists and producers are on the left, and many of them attempt to be fair, they are unable to resist the right-inclined biases which pervade all commercial mass media and which the owners and managers reinforce from above. These tendencies are most clearly evidenced in the bias against the Labour party (usually presented in terms of internal conflict and menacing moves to the left); the inaccurate coverage of nationalised industries as inefficient and wasteful; the presentation of trade unions as strike-prone, of workers as work-shy, of the Welfare State as vulnerable to the dishonest[1] and of the labour movement as responsible – through excessive pay claims and featherbedding – for Britain's inflation record and poor economic performance. Media bias is also shown in the favourable coverage accorded to the media bosses' friends – the Conservative party, big business and the stock market, management, the advertising industry and the entire conservative establishment of Britain (the Judges, Oxford and Cambridge, Whitehall). In particular the media – owned and controlled by big business and the state – fail to report that Britain's poor economic performance derives largely from failures in investment and planning by big business and the state. More diffusely the media – despite a few prominent regional accents and working-class people here and there – still speak largely with both the accents and values of privately educated South of England upper-middle-class middle-aged men. The real working-class voice of half or more of the British people is confined to the sports pages and the comedy shows.

In terms of the previous discussion the criticism is, of course, that both news values and cultural values are in fact Conservative political values. While this critique from the left has been more and more forcibly presented, there are at least two main forms of contradictory critique. One, associated with Mrs Mary Whitehouse, is that cultural pluralist values, especially as operated by the BBC, are – if not left-wing – certainly opposed to, and disruptive of, establishment moral values and religion. Secondly there is an argument often made by managers that news values are anti-management and that managers are in practice placed 'in the dock' by the media – because they only become newsworthy when their company is in trouble. Moreover while the political left accuses journalists and producers of politically centrist views, conservatively-inclined managers are probably correct in believing that most journalists and producers have centre or centre-left political views and are indeed to the left of the Conservative Party.

Bias against trade unions?
The coverage of trade unions happens to fall awkwardly between some of the familiar polarities of the British media. The national/

regional divide means that the national media, looking for conflict-laden stories and national personalities, seize on Britain's national unions and their national officials. This gives a somewhat misleading impression, since Britain's industrial relations are primarily local and harmonious (possibly too harmonious) while local or regional union leaders are often more important than national ones. The provincial media probably give a more 'accurate' picture of industrial relations – certainly within their own localities – but the sensational national press/TV/radio coverage attracts more attention.

The prestige/popular divide in the national press also poses dilemmas. The 'fairest' and fullest coverage of trade unions appears in the serious newspapers, whereas the least and least fair coverage appears in those very papers read by four-fifths of the population and by most trade union members.[2] Moreover the press/broadcast divide means that while reasonably fair and full coverage is available in the provincial press and the serious newspapers, it is the 45-second item on the television national news which, more than anything else, gives the British people their picture (literally) of industrial relations. With such an exceptionally complex field this snap video coverage is inevitably incomplete and often misleading, but – such is television's impression of letting the public see for themselves – few people, and few trade unionists,[3] believe that television as a medium is anything other than neutral.

There is also the *daily* obsession of the British media, and the demand – in a country where conflict tends to be muted – for a daily supply of conflict-laden stories, of interest and concern to a national audience, replete with colourful personalities to quote and newsy events to record and film. On any single day an industrial relations story seems to many news editors to match these criteria fairly well.

The industrial/labour correspondents field came into being in the 1930s. The 1930s were a time of national wage bargaining and strict national union discipline; conflicts between labour and employers were also not hard to find. It seemed sensible then for the dominant national newspapers to cover industrial relations in somewhat the same manner as national politics was covered by Lobby journalists.

The difficulty with answering the common criticisms of industrial-relations coverage is that the criticisms themselves are all upside-down. The common criticism that there is 'too much' industrial relations coverage is, at least in the press, wrong – a sounder criticism might be that the small amounts (and big headlines) inevitably distort complex realities. This criticism is truer of television news; by taking over the press idea of industrial relations as typically the second or third strongest story of the day, television with its shorter bulletins has greatly magnified the proportion of total output which goes to industrial relations.[4] Radio (with its many very short bulletins) probably gives the most 'exaggerated' weight of all, but nobody has yet studied this aspect. The proportion of all industrial relations coverage which is devoted to strikes is also relatively small; in 1975 in the national press it was only 22% – giving strikes well under 1% of all national press editorial space.

The criticisms, at very least, require reformulation.[5] One way of seeing the complaints is that the trade union critics of media coverage in effect are saying that they are indeed covered as though they were national politics, but without the positive coverage of the more bureaucratic, civil service, aspects of government. This analogy can be extended to the local level, where the trade unions are no match for the town hall in generating positive publicity.

The conflict-laden national media and the relatively bland local monopoly media together unintentionally present an *overall picture of trade unions as national organizations dominated by national celebrity personalities*. The reality of British trade unions is much more local than this media picture implies.

The prestige/popular divide means that most trade union members read popular newspapers which largely ignore industrial relations; some survey evidence supports the journalists' belief that public interest in trade unions is limited to major upheavals which affect the public as consumers. Because the popular tabloids devote so little space to industrial relations, while television gives at least some, television does indeed become the dominant source of industrial relations news for the bulk of the population. The grammar and conventions of TV news may indeed tend to penalize trade union members.

But trade union leaders, like managers and employers, also receive rather privileged treatment from television. And the personalities which dominate industrial relations coverage (with press and television) all belong to trade union leaders. These trade union leaders are covered as political leaders, and have often been heavily reported in their role of negotiating with or confronting not employers, but the government. These leaders busily provide statements, 'guidance' and leaks. British national trade union leaders have fewer powers than the TV viewer might think; they preside over mainly rather ramshackle organisations which are most active at the most local and least nationally disciplined level. Most unions lack adequate PR staffs. One of the General Secretary's real and key powers is that he has a national, i.e. media, reputation. National media publicity is a weapon with which to try to beat employers – but equally importantly his own members – into line.

There is thus a missing clause in the trade union critique. Many national trade union leaders – in their personal capacity as publicists and executives – are broadly happy with the present publicity arrangements. But these same men also know that, while they personally may win the publicity battles, this is done at cost of the trade unions losing their publicity wars.

Another way of seeing the union case is as a plea to be treated as the government is treated when its policy documents, its normal bureaucratic functioning (its 'good news') get massive coverage. A further comparison is with management. Both the civil service machine and the business/management machine have greater legitimacy; they are regarded as the 'natural' source of routine news by relevant specialist journalists; they have flotillas of public relations men who pump out good news, while still being conscious of the art (almost unknown in trade union circles) of sometimes staying silent.

Both big business and big government also have advertising and can – if they choose – buy themselves large amounts of publicity. Trade unions do not have such resources.

1979: Winter of discontent and General Election

In the early weeks and months of 1979, immediately previous to the General Election of May, the two main strands – political and trade union – of the left critique, were strengthened and became more bitter. A series of strikes by public sector workers (rail, civil service, hospital, refuse collectors, school caretakers) received enormous media attention, led by highly partisan coverage from the national daily Conservative tabloids (*Sun, Mail, Express*). The Labour–trade union leadership was presented as internally divided; the General Election was duly won by the Conservatives. The use of commercial advertising techniques by the Conservatives further added to Labour bitterness.

Since 1979 newspaper coverage of politics – and national politics itself – has been increasingly partisan, polarized and volatile. The left critique has been broadly accepted by the entire Labour Party; the trade union leaders have increasingly used their still frequent media appearances to attack the government.

Academic studies have also tended to play an ever more prominent part as evidence or ammunition for the left critique. John Hartley, for example, analyses in full semiological detail one television news story on the BBC main news on February 1st, 1979; the story concerned the hospital workers' dispute and included news film shot in a children's hospital. According to Hartley this hospital story (plus accompanying political analysis) presented the hospital workers as the bad guys – opposed to sick children, the government, to decent trade unionism and to 'us' the televiewing public.[6]

However an IBA study conducted in March 1979 indicates that

the London public did not regard such television coverage as unfair. A few aspects of the left critique achieved some popular support – employers' spokesmen were on the whole thought to be more sympathetically presented. But overall the BBC and ITN television coverage was perceived by the public as being broadly neutral.[7] As usual there was no comprehensive study covering radio, national and local press and television.

Male chauvinist bias?

Critiques of male chauvinist bias are as varied as those of right-wing bias, but here is an attempt at a brief summary of the main lines of criticism:

The presentation of women in the media is biased, because it emphasises women's domestic, sexual, consumer and marital activities to the exclusion of all else. Women are depicted as busy housewives, as contented mothers, as eager consumers and as sex objects. This does indeed indicate bias because, although similar numbers of men are fathers and husbands the media have much less to say about these male roles; men are seldom presented nude, nor is their marital or family status continually quoted in irrelevant contexts. Just as men's domestic and marital roles are ignored, the media also ignore that well over half of British adult women go out to paid employment, and that many of both their interests and problems are employment-related.

This bias both reflects and exacerbates ideas generally prevalent in society. It also occurs because in terms of employment the media industries are male chauvinist; women are employed only in clerical or unskilled posts. Programmes are made and newspapers are written by men who work in a male-dominated, drinks-with-the-boys atmosphere. The higher executive levels of the media industry are even more male-dominated. And, last but not least, the advertising industry exerts a powerful influence over the way women appear in the media; the advertising industry wants women to be seen in bed, in the kitchen, in the nursery, and in the supermarket – not striding around the worlds of work and achievement.[8]

We will return to the issue of women as communicators later (Chapter 14). Let us here review some of the existing evidence. On the whole women are indeed depicted in the media as radically different from men – to an extent which goes well beyond actual differences in either paid employment or media consumption. If we consider how women are presented on television we do seem immediately to move into a more gender-polarized and stereotyped world. Women are presented primarily as partners of men, mothers of children, and as bodies. Halloran in an Appendix published by the Annan Committee reports an analysis of British TV drama characters. Taking the six main characters from each of 93 fictional programmes, 67% of main characters were male, 28% female, while the remainder (5%) were cartoon characters of indeterminate gender. For half the male characters marital status was unclear, whereas the women's marital status was almost invariably specified.

What about television advertisements? Two Manchester University researchers studied television advertising transmitted on ITV in 1979. This research indicated a strong tendency for women to be shown as dependent, domestic, consumers of products being advised by men – in vision or voice-over – as to their consumer behaviour.[9]

Why, then, do women put up with this? The answer may be that while the feminists are broadly accurate in their critique of the presentation of women, the anti-feminists, who claim that the national audience of women is relatively happy, seem also to be vindicated. A 1981 study of women and television conducted in London – presumably Britain's most feminist location – does on the whole indicate that women are fairly happy with television. They watch more than men, they watch more ITV than men, and they are more appreciative of programmes in general than are men. There is one exception – sport – but even there women are nearly as appreciative as men. Women are significantly more positive than men about soap operas. This study offers only one important crumb of comfort for the feminist critics; women did notice that some kinds of comedy show were crudely sexist – such as Benny Hill, Dick Emery, Kenny Everett, Monty Python and the Goodies – and they were markedly less well disposed towards such comedies than are men.[10]

Another field in which further research appears to be necessary is the portrayal of homosexuality on British television. One study of *The Naked Civil Servant*, an ITV dramatized documentary about the life of Quentin Crisp as a homosexual, revealed that the programme got the usual size of audience (3½ million) for serious drama/documentary; the majority of the audience had a distinctly positive response to the strong homosexual theme, although a minority did not.[11] This example seems to show both the programme makers and the great British audience in a fairly adult mood. But can the same be said of the bulk of British television? A remarkable amount of television humour seems to involve male comedians either in drag, or feigning homosexuality, or making double-entendus, sex-oriented jokes.

To return to the comparison between the 'right-wing bias' and 'male-chauvinist bias' critiques: there clearly are some similarities, as well as differences. And since women have been around longer than have trade unions, the biased presentation of women clearly has the longer history. From the point of view of showing women in marital and domestic roles, most dramatists – Shakespeare included – are surely guilty as charged.

The conventions of drama do indeed deliberately exaggerate, or emphasize, gender polarities for obvious purposes of dramatic effect and contrast. The problem from the viewpoint of the feminist critique is that similar forces of exaggeration are also at work in news values, in the selective processes of advertising, and in the employment practices of the media industry.

Law and order, police, violence

This is not the place to review the massive (mainly American) literature on the mass media and violence. But it is said that the media are too concerned with violence and with law and order and are too favourably disposed towards the police. An answering critique asserts that the media are obsessed with police wrong-doing.

Certainly there is a lot of crime melodrama on television, but so there has always been in other forms of literature. There is some evidence that the newspaper readers might like more crime stories. Once again both dramatic values and news values emphasize crime, but both also tend to show that the forces of law and order prevail in the end.

Probably at least 80 per cent of what appears in the media about crime and the police broadly reflects the views and interests of the police. In television series the good guys are usually the police, and documentary investigations usually assume that major law-breaking by the police is a distinctly minority activity. The national newspaper reading public probably does not realize that the great bulk of crime news comes from the police at Scotland Yard[12] and elsewhere. It would be difficult to imagine a newspaper in which 80% of the stories came from the criminals, or a television system in which the majority of crime series portrayed heroic criminals dealing, episode after episode, with this week's corrupt policeman. Obviously British television, like Hollywood, Soviet, Brazilian and Chinese television supports the cops against the robbers. The debate is not about this but should be about whether an 80% (or similar high figure) ratio of favourable coverage is too high or too low; secondly are criminals portrayed in some biased way or is some other sub-group identified to a biased extent as being criminal?

Obviously if all criminals were portrayed as being women (when the crime statistics point to men) or as being trade union officials, there would be some vocal protest. But what if criminals are portrayed as being black?

Racist media?

In the United States the black population has in practice managed to negotiate for itself a sort of *de facto* television package deal. In terms of sheer numbers on the American television screen the black population is somewhat – but not much – under-represented as against its numbers in the population. But the other part of the deal is that Hollywood television deliberately under-states the proportion of criminals who are black[13] certainly as compared with the official criminal statistics.

A BBC study conducted in 1971 showed an unexpected side-effect of this Hollywood policy. The study was called 'Non-whites on British television'.[14] Although people of Afro-Asian ethnic origin in 1971 made up about 2·5% of the British population, they accounted for about 3·5% of the speaking parts on British television. However the majority of these were playing characters in imported Hollywood films and series; Hawaians were especially well represented. In British-made television in 1971 'non-white' persons when they appeared at all were usually in non-speaking parts, hovering in the background.

Another study, of the handling of race by British national newspapers in the period 1963–70, discovered a different picture. All national newspapers in the mid and late 1960s gave about 1·5% of space to 'race-related matters'; much of this was devoted to 'race overseas' mainly in Rhodesia and South Africa. Within Britain the major thrust of race coverage by the newspapers focused upon the issue of 'immigration' – race relations problems, immigration legislation, crime, and discrimination. There was a peak in 1968 – the year not only of Britain's first Race Relations Act but of Enoch Powell's emergence as an anti-immigration crusader. The authors also found that many (but not most) ethnic stories had a 'racial cue-word' in the headline – such words as 'immigrant', 'race' or 'West Indian'.[15]

Both of these studies are only rather gently critical compared with what is undoubtedly the most weighty critique of the British media in the ethnic area. This is *Policing the Crisis* by Stuart Hall and colleagues. Sub-titled 'Mugging, the State, and Law and Order', this study accuses the police and the mass media (especially the Fleet Street populars) of having together invented a crime previously unknown in Britain – a crime called 'mugging' committed mainly by young black men on white victims.

The left critique is itself biased?

Bad News and *Policing the Crisis* are the two most important academic studies supporting the left critique. Both studies have drawn blood. *Bad News* does demonstrate that neutral news conventions still allow some extremely hostile television news coverage of trade unions. *Policing the Crisis* shows the police, the Fleet Street tabloids and the Birmingham daily press to have engaged in some highly sensational and overtly racist interpretation of rather ambiguous crime statistics and court cases.

Had they stopped there, both studies might have lent some 'objective' support to the left critique. Both studies, however, engage in interpretative over-kill. The three *Bad News* books total 963 pages, while *Policing the Crisis* runs to 425 packed pages; in many passages each study hands hostages to its opponents.

Both studies build their sweeping condemnations upon the very narrow basis of *Content analysis* over a period of weeks of only one type of news in a few selected news media. Both studies involve a large team of authors – eight in one case, five (really seven) in the other. This authors' collective approach leads to massive repetition and internal contradiction, and a failure to state clearly the main arguments or findings. In addition to the solid empirical base, both studies erect a superstructure of rambling and highly dubious journalistic comment, heavily relying on scissors-and-paste re-interpretation of press coverage. Both claim to be primarily studies of the media output; nevertheless both studies are vulnerable to the obvious critique from journalists and sociologists that they have made little effort to interview, or to understand, journalists, trade unionists, blacks, and the police. Both studies ignore relevant academic and other literature on news, or industrial relations news, on race, and on the police. Both studies are oddly *static*, focusing heavily on their selected weeks in the early and mid-1970s. There is insufficient recognition that the news media and news values change from year to year and decade to decade.

The unintended consequences of these – and other academic studies from the political left – has been to exacerbate yet further the polarization of opinion about 'bias'. Such authors at once document bias in the eyes of the left, while exhibiting themselves as prime examples of bias and inadequate scholarship in the eyes of the unconverted.

CHAPTER ELEVEN
Inequality and ambiguity

Are the media generally *objective*, or do they treat particular subjects (women, trade unions, black people, third world nations) unfairly? Do the media reflect the concerns of western big business? Is it possible for new values in any sense to be either objective or fair? Should people get redress, access, the chance to talk back to the media?

A second major set of themes can be labelled as *ambiguity*. These themes are also pursued in both the public debate and in research. Ambiguity themes dominate the enormous bulk of broadly social psychology research – which stresses audience responses, often the response of children to educational materials or 'action' television series. As voiced by people employed in the media, ambiguity themes include assertions about news values as deliberately giving 'both sides' and thus allowing audiences 'to decide for themselves'.

The present author asserts that in attempting to understand the media in Britain both *inequality* and *ambiguity* must be recognized. Many aspects of the media quite overtly stress, reflect, and help to create, *inequality*. But many aspects of the media also overtly stress, reflect and help to create *ambiguity*. And much of what happens in the media is so muddled, so confusing (to audiences, to critics and defenders, as well as to journalists and producers) precisely because in the very same material both *inequality* and *ambiguity* are overtly present – for example in 'news values'.

Many journalists and producers recognize this. Some academics also have recognized this in their research. For example Jay Blumler and Denis McQuail, while elsewhere quite explicit about the hierarchical nature of news, also analyse the varied 'uses and gratifications' which different members of the audience can extract from the identical TV quiz show. David Morley, while himself favouring one particular left critique of the BBC *Nationwide* news magazine show, also reports that audience groups make several different left-wing critiques, whereas other audience groups make contrasting or conservative critiques of the very same episodes of the very same show.[1]

On the *inequality* aspect: everyone agrees that the media content must reflect the inequalities which exist in the world. Everyone agrees that, say, the Prime Minister's words should receive more attention than those of most other people. Feminist critics do not suggest, simply because certain activities are conducted mainly or entirely by men, that these activities should receive no media coverage; feminist critics do not expect the media suddenly to right all the wrongs of centuries. What they demand is that the media should at worst not increase those inequalities, and at best should reverse them a little.

Those who criticize media inequalities have seldom demanded a totally *equal* media treatment. Typically ethnic groups have at most demanded small amounts of positive discrimination and often have merely wanted their presence in the British urban scene to be recognized.[2] Larger groups have in practice demanded 'less inequality' of coverage. Few trade union leaders or members have seriously denied that management must in general obtain more coverage because on most industrial issues it speaks with more authority.

Such demands for 'less inequality' do however, lead into many logical difficulties. But similar difficulties are experienced by those who, in defending the *status quo*, argue in effect that just about the amount of inequality which now obtains is a fair and reasonable level of inequality. Take the criticism that the mass of the British population is denied the range of media choice which is available to a small wealthy minority. In its most familiar form[3] this criticism claims that in the national press the top 20% of the population have an effective choice of four (very different) national dailies, while the bottom 80% of the population have a choice of only five (very similar) national dailies. In some respects the top people have an even bigger unfair range of choice, it can be said, because they also tend to read the pop papers (giving them an effective choice of nine) whereas the 80% underprivileged cannot understand the four more weighty dailies or afford their higher cover prices. This argument is also extended into radio that the top 20% have their own two national radio channels (BBC radios 3 and 4). Of television it can be said that roughly half of the output of four national channels is aimed primarily at the same educated minority, who happen also to be light viewers of television. Thus, *Panorama*, the BBC's flagship programme, is seen not by 20% but about 6% of British adults.

Newspapers with affluent audiences are especially attractive to advertisers, who thus enable 'up-market' national daily newspapers to exist with sales of not 3 million but 300,000. The same thing also happens in television because advertising, prestige, 'balance', and the urge for 'minority' channels in practice also mean that not all viewers or licence fee payers are equal. There is clearly something in this argument.

But only something. Even if one accepts the general argument that the top 20% get the same range of choice as the bottom 80%, does it not still mean that everyone gets about the same range of choice? In some other contexts this is widely applauded; Britain, like other European countries, has an accepted tradition of taking television to remote and mountainous areas, on widely accepted grounds of 'equality'. Or is it even true that the bottom 80% do not have an effective choice to read, or tune in to, the 20%'s up-market media? In practice all of the 'serious' papers do have readers from the lower occupational categories (Figure 6) and all four national TV channels have an audience widely spread by class/education/ income. Critics of this argument can say that this is just the old familiar wish for a Labour party national newspaper, whereas the death of the *Daily Herald* shows that there is no popular demand for it. If there is a sufficient demand even a Tory-owned newspaper (like the *Daily Star*) will 'vote' Labour . . . and so on.

The centrality of ambiguity

Inequality certainly exists, and there is survey evidence to suggest that significant minorities of businessmen and other up-market persons believe both the provincial press and the BBC to be biased in their direction.[4] The present author agrees that there is *some* 'bias to the right' but less than most left critics assert, and indeed impossible to quantify or estimate. Impossible because of built-in ambiguity. (Of course it is also true that if a less right-wing press were to appear it would only need to push the national electorate a few percentage points leftward in order to register a major political readjustment.)

The very goals of media organizations are ambiguous. In newspapers this includes the sometimes contrary requirements of circulation, advertising, prestige and partisanship. The BBC enshrines ambiguity in its vague and apparently contradictory traditional goals of education, entertainment and information. News values historically relate to 'both sides' reporting – first the government view, then the opposition refutation. Conflict is also as old as drama, and ambiguity is often further enhanced by such old devices as the flawed hero, the appealing bad guy, and the 'good bad girl'. Typically the media both glorify – politicians, money, power, beauty, violence – and also denigrate them.

Finally the audience level introduces new ambiguities, quite apart from 'messages' which either carry no message, several messages or deliberately contradictory messages. 'Selective perception' is well documented – on the whole people perceive what they want to perceive; in the media 'selective exposure' adds to this – people follow that they already like and agree with.

The idea of an anti-prejudice programme which deliberately puts racist statements into the mouth of a bigoted character appeals to a scriptwriter and to the BBC. Research also showed that it appealed to bigots (who agreed with the bigoted view) and anti-bigots (who agreed with the scriptwriter that such views were absurd). *Till Death Us Do Part* (from which *All in the Family* and *Archie Bunker* were derived) thus achieved the BBC's ambiguous goals of entertaining, informing and educating and (a cynic might add) maintaining the *status quo*, all in one deliberately ambiguous package.[5]

The repeat viewing problem: more ambiguity

One relatively calm but significant area of controversy is that of repeat viewing. Goodhardt, Ehrenberg and Collins published in 1975 data about the propensity of television viewers who view one episode of a series to see subsequent episodes.[6] In several re-analyses of ITV/IBA data they have discovered that of people who watch one episode, about 55% will watch the next episode. This broadly holds true for anything, whether daily or weekly series, whether first runs or repeats, whether the BBC main evening news or a soap opera. Very popular series get a higher figure – 60% or 65% watch the next episode – while below average rating shows get a lower repeat viewing level – perhaps 50% or 45%.

But there is a pronounced clustering around 55%, which makes a remarkably neat conclusion to some complex data. How interesting is such a finding? Once again, we are back to ambiguity. How interesting the '55% repeat rule' is depends upon what sort of questions about television happen to interest you. The authors themselves have business school backgrounds and not too surprisingly their findings probably are of most interest to advertisers and their agents. Typical television advertising campaigns pursue their target audience by buying into an appropriate time in the ITV schedule and by repeating the advertisement a number of times at a daily, weekly or some other interval in order to achieve weight of repetition and 'reach' across the target audience. Much advertising is bought within large time blocks of programming but it is possible to pay a premium price for a specific location – such as in the first commercial break *within* a particular time slot. Repeat viewing data thus help advertisers to make detailed cost-benefit calculations.

One might also think that schedulers, the people who plan entire networks, would be most interested in such data. But schedulers probably did know it before and also did not find it too interesting. Schedulers – the managing director of BBC television for example – have long had the power and money to commission such studies, even though the traditional daily BBC quota sample could not produce such data. But schedulers are more interested in the audience flow across programmes and channels.

These authors have given seminars for producers. But again the reaction was bound to be: we knew it before and/or it is not very interesting. Producers only knew it approximately before but such evidence strongly affects only series with continuing plots; series with separate episodes or topics already assume lack of audience continuity.

Some soap operas, including long running radio serials with continuing plots like *The Archers*, have long had both a daily and a weekly repeat to solve the plot continuity problem. This problem is perhaps most severe in that characteristic British product, the short series. With a successful dramatic series of say seven episodes, the research tends to show that about 50% of the public see no episodes, while the half of the British population which does see any episodes is fairly evenly spread between those who see 1, 2, 3, 4, 5, 6, or all 7 episodes. Less successful series have somewhat more seeing none, or one, or two episodes; more successful series have more seeing 5, 6, or 7 episodes but even then probably less than 10% of the population see all seven episodes. Expressed this way the audience does look like a confusing target for the producer to aim at – whether he assumes high previous knowledge, or some, or none, will it not in fact be untrue of about two-thirds of those viewing? No, not so. Even if only 8–10% of the population see all seven episodes and another 8–10% see all but one, these two categories bulk much larger in each week's audience – in fact typically accounting for over half the total audience (or rating) for any one episode of a successful series – which might be around 25% to 30% of the population. To put it the other way around, the producer can largely ignore the perhaps 15% of the population who see only one episode, because they are spread once only across all the episodes. The greater (or smaller) *majority* of those viewing any episode will see the greater (or smaller) majority of all the episodes.

In practice the producer is probably more worried by other problems which arise from other conflicting requirements – and of course it is the *mixed* audience goals of British TV channels (which encourage channel switching) that lie behind these repeat viewing figures. If (and when in the future) TV channels are scheduled on a more specialised basis (as radio channels are) you will get the combination which is so far unknown on British TV – low total audience, but high repeat/loyalty level.

Ambiguous images of newspapers and broadcast organisations
There is evidence, also, of considerable ambiguity and ambivalence in public attitudes towards broadcast organizations and towards newspapers, even by their readers.

According to replies obtained in 1975 in research for the Royal Commission on the Press, the prestige national dailies appear to have a more loyal audience. In terms of ambiguity the replies by the readers of *The Sun* are perhaps more intriguing; in 1975 *The Sun*'s circulation was 3·4 million copies daily and was still rising. But these survey replies (from 472 readers of *The Sun*) seem to indicate a rather low opinion; *The Sun*'s readers apparently saw it as containing little news, as being prone to sensationalism, as getting its facts wrong and using trivial stories. Less of *The Sun*'s readers said they would miss it than was true of most other dailies.[7] Why, then, did its readers read *The Sun*? Presumably the answer lies in the high proportion of readers who found *The Sun* 'enjoyable'. Half of its readers said they spent less than 30 minutes a day reading it. *The Sun* scored poorly on most of the sober serious news questions favoured by the Royal Commission, but it scored well on providing an enjoyable 30-minute read – a service which, however, its readers would not greatly miss (or think could be provided by an alternative). That interpretation is consistent with *The Sun*'s high casual non-home-delivered sale. Or do *Sun* readers doubt the whole concept of 'news', or are they responding apologetically to the questions of middle-class interviewers clearly interested in a middle-class serious view of newspapers? While the sex, crime, sport and sensation formula is obviously packed with human appeal, the precise nature of the appeal is more mysterious. How can such an obviously male chauvinist publication as *The Sun* retain the typical ratio of 45% of its readers being women? How can such a paper, apparently aimed at the very lowest levels of taste and intelligence, in fact have over two million middle-class/white-collar readers?

The BBC's image provides a different problem but one equally strong in ambiguity. A 1979 study done for the BBC about its own image, is rich in evidence of ambivalent attitudes. People in other countries may, perhaps, have a clear image of the BBC as a bastion of public service broadcasting and political independence – but the attitudes of the British people are more complex. Many Britons do not apparently think of the BBC as the great television *and* radio organization; they tend to think of BBC television separately from 'the radio'. The BBC's image seems to be getting worse, with only 55% of Britons thinking they can always trust it and only a similar percentage believing the BBC to be in touch with ordinary people. About as many thought that it is controlled by the government (30%) as thought it independent of government (34%), while 36% did not know or would not say. Although 60% thought the BBC was not politically biased, 22% thought it was. Among both working-class and middle-class respondents more thought it was biased in favour of the Conservatives.[8]

Overall the survey makes fairly clear that the middle class and those over the age of 55 have the best opinion of the BBC, while the working class and those under 44 have the least favourable view. Clearly such opinions correlate with viewing and listening – the middle class and the elderly view and hear BBC programming more than does the rest of the population. But any attempts at further interpretation are quickly bogged down in ambiguity. Is it inevitable that a public service broadcasting organization seems to lean to the right? Or is this mainly a matter of image, the BBC's traditions and reputation getting in the way of its actual performance? Does a licence-fee-financed system have no need to lean towards the bulk of the population – since they have to pay up anyhow – while it does need to learn towards the establishment for legitimacy and licence fee increases? Or can it be that the forces which exert pressure from one direction (the Labour party, the trade unions, ordinary people) are simply less effectively powerful than the forces from the other direction (the Conservatives, the establishment, the middle class, public service and artistic pressure groups)?

Ambiguity once again: television programme categories
Table 19 shows how the BBC and IBA described and quantified their national television transmissions for 1981 2. The BBC and the IBA clearly use different categories and definitions, which thus make precise comparisons impossible. How much of this ambiguity follows inevitably from the different characteristics of BBC and ITV and how much is designed deliberately to confuse and to conceal? The answer seems to be some of each.

What are the BBC and IBA trying to conceal? Both are probably being traditionally cautious about the delicate issue of imports. Both are trying to emphasize their hours of 'informative' or serious output. The BBC is perhaps being a little shy about its fewer hours of daytime transmission; the IBA is being shy about advertising – the real figure was 9½ hours of advertising per week on one ITV channel.

But only some of this ambiguity is deliberately contrived. There are indeed major differences between the BBC central command system and the federal IBA system; and these differences may require different classifications.

The categories and the percentages change from year to year. These were the last figures before breakfast television and Channel Four added further complexities. These additions now further exacerbate the contrast between some 50 hours a week of big audience television (evening peak hours on BBC1 and ITV) and, from 1983 onwards, some 300 hours of small audience television available in British homes. To be meaningful it is increasingly necessary to show these programme categories together with audience data – to substitute millions of audience hours per category for

TABLE 19

BBC AND ITV PROGRAMME DEFINITIONS AND OUTPUT, 1981–82
(*April 1981–March 82*)

BBC Definition	BBC1 %	BBC2 %	ITV %	ITV Definition
News	6·1	1·8	11	News and news magazines
Current affairs, features and Documentaries	14·8	22·8	12¼	Current affairs and general factual
—	—	—	1	Arts
Religion	2·6	0·2	2¼	Religion
Continuing education	4·8	2·3	2¼	Adult education
Open University	5·4	21·9	—	—
Schools	7·5	0·1	6½	School programmes
Children's programmes	11·9	2·9		
—	—	—	2½	Children's informative programmes
—	—	—	7¾	Children's drama and entertainment
—	—	—	1½	Pre-school education
Sport	12·1	16·2	9¼	Sport
Drama	4·9	4·5	21¾	Plays, drama, TV movies
British and foreign feature films and series	15·7	16·0	—	
—	—	—	8	Feature films
Light entertainment	7·9	5·9	14	Entertainment and music
Music	0·3	2·3	—	—
Programmes in Welsh	0·8	—	—	—
Continuity	5·2	3·1	—	—
TOTAL	100	100	100	TOTAL
Average weekly total programme transmission hours	101·6 hours	84·2 hours	102 hours	

Source: *BBC Annual Report and Handbook 1983*, p. 116; IBA, *Annual Report and Accounts 1981–82*, p. 37.

simple hours of transmission. But even if, or when, that is done the existing programme categories – and any alternatives – will still be ambiguous.

Consequently there is not – and there will not be – an entirely satisfactory answer to such a simple question as: How is television output split between entertainment, education and information?

Is television the dominant source of news?
Television, it is often said, is the main source of news for the British people – as for the people of other comparable countries. Survey evidence started to show in the 1960s that the majority of the public increasingly identified TV as its 'main' source of news and also as more 'reliable' than the press. Since the 1960s, as the number and length of television news bulletins has expanded (so also has current affairs coverage) such evidence seems to reveal an ever increasing dominance of television as the main source of reliable news. Both defenders and critics of TV news, in discussing this 'dominance', quote the same survey data. For example, the Glasgow *Bad News* authors in 1976 quoted one of the first such BBC surveys conducted in 1962 'which demonstrated that 58% of the population use television as their main source of news.'[9]

There is, however, one rather important weakness in this argument. Studies have repeatedly shown that those people who see any main evening television news bulletin on a typical weekday evening are only about 50% of all adults. There are two other relevant findings: first these figures relate to *weekdays* only; at weekends the TV news bulletins are briefer. Secondly, research also shows that especially for the *early* evening news bulletins provided by BBC and ITN, not all 'viewers' are devoting their *primary* attention to the news. In other words the proportion of British adults who devote their *primary* attention to all, or even most of, any main evening TV news on a typical day is about 45% of all British adults. Meanwhile press readership evidence indicates that – despite circulation losses – about 75% of British adults read a *morning* newspaper (mostly national) on a typical weekday; and another 10% do not read a morning, but do read an evening, daily. This gives us about 85% reading a daily on weekdays. The average weekday time spent reading is around 30 minutes or a little higher. On Sunday the sales penetration of Sunday mornings (there being no evenings) is again around 85% when the few provincial Sundays are included. The only day on which this figure is significantly lower is Saturday.

Thus on six days a week the proportion of British adults who read a daily paper is twice, or almost twice, the proportion who give their primary attention to one main TV news bulletin. People typically also spend slightly longer on the paper than the TV news lasts,[10] and other evidence suggests that most people read at least twice as many words in half an hour as a newscaster does on television.

So what is happening here? Is it simply that the *visual* character of

TV, plus perhaps the prestige of the BBC and ITN, makes people regard TV news as their main and most reliable source of news, although in fact twice as many people read daily newspapers and each takes in twice as many words there? The BBC research report on TV news in 1962, to which the *Bad News* researchers (indirectly) refer, warns:

> It must be pointed out that these figures do *not* indicate the relative circulations of each medium. They should be regarded as expressions of a preference – of the source which the informant regards as of 'most importance' to him.[11]

The very high level of ambiguity in this line of questioning was clearly evident to the BBC researchers in 1962 and presumably it was this very ambiguity which led the BBC largely – but not entirely – to leave the topic to others. Most of the 'studies' which are quoted in fact derive from commercial television, especially in the United States.

In Britain the main comparison in practice is between BBC and IBA channels on the one hand and between the popular tabloids and provincial evenings, which together account for well over four-fifths of all daily newspaper reading. So, when people say that they find TV news their 'main' and most reliable form of news they may be – in a different form – repeating what we quoted earlier about *The Sun*. More people actually read (mainly popular tabloid) newspapers which they find enjoyable but not over-full of reliable news. They are somewhat less likely to watch BBC or ITN news; however the great majority do watch TV news less than everyday, but at least weekly, and they acknowledge that it is more 'reliable'. If you positively want some 'news', then yes you would switch on the TV news.

But clearly like is not being compared with like. On the whole TV news is much more cautious – it has a legal requirement to be neutral – and, while saying fewer controversial things, is likely to seem more 'reliable'; the popular press deliberately surrenders 'reliability' in search of excitement. Television news – presumably because its pictures hold audiences – is able to get away with relatively dull coverage. For example two minutes might go to a visiting head of state arriving in London, then arriving at 10 Downing Street, and then reading a prepared statement; this could take up 10% of an entire TV news bulletin but in a newspaper it might be worth say half a column, or 0·5% of all editorial space.

Ambiguity is also present in terms such as 'news on television'. Many people are not aware of the distinction between 'news', 'current affairs' and 'outside broadcasts' and 'documentaries'. On television there is indeed a great deal of material which contains some news and politics; if one includes light magazine shows like *Nationwide*, plus documentaries and current affairs, plus the late news, then on many nights of the year each of the main channels is showing between two and three hours per evening of 'news' (or actuality). Clearly this definition – some ten hours of 'news' per weekday evening – will raise the amount seen by a typical viewer.

In addition some people when they hear the interviewer mention 'BBC TV' may in fact include their radio listening. Typical upper middle-class Britons hear about as much radio news (mainly Radio 4) as they watch TV news; and large proportions of working-class people frequently hear radio news bulletins – some of them 15 minutes long – on BBC radios 1 and 2 and on ILR. There are also of course short news offerings on television.

Many, many ambiguities here are unresolved. Little research exists on different sources of news, because – although many people would be quite interested – those who pay to have the research done are located either in the press, or in broadcasting, or in advertising, and commission research accordingly.

The patterns of overlap between different media are highly complex. On the whole serious newspaper readers seem also to be interested in electronic news of all kinds; and a large section of the working class, which basically finds news boring, manages largely to avoid 'news' apart from the occasional 2 or 3 minutes half-heard, seen or read, on radio, or TV or in the tabloid press.

There certainly is a social class division – those most interested in news following it in all media, but especially in the press and on radio; there is a large middle mass who are the main audience of TV news and who have a moderate interest in news attractively presented; there is also a large low-news-diet, mainly working class, segment of the national audience.

The TV news audience has a disproportionate number of the retired and of people aged over 55 – mainly because younger people are more likely to be out of their homes at the news times and middle-aged people are more likely to be busy putting children to bed, working, cleaning, and so on.

Television news, while obtaining its reputation as the dominant mass communication force in political fields, has paid two prices: first, its news and politics are wrapped up in a popular format which stresses political celebrities, personality presenters, and dramatic news film. Even so, the bulk of the public still stick to popular newspapers (despite, or because of, their lack of 'news'). Secondly the audience which does follow TV news is heavily weighted in general with people who are only moderately interested in news, and in particular with retired and elderly people who are heavy viewers of all television including news.

The very largest news audience is still that reached by the most popular newspapers, but these are also the 'news' media which in fact carry the least news. Newspapers do begin to show up better if questions are asked about more specific and detailed areas of interest; obviously the vastly greater number of words in a newspaper allows more local news, more economic news, more lobby news, more about particular industries, countries and sports. However, on the whole, these more specialized topics are more suitable either for local media or for the serious national newspapers. There are not many specialized areas in which tabloid newspapers can clearly beat television. One of the few areas in which newspapers score higher is horse racing news, at least amongst those strongly interested,[12] because those who bet on horses require the detailed advance information which newspapers provide.

But there remains a fundamental aspect of class and education inequality in the whole concept of 'news'. The detailed and weighty kind of news is clearly carried only in the serious newspapers – which the bulk of the population cannot or do not read. Television succeeds in presenting short news summaries with the strong *human* appeal of news film and on-camera interviews with celebrities in the news. But when television moves on to more serious coverage – of Afghanistan or Zimbabwe, or aerospace or zoology – in current affairs and documentaries – the popular audience largely loses interest, whereas the educated audience fresh from much fuller newspaper coverage also moves on to dominate the audience watching the fuller kind of television news/actuality. Many people find TV current affairs especially boring and place *Panorama* – long the BBC's leading current affairs show – top of the list of boring programmes.[13]

The Reithian approach of general television channels with mixed programming does still obtain for the news and the more popular current affairs output audiences which are widely spread across the social class spectrum. The move to more specialized programming and news-and-talk channels tends to make the news channel into a middle-class preserve. The reduction of the news content of the BBC's more popular radio channels and their concentration on to a single news-and-talk channel (Radio 4) led between 1962 and 1971 to a reduction of one-third in the total working-class audience for main radio news broadcasts, and an increase of over 40% in the middle-class audience.[14]

The concept of news has built-in audience implications for social inequality. Also paradoxically one of the most well-known findings of all media research – the dominance of TV news – is poorly founded; most of this 'evidence' in fact derives from people who are less interested in news than in selling advertising. Remarkably little is known in any detailed or reliable way either about how the British public regards the overall news menu or about how particular groups make up their particular news diets. Further research is indeed necessary. Meanwhile inequality and ambiguity go hand in hand in this as in most other aspects of media content and media audiences.

Inequality, ambiguity, and Channel Four

When Channel Four began transmission in November 1982, it attempted to tackle some of the previous inadequacies in the television coverage of trade unions, of women, of ethnic minorities. The new channel appeared to lean to the political left; and it also was the first British television channel to schedule a full hour of news in prime evening time.

As usual the new programming efforts were accused both of going too far and by others of being the same as usual. A central dilemma of 'minority' programming was quickly evident – the small audiences for nearly all the more ambitious efforts, including the hour-long news. A second core dilemma is the relatively small size of some of the more obvious British minorities; within a four-channel television system this leads to yet another truly British compromise – 'minority' programming which aims to appeal both to the particular minority and to a majority of general viewers.

Channel Four itself is probably an intermediate stage between the very limited channels of the past and the multi-channel future. Meanwhile it suggests that ambiguity will still have a long life; so probably will inequality.

PART D
Media industry

CHAPTER TWELVE

Finance, power, conglomerates

We now move away from particular media products and audiences and look at the media as an industry. We will consider questions of power and control, of monopoly and competition, of ownership and trade unions, both at the level of the press and broadcasting and in the context of a British media industry which is also part of a wider international media industry.

These chapters will be followed by a concluding batch on 'media policy'. But in the media, as with any industry, government policy is enormously important and the distinction between 'industry' and 'government policy' is rather arbitrary.

Many other themes link these next two sections. One such theme is the central importance of the arrival of commercial television in 1954–56 and the tendency for early decisions and early consequences to stick permanently. Another continuing theme is the combination of both the commercial and the non-commercial in a whole series of uneasy and shifting compromises – with unclear goals often leading to ambiguous consequences.

One important area in which compromise is widely thought desirable is between monopoly and competition. The British media seem to exhibit some fairly extreme examples of no-holds-barred competition and of fairly complete monopoly. Is there something about the British media which makes them oscillate between extremes of monopoly and competition without ever settling at the 'truly British' position in between?

Another pair of opposites are concentration and fragmentation. Media power and ownership become increasingly *concentrated* into state agencies like the IBA or into mammoth international media conglomerates, but at the same time *fragmentation* also seems to increase. Many people in the media will deny that there is any such thing as a media industry; there are, indeed, many small and highly specialized companies, and media policy-making also is fragmented between an almost endless number of government departments, agencies and committees.

A further contrast within the media and within media policy is the sense of extreme volatility – financial and technological especially – while at the same time nothing much seems to change.

Another recurring theme is the centrality of *imagery* within the image industry and also in media policy-making. The media industry has many aspects, much output, many audiences. While the mass media are indeed massive, time – especially for busy people – is short. Few media executives or media policy-makers read all nine national daily newspapers, or listen to the radio all day, or carefully sample the over three hundred hours of television on offer each week. Within the media industry and in media policy, people inevitably operate on the basis of the 'pictures in their heads' (to use Walter Lippmann's astute phrase). Attempts to influence these images – public relations – are nowhere more actively pursued than in the media industry itself.

Advertising, prestige and financial volatility

Reliance on a single and vulnerable source of revenue makes all media managements insecure. There is concern that the single source is highly vulnerable, not simply to unpredictable market forces, but also to related and equally unpredictable government policies.

Not only BBC licence fees and the ITV levy, but press revenue is subject to government economic policy. The provincial press is very dependent on job, house, car and retail advertising – all highly sensitive to government economic policy. Press sales revenue has also at times been dependent on government permission to raise prices. The different single sources of revenue can also get out of phase. The same inflation which fuels ITV revenue increases may lead to political motives for restraining the BBC licence fee.

In the mass media everywhere the economies of scale tend to operate in an extreme form; fortune favours the market leader. Another major constraint in Britain is the strength of media trade unions. Union resistance can easily mean that a management cost-cutting exercise creates more extra costs (or loses more revenue) than it saves.

Political aspects of the media political economy fall unevenly as between different media. In the case of broadcasting the government and its agencies (such as the IBA) set the rules, and, in awarding franchises, choose the players. In the press the government neither makes the main rules nor chooses the players – until a player seeks to pass on his hand to another. Equally the *prestige* factor falls unevenly between the media. There is more prestige (and power) in losing money on a serious publication than in making money on a popular publication.

As described by Marxist critics, advertising ought to make running the capitalist media relatively easy. Television is undoubtedly the strongest advertising medium, but, even so, the bulk of expenditure still goes on the press. Indeed in the early and mid-1970s the regional press alone attracted more advertising expenditure than did television. Television is the heavy artillery of advertising – big in impact, expensive to fund, difficult to aim, and inclined to scatter its effect well beyond the target. But television's impact is believed by advertisers to be enormous; the larger advertisers – mainly of packaged consumer goods – tend to use primarily television. The larger advertising agencies, whose typical clients are large spenders, also use mainly television.

But most advertising is placed by smaller or medium-sized advertisers and these use mainly the press (as do smaller advertising agencies). Classified and retail are easily the largest two categories and both of these go mainly into the press.

The press in general is capable of much finer tuning and is often cheaper; for example an advertiser can buy full pages in several national daily newspapers for the cost of one peak-time 30-second national television commercial. Most products are aimed either at working-class or middle-class people, at men or women, at the young or housewives; there are suitable press media – or pages within media – which select out all such categories. It is, of course, these specialized categories – and the classified readers – whom the new electronic media seek to take away from the press.

Working-class newspapers are said to be starved of advertising. In fact more significant than quantity is the *price* that newspapers of different sorts can charge. At least since 1940 popular newspapers have not gained enormously from carrying advertising because their relatively low rates have meant that the bulk of advertising revenue has gone into the paper and other costs of producing the advertisements. One calculation is that in 1960 popular Sunday newspapers obtained only 21% of their revenue from advertising – after deducting the resultant costs – and popular national morning papers only 29%. The comparable figures for 'qualities' were 62% (Sundays) and 68% (dailies).[1] The serious papers could charge several times more per (more affluent) reader.

During a time of rapid paper price increases in the 1970s it was widely believed that Fleet Street populars were actually losing money on printing advertising. Numerous complexities cloud the outcome of such calculations – for example bulk discounts on both advertising sales and paper purchases. Readers also tell researchers that they prefer a newspaper containing advertisements – both classified and display.

Most advertisers do not simply want to reach everyone at the cheapest cost (although some advertisers do, especially those in local newspapers and freesheets); advertisers want to reach realistic prospects for buying their goods or using their services. There is the general factor of *prestige*. Prestige may be another name for being taken seriously by politicians – i.e. power. But *prestige* is also linked to *advertising*. Both considerations point 'up-market.'

Foreign correspondence is a classic example of prestige. Good quality comprehensive world news services are available from news agencies at bargain rates; having a team of your own foreign correspondents costs several or many times as much and cannot easily be justified on any cost-benefit basis. It was noticeable that during the 1970s British newspapers such as the *Daily Telegraph* cut down on their previous lavish provision in this department. The *Financial Times* has expanded its foreign correspondent team for several reasons. They do produce specialized financial news; they confer prestige and get the paper taken seriously as more than just a financial news sheet; finally *Financial Times* foreign correspondents do partly attract advertising – those admirable 'supplements' on Banking in Saudi-Arabia and the Construction Industry in Brazil.

The BBC continues to shoulder the white man's burden of a large and expensive team of staff foreign correspondents – who are difficult to use, even in the BBC's innumerable slots on 6 national channels. Nevertheless at the BBC prestige equals licence fee; BBC executives may also perceive that politicians are busy people with short memories who tend to remember dramatic foreign events – thus it may be worth stationing permanently in a foreign capital a correspondent who sends mainly radio feature pieces, but is ready for the occasional drama which will thrust 'our correspondent' – instant and expert – on to the television screen.

Although some cheap-to-make programmes (notably TV quiz-game shows) are very popular, and some expensive material (like serious live music and foreign correspondence) is not very popular, there is nevertheless a correlation between costs and audience attraction. Comedy shows exhibit a tendency for costs to rise with popularity. The more popular a comedy team are the more pay their agents want for the stars and the more pay the ever expanding staff of writers also require.

A somewhat similar process occurs in Fleet Street. When Rupert Murdoch acquired *The Sun* in 1969 it was on the verge of death and he achieved big savings in labour costs; as *The Sun* revived and expanded, its costs also escalated. The mechanisms are well known; extra work in Fleet Street brings into play massive overtime and other special payments, armies of 'casual' workers and numerous related exotic payments.

On the other hand the very popularity of the most popular media makes them cheap per large audience reached. On television some of the most popular material is entertainment – such as variety shows and comedies. These shows are amongst the more expensive to make, but simply because they do reach such big audiences they are cheap in relation to audience reached. Similar economies of scale operate in national newspapers.

Some serious programming on television is also amongst the more costly to make – especially one-off serious plays and once-a-week current affairs shows such as BBC's *Panorama* and Granada's *World in Action*. These latter shows have traditionally spent lavishly, especially on foreign filming and are not on the air for many hours per year. Even in the past they were expensive programmes with medium-sized audiences. These programmes had prestige and both BBC2's and ITV's pursuit of prestige led to many more such programmes in the late 1960s and 1970s. The medium-sized segment of the audience which wants to watch serious current affairs is now spread between a much larger number of shows; this reduces the average audience, which leads to attempts to hold down production and foreign film costs, which may reduce audiences further. In any case the smallish average audiences reached ensure that current affairs programming is indeed expensive per viewer.

Media concentration: Marxist and pluralist views

Marxists argue that the British media are not merely highly concentrated under the control of very few dominant ownerships – and close to big business and the Conservative party – but they also point to the importance of conglomerate and international ownership elements as evidence that the British media are owned and operated by, and for, international capitalism.

Curran and Seaton in *Power without Responsibility* (pp. 104–8) published a group of tables along these lines. One showed that around the late 1970s six British media companies – Reed, Pearson, Thomson, News, Trafalgar and British Electric Traction – were also involved in a major way in other industries and other countries; a second table shows just three companies controlling well over half of all *national* newspaper circulation. Another table indicates that even the provincial press is highly concentrated – over half of all regional daily circulation being owned by five chains. A separate table reports the share of the five largest companies in ten separate media categories; five companies – the table suggests – control around three-quarters of each market. Yet another table includes seven, by now familiar, companies, and lists their holdings in newspapers, commercial TV, commercial radio, magazines, books and foreign media. Each of these seven companies on average owns interests in 5½ of the six media fields. Four companies are involved in all six media fields. Table 20 from the Marxist *Labour Research* shows the ten leading newspaper ownerships and their radio and TV interests.

For some Marxists this detail may prove the case that the media are part of international capitalism. There are exceptions – small independent companies exist in most fields, and there are a few brave left-wing voices – but these are only exceptions which prove the rule, exceptions which capitalism can easily afford (or perhaps actively encourages) as part of its practice of repressive tolerance.

᠈ The pluralist argument, of course, takes the 'exceptions' but argues that these are centrally significant. Around 50% of regional evening sales may be controlled by five companies; but even these are run in a decentralized manner with much local autonomy, and some 35% of regional evening sales belong to newspaper companies not in the top ten whose future is protected by monopoly legislation. Some large media companies do not support Conservative policies; in practice big companies are too sophisticated to dictate to subsidiaries on detail, but merely lay down financial guide-lines and profit targets. Prominent journalists and communicators cannot be dictated to. Nor will commercial managers welcome political interference which might impede achievement of financial targets.

Moreover these lists of five or ten dominant companies conveniently leave out the BBC and the IBA. Such lists also neglect that these are not the same five companies in each case. The total number of companies which occupy the five market leadership slots across ten separate media fields is not five but about 25 companies. 'Dominance by 25 companies' – the pluralist can claim – may not be perfect, but scarcely justifies the Marxist case of monopoly capitalist control.

If you specify any particular narrowly defined field such as national newspapers by circulation (thus omitting both low-sale prestige nationals and provincials) then a huge major slice of the market is indeed controlled by three, four or five companies. If you define the media at large in revenue terms, then ten organizations (including the BBC) do account for well over half the revenue. But if you specify the top five market slots in ten media fields, then some 25 organizations are involved.

Beyond these 25 or so 'dominant' organizations there are further companies which occupy slots between number six and ten in terms of market (revenue) leadership in their own fields, but which are still quite significant companies. Examples of such companies would be the second five ITV companies such as Anglia or Scottish; or one of the companies which own 20 or 30 specialized trade magazines. Such companies in the early 1980s had revenues of around £50 million a year. So did the tenth largest newspaper grouping – the Liverpool Daily Post and Echo company, which owns the two daily papers in Liverpool plus a string of weeklies. Another company of this size – East Midlands Allied Press – owns two daily newspapers and some 30 magazines. Some of these important regional com-

TABLE 20

THE TEN LARGEST NEWSPAPER OWNERSHIPS, 1981

Company	National daily and Sunday newspapers		Provincial daily newspapers		Commercial radio	ITV
	no. of titles	*% total circu-lation**	*no. of titles*	*% total circu-lation**	*no. of stations in which interests held*	
News International	4	*29·6*	2	*0·8*	—	1
Reed International	3	*33·6*	1	*8·0*	2	—
Trafalgar House (Fleet Holdings)	3	*19·0*	1	*2·8*	2	1
Associated Newspapers	1	*5·8*	17[1]	*15·5*	8	1[2]
Daily Telegraph	2	*7·3*	—	—	—	1
Guardian & Manchester Evening News	1	*0·1*	2	*3·7*	1	1
S Pearson & Sons	1	*0·1*	12[3]	*7·2*	1[4]	1[4]
Lonrho	1	*3·0*	3	*3·8*	2	—
Thomson Organization	—	—	12	*13·8*	1	
United Newspapers	—	—	8	*7·9*	2[5]	2[5]
TOTAL for 10 companies	16	*100*	58	*63·6*	13†	6†
					Total no in operation	
TOTAL for sector	16	*100*	98	*100*	26	15

* For period Jan–June 1980.
† Overlapping interests.
[1] Also owns a quarter of Bristol Evening Post with 2 provincial dailies (2·3% of total circulation). [2] South TV, which loses its franchise at the end of the year. [3] Also owns 38·5% of BPM Holdings, with 3 provincial dailies (4·6% of total circulation). [4] Via BPM Holdings. [5] Via Trident Television (8·2% owned).
Source: *Labour Research*, April 1981, p. 75.

panies enjoy a marked degree of local press monopoly control and hence monopoly profit. But this poses a problem for the Marxist argument. Yes, such companies are local monopolies; however, this strong element of monopoly is a source of commercial strength which favours their long-term viability (despite the prevalence of larger national companies) and this local monopoly can be said to weaken the evidence for national concentration. This, of course, takes us back to an earlier point about a central ambiguity: Genuine monopoly co-exists with equally genuine competition.

Large media enterprises and media power

Leaving aside any precise problems of defining what exactly is
meant by the *largest* British media enterprises, there still are several
ways of classifying them. One form of classification would distinguish between the mainly print companies (Reed, Pearson,
Lonrho, Trafalgar-Fleet, Thomson, Associated and News) and
the mainly *electronic* companies (Thorn-EMI, Central, Granada,
Yorkshire, London Weekend); the *wholesale-retail* companies (W.
H. Smith and John Menzies); and the *non-profit* enterprises (the
BBC, Press Association, the IBA and its affiliates).

Another possible form of classification could be constructed
along the *conglomerate* dimension. In some cases (e.g. Lonrho) the
company is a genuine conglomerate whose media interests are
relatively small. The opposite type of company is overwhelmingly
confined to a *single mass medium* – such as Yorkshire and London
Weekend, both consortia designed for and still heavily confined to
operating a major ITV franchise. In between there is a big variety of
companies, including several in which the media activities make up
a large minority of total activity; for example Pearson – despite its
major newspaper interests – obtains more revenue from books,
banking and other activities; Granada – despite being a major ITV
contractor – gets more revenue from television set and related
rentals; Thorn-EMI – despite being a record major and owning half
of Thames – is primarily an electronics company; British Electric
Traction which controls the other half of Thames and has major
press interests is primarily an electronics and transportation company.

It would also be possible, thirdly, to classify media companies
according to the percentage of revenue obtained from Britain
and/or from British media. Some companies get the vast majority
of their revenue in Britain – for example Anglia's non-British
earnings are confined to a few overseas sales of its television programming. But Reuters obtains over 80% of its revenue outside
Britain. Other companies are foreign owned (to which we return
soon).

In terms of power and control, there are many possible forms of
classification. In the ensuing chapters the following two main sorts
of power will be considered:

First, *power within the media industry*: in this category power may
be exercised by *business*/conglomerate/capitalist interests; or by
public bodies presided over by 'public figures' (or 'amateurs') such
as the BBC governors; or by *communicators* such as TV producers
or journalists; or by *trade unions* of printers or technicians. We will
consider all of these in this block of chapters.

Secondly, *power outside the media industry* may be exercised by *politicians*, or by *civil servants* – we consider these people again in the closing chapter on 'media policy'. But also outside-the-industry power might be exercised by the *mass public* or the electorate; finally – power may be exercised by the *professionally articulate* public – perhaps 2% of the total population and disproportionally drawn from 'professions' such as the law, medicine, academia.

New entrants?

Ease of entry is usually regarded as indicative of the degree of competition or monopoly. Since 1945 the most common form of press new entry has been to buy existing publications. Such completely new publications as are launched are, with few exceptions, launched by existing press groups. The other main channels of new entry have been ITV and ILR companies.

In the national press two Sundays – the *Sunday Telegraph* (1961) and *The Mail on Sunday* (1982) – and one daily – *Daily Star* (1978) – have been launched, but all by existing groups wanting to use spare printing capacity. For provincial evening newspapers the 1977 Press Commission report concluded that the prospects for major new entrants were virtually nil; even when the new evening was launched from an existing base of weeklies or another evening and faced no daily competition, it took four or five years to break even, after a loss of up to one million pounds.[2] With each year since 1977 the sum required to launch a small provincial daily must have been rising, while the chance of ultimate viability has been falling.

For new weekly paid-for newspapers the prospects were nearly as gloomy. Almost invariably new weeklies were launched by existing weekly groups. Prospects for launching new periodicals were a little better. Nevertheless among 33 successful sizeable consumer magazines which the Commission identified as having been launched in the period 1966–74, half the total were launched by just four big companies, with IPC far in the lead.

Britain has had very few significant 'new entries' since 1945 – certainly by comparison with both the rest of Western Europe and the United States. The obvious contrast with New York and Paris is that there newspapers died and were partly replaced by quite rich magazines.

All of the above points can be taken to support two arguments about Britain's exceptionally concentrated media and the difficulties of 'new entry'. First, the British national press has – since 1950 – in contrast to Paris or New York – 'refused to die'; if several Fleet Street publications did die, they might unleash reader and advertiser support for a wave of new publications. Secondly, the evidence can be interpreted along more Marxist lines: new entry is virtually impossible because the existing media are deliberately kept in place by the capitalist state; when major new openings arise – as with commercial TV and radio – these are filled by the existing media in alliance with the capitalist state.

This discussion turns partly upon the interpretation one chooses to place on the decisions of the ITA/IBA (see Chapter 14). There is some evidence for the argument that monopoly does eventually attract successful competition. The four most important areas of monopoly in the British media in recent decades have probably been: the BBC, the market for regional and local advertising, women's magazines, and press wholesaling.[3] Apart from the last case, there has been a major reduction in monopoly in the other three. The BBC has lost its monopoly in television and radio; the strength of IPC in women's magazines has at least reduced.

At the regional level both press and electronic advertising have been largely monopolies. In recent decades the incursion of freesheets and commercial radio have made major differences. Certainly provincial newspapers now face more competition. However, a counter-interpretation is that the newspapers won compensation by being allowed to buy into both ITV and ILR. Secondly the freesheet phenomenon, while it has indeed made millionaires out of some local printers, has in fact not led to significant added choice for readers (as opposed to advertisers), while the conventional newspaper groups have themselves ended up owning over half of the freesheets. Finally, it can be said, the biggest and worst monopoly – the ITV companies, each of which has a local monopoly of the premier advertising medium – had actually been strengthened and extended by the IBA decision against full commercial competition between its two television channels.

The pluralists can argue that even if media competition leads to monopoly, then monopoly will lead back to competition. But the Marxists also have some evidence for their monopoly-competition-monopoly case.

Conglomeratization

The process of conglomeratization has occurred in two opposite directions. Some media companies became mini-conglomerates, but in addition major conglomerates acquired media companies.

Media companies move in the mini-conglomerate direction because they have nowhere else to expand. Major press companies are (at least formally) barred from significant acquisitions in the press. Commercial television companies cannot acquire a second television franchise and their surplus profits were used to buy into neighbouring areas – such as television set (and later video) rentals, recorded music, book publishing – where they hope to find a less volatile cash flow.

But the volatility of media companies seen by major conglomerates looked rather different. This was a high risk/high return involvement – qualities which may be quite appealing as part of a calculated policy of running a conglomerate with a diverse portfolio. The prestige factor is a potential bonus. Another appetising attraction for conglomerates was that some media companies were under the control of eccentric and dominant individuals who led them into trouble. Such companies can be cheap in relation to their rich assets. The difficulties of managing a media company include the need to balance sound financial control with 'creative' and political skills, and handling an aging and highly unionized work force while still appealing to young audiences. Conglomerate companies may well think that they have the necessary professional financial and management skills.

Northcliffe at the start of the twentieth century established the pattern of eccentric personal management which tends to get into severe trouble as the tycoon becomes less perceptive, less young, and less lucky. Examples in recent years include Lord Beaverbrook with his Express Newspapers, Sir Ted Lewis of Decca, Sir John Davis at Rank, Sir Philip Warter at ABPC, Cecil King at IPC, Lord Lew Grade at ACC/ATV, and Lord Hartwell and his Telegraph newspapers. Compared with this pattern of eccentric management, the BBC's pattern of management succession many seem to be one of great rationality; the BBC Director-General is typically appointed in his early fifties with a track record of executive achievement and he retires compulsorily at age 60.

Paradoxically the IBA's anxiety to prevent takeovers of its key but (by general standards) smallish companies had led to the practice of non-voting shares with a small inner number of rigidly held voting shares. This pattern can merely protect eccentricity, and the very devices intended to prevent takeovers – which allow an ITV company to diversify into disaster – may also lead to takeovers.

The final attraction of media companies to conglomerate takeovers is their assets. Old newspaper offices, cinemas, and studios typically sit on very valuable sites; often a media mini-conglomerate has a lot of scattered investments which it has not fully digested. The major conglomerate – with a successful record of discarding losers and of realizing the true profit potential of strong assets – must find such a company an appetising prospect.

Internationalization

Just as it is difficult to point to one moment in time as the beginning of conglomerate ownership, so also with the internationalization of media. Both can be traced back to 1955 and the launch of ITV; but one can also point to the Canadian Lord Beaverbrook, to the emergence of Hollywood, or to the nineteenth-century news agencies.

Nevertheless several major sales of British media companies which occurred around 1980 did seem to have some new characteristics. These transactions did not follow the pattern of one large company buying up one small company. A common theme was of two large and internationally minded companies – one selling and one buying – but each in its way pursuing not just a national but an international media strategy.

Perhaps the most dramatic of these sales occurred in February 1981 when *The Times* and the *Sunday Times* were sold by Thomson to Murdoch. The Thomson interests were held in two major companies – Thomson Newspapers (confined to the Canadian and US newspaper interests) and the International Thomson Organization; both companies were Toronto-based but the latter company contained the current major profit centre – the British North Sea Oil interests which Lord (Roy) Thomson had been led into via his British newspapers. But now ITO[4] was quite explicitly pursuing a strategy of investing these largely British-earned profits within the USA and Canada – in newspapers, book publishing, data and information systems, travel, and oil. Within this strategy Times Newspapers of London had no place. But News International – Rupert Murdoch's company – was pursuing its very different British-USA-Australia strategy, largely confined to newspapers, by purchasing Times Newspapers; Rupert Murdoch was acquiring valuable assets and a chance yet again to transform a problem newspaper enterprise.

However, a second 1981 transaction involved News International as the seller – divesting itself of Berrow's (a group of daily and weekly newspapers in the West of England) to Reed International.[5] This sale was presumably part of a change of emphasis in Mr Murdoch's British interests; but also the acquisition of relatively few large publications in three countries seemed to fit with his particular management style.[6] Meanwhile, the purchasers, Reed International, saw this as part of their British policy of strengthening their previously weak position in provincial newspapers. But Reed also is a major international company with large paper and other interests in Canada and USA.[7] In 1981 Reed's US magazine company – Cahners Publishing – was the 59th largest media company in the USA.[8]

A third transaction in 1981 was the sale of *The Observer* by the Atlantic Richfield company of California to Lonrho, a British conglomerate. Atlantic Richfield decided that for a large oil-metals company to own a single foreign newspaper was a mistake. But Lonrho – according to its chief executive, Mr Rowland – had long coveted *The Observer*. Lonrho was a classic conglomerate involved in many industries and many countries, and with its African and Scottish newspapers a small fraction of the whole.

A fourth transaction in 1980 was the purchase of EMI – the international recorded music major – by Thorn. EMI had long been particularly dependent upon world-wide record sales; in the late 1970s it ran into major difficulties in the US market with its entire product range, not least its records and its medical electronics. Thorn, already Britain's largest manufacturer of TV hardware (Ferguson) acquired a massive list of new assets, many of them in software – a world-wide record business, an inventory of 1,700 feature films, half of Thames Television and much else. These acquisitions were seen by Thorn as highly relevant to its *international* ambitions in the satellite age; in 1981–82 of the newly merged Thorn-EMI's £2·6 billion worth of business, foreign based operations (apart from exports) accounted for a full one third.[9]

Fifthly in 1982 there was the remarkable takeover of Lord Lew Grade's Associated Communication Corporation by Mr Robert Holmes à Court and his TVW Enterprises of Perth, Western Australia. ACC was a much smaller company than EMI, but ACC also had run into trouble in foreign markets in general and in the American film business in particular (*Raise The Titanic* finally sank the titanic Lord Grade); ACC was also heavy with assets – music, films, theatres, cinemas – and it had once owned all, now half, of a major British ITV networking company (ATV Network). Mr Holmes à Court's remarkable takeover battle was fought by a smaller company; he clearly saw in ACC not merely its rich assets but also its existing *international* involvement and the opportunity to extend this into another Australian-British-world communications company.

We will return to the IBA's apparent impotence (Chapter 14) and the wider issues of British media exports and participation (Chapter 18). But for the present the main points are the *international* aspect in general and the United States aspect in particular.

A final concern is the relevance of all this for Marxist v. pluralist arguments. As ever there is ambiguity here. Just because media organizations become more international it does not automatically make journalists, for example, less autonomous; the reverse could be the case. Nevertheless, it would also seem fair to add that while such developments do not destroy the pluralist arguments, they do make life harder for those who would argue the pluralist case.

CHAPTER THIRTEEN

Control in the press

Marxist media critics, old Hollywood movies, and journalists telling anecdotes in pubs, often seem to share a common melodramatic view of press freedom and press power: on my left the battling journalist trying to nail society's wrong-doers, and on my right the newspaper owner, a bruising businessman who seeks to protect his own kind.

A more sophisticated view of press power is reflected in the two reports of the Royal Commission on the Press of 1974–77. From this perspective it is difficult to say very much with any certainty about British journalists (a majority in the selected sample refused to answer the Commission's questionnaire); it also seemed easier to compile details of the (rapidly changing) conglomerate ownership structure than to draw any conclusions about its significance.

On the other hand the Royal Commission found itself confronted by a massive press industry. Fleet Street in 1975 had about 2,700 journalists – a mere 2% of the 135,000 people employed in British newspaper and periodical printing and publishing; 55% of these latter were employed in London and the South East, with the North West (Manchester) and Scotland the next largest centres. Not only did the Royal Commission find itself confronted with this large industry, but it quickly discovered that most of its witnesses saw the press largely in terms of management versus unions. Some senior managers claimed to spend the majority of their time dealing with trade unions, and even some editors apparently saw their main problem as a threat from the National Union of Journalists. Some Commission members were also startled to discover that the production of newspapers and magazines was in effect contracted out to be operated by trade unions.

The present author worked as a consultant for the Royal Commission[1] and tried, unsuccessfully, to persuade its members that their 'sophisticated' view was less sophisticated than it seemed. This chapter will argue that while the management versus printing trade unions struggle is of some significance, the real power of the press is shared between its owners and the journalists.

Types of press power
Let us briefly indicate the main powers executed by the four main categories of power holders outlined in the previous chapter:

1. *Businessmen, owners and conglomerates*, as already discussed, can and do buy and sell publications; existing owners in practice have the main opportunity to launch new publications and they similarly have the power to close publications. In addition to these powers of life and death over publications, owners and senior executives have one other major power – the power to establish financial guide-lines and strategies. The power to set profit (or loss) targets also involves decisions about the number of pages, the ratio of advertising to editorial, cover price policy, circulation policy, the promotion budget. All of these things are absolutely crucial to the existence of a publication and its purpose: is it seeking prestige via aggressive journalism, is it filling up spare printing capacity, or is it deliberately exploiting a monopoly situation in order to create a positive short-term cash flow?

2. *Trade union power* certainly exists and has indeed been used to prevent, or at least to delay, the introduction of new technology. However, the power of trade unions is somewhat less than popularly supposed. Comparisons with American publications are not valid. The most exotic labour practices occur in Fleet Street's national newspapers, but even here not all workers are very highly paid and/or underworked. Five-sixths of the newspaper and magazine labour force do not work on Fleet Street newspapers. Trade union power is almost entirely focused on traditional trade union goals, and the fairly rare examples of union interference with editorial are usually confined to stories about, or cartoonists' caricatures of, the union in question.

3. *Public bodies* of the BBC and IBA kind do not exist in the press; the most important relevant body with some of these 'public' and 'amateur' characteristics is the Monopolies Commission (see Chapter 18).

4. *Communicators*, in the form of journalists, are the people who operate much of the power of the press as usually understood. This may include a decision as to whether a particular person, company or sports team is 'worth a story', or whether the publication should express support for a particular policy of the current government.

Newspapers and magazines, of course, differ radically from radio and television since the latter have a legal requirement to behave with political neutrality. Thus while a broadcast producer can only be partisan with stealth, a print journalist is often free to be as partisan as he or she likes so long as the result is a 'lively' story. The convention of reporting even 'two sides' of the story is in the British press vague and only intermittently observed.

Electoral endorsements are often thought of as the key power of newspapers. Little is known about how or why endorsements are made in Britain and whether they have any effect. This clearly is a power sometimes exercised by chief owners or executives. However, the British provincial press has largely given up endorsements – monopoly now suggests cautious neutrality. In much of the national press the party allegiance is traditional and, since more or less actively shared by much of the readership, cannot easily be altered. Examples such as Mr Murdoch's two switches of allegiance of *The Sun* in the two elections of 1974 are, if not rare, certainly not the predominant pattern.

More important, probably, than the electoral endorsement itself is the extent to which it is reflected in general news coverage. Journalists do not need to be told by editors or publishers what policy is – they are the most eager readers of their own paper.

The main power of the press probably resides in its general approach – its selection of stories, its conferral of legitmacy on some and not on others, its patronage of arts and sports, persons and performances. Much of this power is fairly particular and special-ized – it carries great weight and significance but only within the specialized world to which it applies; often only a fellow member of the world in question will even recognize that choice is being exercized. This kind of power resides largely with journalists and is exercized by a daily newspaper hundreds or thousands of times a week. The conglomerate chief executive has not the time, knowl-edge or inclination to notice that a certain obscure politician or football player receives regular attention from a particular journal-ist. Some years later the publisher may discover that the obscure politician is now a minister, the football player a superstar and the journalist also has a name, a reputation – and autonomy – to match.

To a considerable extent the interests and powers of businessmen or conglomerate executives and of journalists are indeed separate. The businessman exercises *industrial* power; the journalists exer-cise most of the power to withold or confer *news coverage* and comment.

Managers versus unions

The connection between printers and management is an old one; many nineteenth-century newspaper owners had themselves been print workers. The small scale of operations and the real prospects for ascent meant that print workers – despite the very long history of their crafts – were far from fully unionized. The 'Northcliffe Re-volution' converted newspaper production around 1900 into a relatively large-scale industry; as a consequence the craft element was greatly strengthened, but so also were less skilled and casual elements.

No established career or cadre of efficient newspaper managers has ever existed in Britain. The admirable H. Yeo in his *Newspaper Management* (1891) gives a picture of quite astonishing chaos and incompetence prevailing at that time; many newspaper owners, he writes, have still not got to the stage of double-entry book-keeping. Newspaper directors are often politicians, parsons, shopkeepers and others who neither know nor learn anything about sound newspaper management; 'managing editors' while often adequate as 'literary men' and editors, are bad managers. The compositors are 'a very intelligent class of men' often made to work in disgracefully poor conditions. Newspaper owners, Yeo tells us, are infatuated by advertising – but remarkably careless about collecting advertisers' money.[2]

In the 1930s many such earlier weaknesses still continued. The highest salaries were paid to advertising managers. The 'publishing' side of newspaper production was badly paid, with casual labour predominant. The compositors, however, who had made their first national agreement only in 1896, now were the leading example of highly paid national newspaper workers. Already the device of a highly complex payment system was being used to baffle employers:

> The earnings of London compositors are calculated on piece-rates by methods of incredible complexity. The 'London Scale of Prices for Compositors' occupies a hundred closely printed pages, and on one London daily it takes four whole-time clerks to work out the wages of fifty compositors.[3]

The second Press Commission (1961–2) and the third (1974–7), as well as numerous other reports in between, documented the extraordinary ascendancy of the craft unions in national newspapers. Previously concern was expressed about overmanning and high pay; but during the 1970s the focus turned towards 'new technology' – the electronic revolution which came from the United States. It revolutionizes the interface between journalists and compositors by abolishing the latter; the journalist's typewriter and the compositor's linotype are combined into a single electronic keyboard on which the journalist sets the final version. This revolution was by 1980 nearly complete in the United States and was well advanced in the British provinces, with the major modification that, while the electronic equipment was used, the compositors remained to use it.

The 1974–77 Press Commission in its Interim Report called on the Fleet Street unions to accept the 'new technology' but the

memberships later balloted not to do so. Were the union members
burying their heads or using them?

Within the press the house level, that is the layer of the unions
within an individual employing organization, is called the 'chapel' –
one of many quaint expressions going back to the medieval origins
of printing. Fleet Street alone – including magazines – has the
incredible number of some 360 separate union chapels; in Fleet
Street union power is chapel power. The complexity of payments
systems, the astonishing anomalies – with people doing similar work
often paid very dissimilar amounts – all this focuses upon splits not
merely between a number of warring unions, but between warring
chapel factions within a single union. A favourite tactic is the
'chapel meeting', effectively a lightning strike close to a production
deadline; if the management does not concede it may lose an
edition, – with its sales and advertising revenue – and if it does
concede it will pile up yet one more weird extra payment on to a pile
already so high that in some cases earnings are three times the basic
rate.[4] When this happens chapel power is increased, management
confidence and competence are challenged, and other unions and
other chapels are set new targets.

The PEP report on the *British Press* in the late 1930s found that
there was no career structure in any of the main management fields;
advertising departments at that time normally recruited bright
young men from the accounts department – thus perhaps ensuring
that both advertising and accounts were poorly managed. Various
reports conducted for the 1974–7 Press Commission found the
quality of management improving only slowly. The ACAS report
on the national newspaper industry found that still in 1977 few
managers had worked outside the national newspaper industry and
they were thus used to static technology; management was excessively sectionalized and not well informed on general management's
objectives or even on union agreements.

Graham Cleverley subtitles his book *The Fleet Street Disaster* 'a
case study in mismanagement'. He points out that managers in Fleet
Street not only lack a career structure and adequate experience or
qualifications; besides not being very competent, they are actually
quite insecure. They can be sacked. In Fleet Street even 'managers'
are expected to belong to a trade union. The union they belong to is
NATSOPA, the larger of Fleet Street's 'unskilled' unions.

The sovereign editor myth
A peculiarly British myth holds that the chief editor of a newspaper
both can and should have sovereign control of editorial content.
The chief editor is head of the editorial department and some
editors – through a mixture of luck, commercial success and support

from above – do indeed achieve a high degree of autonomy. But in quite large-scale national news organizations, employing perhaps 300 journalists and generating annually tens of millions of pounds of revenue, it is inevitable that much of the power is exercised by others below, to the side of, and above the editor in the organization's hierarchy. On national dailies, the chief editor only actively edits the paper on a little over half the 300 days of publication each year; he has a high load of administration of a personnel management and general sort; he has major duties of liaison with the business departments. On both *The Times* and the *Daily Telegraph* in the 1960s and 1970s the editor's authority was largely confined to the opinion and non-news pages and he was not responsible for making the most senior editorial appointments. On local and regional newspapers again the editor's autonomy has even stricter limits.

Why then does everyone seem to have an impression that the editor is in sovereign control? One answer is that at the level of day-to-day journalism the editor and his deputies are in charge. Secondly politicians and other news sources usually are involved in tacit bargaining with lower level journalists such as political correspondents, and in relation to this common source–journalist relationship the editor is perceived as a remote and very elevated figure in the distant background.

But thirdly the editor *seems* to be in charge because it is one of his tasks to seem to be in charge. The editor is usually the public face of the publication. It is part of his job to appear on television and radio talking about 'my' paper, 'my' journalists and even 'my' management. Similarly most Fleet Street editors and provincial daily editors also see it as part of their duty to accept invitations from senior politicians and other prominent persons. Moreover, far from the editor being in endless conflict with the business management, probably most editors most of the time see co-operation with business management in a positive light. The editor is in favour of more or better circulation, and more or better advertising because the extra revenue promises extra pages and resources for editorial. The editor also needs the co-operation of the business departments even for his most ambitious and idealistic efforts – for example a series of 'investigative' articles, if it is to achieve its maximum effect, may require special advertising and promotion. Consequently the editor sees no conflict of interest in enthusiastic co-operation with the more public aspects of business policies.

This public relations aspect of editorship has been present throughout most of the 200-year history of *The Times*. So well is it understood that one of the editor's main tasks is to be the paper's public face, that editors are partly chosen on dramatic casting principles – as looking and sounding the part. One of the strongest impressions from a series of interviews with British newspaper editors, both national and provincial, was that they seemed to personify the paper, or the attributes and virtues which senior business executives would like to stress. Newspapers are often said to have 'personalities' and the editor's own personality needs to match.[5]

Journalists – more or less powerful?

Are journalists getting more powerful? Is journalism at last becoming a profession?

In the nineteenth century the press was highly partisan and journalists were part of the national political apparatus, in effect clerical assistants taking down speeches and the like. But a few of them – mainly editors and leader-writers – were prominent political advisers and consultants. Today very different kinds of politics and political journalism mean that journalists retain political functions. Arguably these functions are more important, because the enormous complexity of modern politics and government places a great emphasis upon the functions of political and semi-political journalism – disseminating and summarizing information, focusing attention on current issues and agendas, defining 'crises', acting as go-betweens.[6]

Thus journalists have become more important with the steadily growing salience of the mass media. Journalists indeed are most powerful, not in the press at all, but in running the BBC (next chapter). Within the press two of the most important changes have been the enormous increase in numbers and the related increase in specialization. Britain had less than 2,000 journalists in 1861, about 10,000 in the late 1930s, about 20,000 in the late 1960s; the definition of 'journalist' is getting increasingly vague. But despite the problems of newspapers on almost any definition the total number of journalists further increased in the 1970s – especially in television, radio, trade publications, and freesheets.

Along with this has gone specialization – until 1939 this was primarily in political and sports journalism only. By 1970 there had been an enormous expansion and it has continued with for example environment, energy and technology correspondents in the national press. The specialists inevitably acquire a good deal of tactical autonomy, based on their knowledge, their reputation and byline, their specialized sources of information, their personal choice (in most cases) of which stories to cover, and their membership of an informal group of 'competitor-colleagues' who in practice define the specialist field's current story agenda.[7]

The editor's task is transformed by these two developments. The

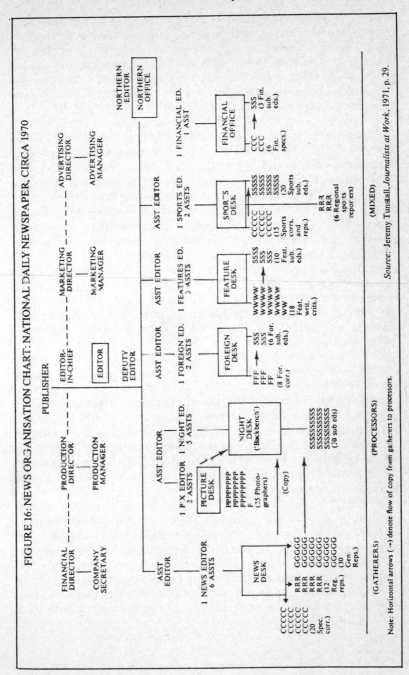

FIGURE 16: NEWS ORGANISATION CHART: NATIONAL DAILY NEWSPAPER, CIRCA 1970

Source: Jeremy Tunstall, *Journalists at Work*, 1971, p. 29.

Note: Horizontal arrows (→) denote flow of copy from gatherers to processors.

Victorian editor perhaps had a staff of twenty journalists; the editor wrote his own editorials and was also in effect the paper's only or senior specialist reporter. A present-day national editor with 300 journalists – including specialists in a bewildering array of fields – inevitably is much more of a departmental manager; the editor is also a personnel manager,[8] with the allocation of specialists – and filling in the gaps made by moves – one of his major tasks.

In this age of celebrity and electronic media, journalists have shed their anonymity and any national newspaper now contains a number of celebrity journalists – mostly specialists and columnists – who may well be better known than the editor, and may also (with, for example, extra television earnings) earn more than the editor.

Journalism has not merely colonized other fields – television, radio, public relations as well as the old favourite of politics – but these fields, by creating alternative career ladders and opportunities, have given the most prominent press journalists more bargaining power.

Journalists are also now better educated. Although *The Times* recruited Oxford graduates in the early nineteenth century, this was for a hundred years a minority pattern. As late as 1965 only 5% of the intake of young journalists into provincial newspapers were graduates. By 1980 this figure was 31%, with a higher figure for periodicals.

All of this means that while journalism is not, and will not be, a 'profession' in the traditional sense, it has increasingly become 'professional' in the looser sense of being an occupation which stresses a combination of education, experience and knowledge. A 'professional' (in the loose sense) elite has tended to develop consisting of, at most, a few thousand journalists. Definitions of such an elite are debatable but the general point is that the concept of 'journalism as a powerful profession' is limited to a small minority of all press and provincial journalists, and a larger minority of all broadcast journalists.

While perhaps two or three thousand journalists can look politicians, publishers and editors in the eye, there are also contrary forces at work. As well as professionalization there is deskilling and declining status. As the Fleet Street populars have become more entertainment oriented, so have their journalists. Provincial newspapers – traditionally the main field of employment – scarcely bring the bulk of their journalists into the national elite; the advance of freesheets also threatens both jobs and minimum standards of editorial performance.

The National Union of Journalists

The National Union of Journalists (founded 1907) in its early days was a deliberate rejection of the 'professionally' oriented Institute of Journalists. However the NUJ also modelled itself partly on the teachers' unions; the NUJ quickly outstripped the IOJ and in effect it has defined journalism as having much in common with bank clerking – responsible white-collar work, within large impersonal employing organizations; this was how provincial journalism increasingly developed and it was in provincial journalism that the core of the NUJ was located.

But the craft model has always also been a seductive one, and a common complaint has long been that print compositors earned more than journalists. From the 1920s well into the 1940s the NUJ's proportion of journalists in membership stayed around 70%.[9] But gradually this proportion was increased and largely by using craft union tactics. The craft union tactic of controlling apprenticeship and entry was pursued through the training scheme, by forcing all newspaper recruits to start in the provinces where the employers' miserly pay offerings made recruitment to the NUJ easy. The 'closed shops' which the NUJ most envied were those of the high-paid London craftsmen – and the NUJ set out to obtain closed shops in both national newspapers and magazines.

Many factors lie behind these changes – including management ineptitude and the national/provincial divide. The craft approach has proved an effective coalition strategy for holding together not only an occupation which retains managerial, professional and clerical elements, but also an NUJ increasing proportions of whose members work in magazines, in broadcasting, public relations and in book publishing.

The NUJ itself has contributed to journalism as an occupation becoming both stronger and weaker. After a slow build-up in the 1960s, NUJ 'chapel power' emerged in full strength at the *Daily Mirror* with a claim for a 97% pay increase over two years. This kind of militancy led to Fleet Street journalists in the 1970s becoming fairly well paid. But it has had other consequences, including an increasing distance between the national elite and the smaller provincial publications. The latter have come to employ increasing proportions of young women – but this indicates as much about the low rates of pay as about the advance of women in print journalism.

Journalists continue to see themselves as belonging to a craft occupation with strongly male, if not *macho*, overtones. These occupational realities and myths do not greatly aid the advance of women or members of ethnic minorities, despite the left-wing rhetoric at NUJ annual delegate meetings.

The odd combination of power and weakness may well increase

as the NUJ continues to reflect the contrasts and the frustrations
within journalism. The NUJ is somewhat unusual – in comparison
with the USA, France or West Germany – in having succeeded in
enrolling about 90% of all British journalists; the growth of the
mass media plus the inevitable advance of 'direct in-putting' by
journalists into computers may seem to offer the NUJ the potential
for industrial domination. Already it has left the Press Council (see
Chapter 18) and taken part in a number of bitter strikes. But
paradoxically the craft trade union may in practice most help those
elite journalists who least need its help and are least active in the
NUJ – simply because real bargaining leverage is so unequally
distributed. Those who benefit most of all may be the few hundred
journalists in television; the biggest impact of the NUJ may indeed
be (as managements proclaim) to threaten the weakest parts of the
provincial press.

The case of Times Newspapers
Times Newspapers around 1980 again illustrates the ambiguity of
events:

- From November 1978 to November 1979 *The Times* and *Sunday Times* were silenced by a dispute over electronic technology
  between the Thomson management and the unions.[10]
- Early in 1981 International Thomson completed the sale of
  Times Newspapers to Rupert Murdoch's News International.
- Harold Evans, editor of the *Sunday Times* 1966–81, was
  appointed editor of *The Times*. After 12 months as editor he
  was removed by Murdoch in March 1982, and replaced by his
  deputy, Charles Douglas-Home.

These events demonstrate fairly unambiguously the power of chief
owners to buy and sell famous newspapers and to hire and fire
famous editors. The contemporary coverage by the press itself
tended to dwell on 'union power' in the early events and the
arbitrary dismissal of the editor in the later events.

Less attention was paid to the fact that as editor of the *Sunday
Times* Harold Evans had had an editorial superior, Sir Denis
Hamilton – a role which Rupert Murdoch himself evidently decided
to adopt. These events could also be seen as emphasizing not only
the continuing less than complete autonomy of editors, but also the
continuing collective power of journalists. The Thomson management had had to face an NUJ strike which closed both Times
newspapers and may have been – seen from Toronto – the last
straw. Subsequently there were some signs that Harold Evans as

Times editor had less than the full support of the other senior journalists, one of whom was appointed to succeed him.

The fragmentation of press power
The fragmentation of power within the press does not improve the press industry's chances of surviving unscathed. Just as there are several printing unions each made up of warring factions, so there are several employers' organisations each made largely impotent by internal conflicts. The National Union of Journalists, for all its many obvious faults, is the most important single organization within the British press and about the only one giving any serious thought to the future direction and survival of British journalism. The Newspaper Publishers Association is made largely impotent by its current fears and by ancient rivalries between its members, the Fleet Street newspaper owners. The ultimate power of press owners may simply be self-destruction. The ultimate power of the senior journalists is that, whether or not newspapers survive on any significant scale, journalism undoubtedly will. Indeed the power and importance at least of the few thousand senior journalists seems likely to increase.

CHAPTER FOURTEEN

Control in television and radio

In British television and radio, power is more widely spread than in the press. Much more power is exerted over broadcasting from outside. Politicians no longer exercise formal control over the press (although there are a few key informal exceptions); but clearly *politicians* do legislate on broadcasting and the responsible minister must also approve significant new projects and capital expenditure. In this and other ways *civil servants* also exercise power in broadcasting.

In contrast to the press, clearly public bodies and amateur public persons do – as BBC governors and IBA members – have some significant powers. The BBC governors, for example, select the new director-general, and the IBA members award franchises to both commercial television and radio companies. However, this chapter will argue that despite great potential power, these 'amateur' public servants at least up to and including the franchise decisions of 1980–2 have only been the fourth most important wielders of power within broadcasting.

Somewhat more powerful have been the trade unions, which – unlike those in the press – do have a considerable influence over what goes out to audiences.

The second most powerful group, this chapter will argue, are business/capitalist/conglomerate interests, whose power is considerable within, but is confined to, the advertising financed side of broadcasting. It has no significant influence upon the BBC.

Finally, the most powerful single group are the communicators – such as producers, directors, journalists and writers – including those ex-producers and ex-journalists who occupy most of the top jobs in the BBC.

The BBC

Table 21 shows the BBC's biggest categories of employment and the 1962–76 changes. The arrival of BBC2 in 1964 is shown in the greatly increased number of salaried staff in television. Apart from local radio perhaps the other most spectacular growth was in Personnel. The number of manual employees in the BBC is small especially in contrast to the sizeable armies of unskilled manual workers involved in the physical *manufacture* of newspapers.

Figure 17 indicates the complexity of BBC senior management in

TABLE 21

BBC PERSONNEL BEFORE AND
AFTER THE SECOND TV CHANNEL, 1962–76

Salaried Monthly Staff	March 1962	September 1976	1962	1976
	Numbers		*Percentages*	
Radio	569	844	3·2	3·7
Local radio	0	453	0	1·8
Television	1,136	3,012	6·4	11·7
Open University	0	162	0	0·6
External	1,090	1,259	6·2	4·9
Regions	699	1,536	4·0	5·9
News	299	508	1·7	2·0
Engineering	3,684	5,450	20·9	21·9
Personnel	285	700	1·6	2·7
Public Affairs, including audience research & libraries	232	458	1·3	1·8
Finance	115	137	0·7	0·6
Monthly staff, Total	8,109	14,519	46.0	56.2
Secretarial, weekly	9,537	11,328	54.0	43.8
TOTAL	17,646	25,847	100.0	100.0

Source: *Report of the Committee on the Future of Broadcasting*, 1977, p. 98.

1979. Only two of the posts which reported to the director general were reserved for technical specialists – the directors of engineering and finance. The BBC organisation is sufficiently complex that it can, of course, be divided in various other ways. Television accounts for the bulk of BBC expenditure. Reporting to the managing director of television, the channel controllers of BBC1 and BBC2 have the task of composing the schedules and thus determining what programming is made. The allocation of a time-slot in the schedule also largely determines whether the programme will be cheaply or expensively made.

A BBC producer can call on more than 100 different specialized services within the BBC to help or hinder him. The BBC makes the great bulk of its own transmissions; in sheer numbers of hours of material the BBC's 1981–82 production of over 8,000 hours of television for its two national networks makes the quantity of material produced by Hollywood in its golden film years pale into insignificance.

FIGURE 17: BBC PERSONNEL 1979

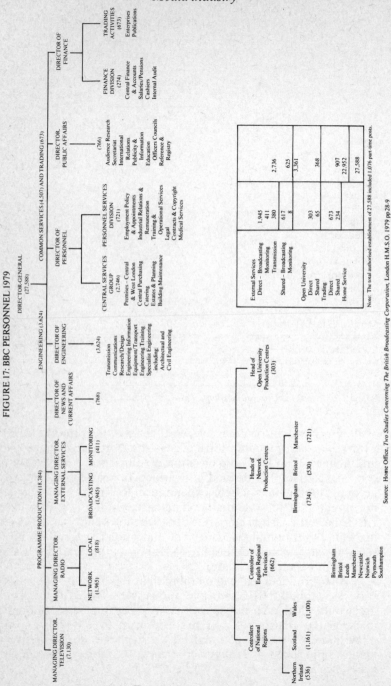

Source: Home Office, *Two Studies Concerning The British Broadcasting Corporation*, London H.M.S.O. 1979 pp28-9

The BBC puts out a bewildering array of drama, news, entertainment and current affairs programmes; in addition to its national and local radio, it transmits 700 hours a week of external radio in English and 35 other language-services.

The BBC has three major locations – Broadcasting House for radio and central administration, located near Oxford Circus; Bush House for external broadcasting in the Aldwych; and Television Centre a few miles west at Shepherd's Bush. There are many lesser locations. The BBC is full of backwaters, exotic and mundane. But it is a single organisation; it has a strong central administration, and a single system of formal salary grades and promotion procedures. The bulk of its employees – including all the senior ones – are based in London. The BBC is, indeed, as Tom Burns has said, a cultural bureaucracy;[1] despite its considerable complexity, and its very wide variety of output, the BBC is distinctly bureaucratic and hierarchical. Charles Curran, writing about broadcast policy after his retirement as BBC Director General called his book *A Seamless Robe*.

There are just two major functional categories of employee – the engineers and the programme producers. And the BBC is run primarily by the programme producers. There is a single career structure and a single programme-making ethos stretching from the junior radio producer with a tape-recorder over his shoulder up to the director-general (usually himself a promoted producer) in the famous third-floor office in Broadcasting House presiding proudly over the BBC, its budget, its 28,000 personnel and its world reputation.

The unitary nature of the organisation – programme production and networking combined – makes the BBC at once difficult and easy to control. Decision-making is in practice devolved downwards to hundreds of quite junior producers and directors, but these people in turn accord legitimacy to the senior management partly because they know that the senior managers held jobs similar to theirs ten or twenty years earlier. These characteristics make the BBC difficult to control from outside.

BBC governors, director general, board of management
Because of its formidably unitary character it would take an extremely determined collection of part-time governors to impose their distinctive will on the BBC.

The attempt appears to have been made only twice. Once with the very first chairman – the Earl of Clarendon (1927–30); but neither he nor John Reith was really in charge, despite Reith's authoritarian management style. The real power then still lay outside the BBC with the government, the parties and the press.

Media industry

One other chairman, Lord Hill (1968–72) might be said to have imposed his will also. Lord Hill had quite an exceptional store of previous experience; he had been Secretary of the British Medical Association; he was a famous radio broadcaster; he had been the responsible government minister (Postmaster-General) during ITV's difficult early days in 1955–57. He had been in the Cabinet as co-ordinator of government information, and he had previously been chairman of the Independent Television Authority (1963–8).[2] However, even Lord Hill admitted that his reign at the BBC was less serene than at the ITA. Having chased one director-general (Greene) away and appointed the obvious successor (Curran), there still was not a lot the BBC chairman could do.

Some BBC chairmen have been willing to admit their lack of real power. One of these was Lord Simon (1947–52) a university vice-chancellor.[3] Another academic example was Sir Michael Swann (1973–80), plucked from a career in medicine and university administration in Edinburgh.[4]

The chairman of the governors is normally the key figure because although usually an amateur, typically meeting broadcasting for the first time in a major way relatively late in life, he at least in practice does the job on a more or less full-time basis. The other governors are amateurs both in the sense of being outsiders and of being part-timers covening once a fortnight.

Asa Briggs tells us that of the 85 governors who served in the BBC's first fifty years (1928–78) most were politicians (usually retired), educators, business people, diplomats, social service administrators, trade union leaders, authors, journalists, lawyers or retired military officers. 56 out of 85 were graduates, 40 from Oxford or Cambridge.[5] The BBC governors exemplify the 'great and the good'. Such people, even if they had the time and resources to exert their will on the BBC, might not have many ideas or ideals radically different from those of the senior full-time BBC employees on the Board of Management.

It is often said that the one key function of the governors is to select not only the new director-general but also the occupants of other senior posts. Asa Briggs himself reveals little about this and clearly confidentiality surrounds such an appointments system. But Charles Curran's discussion implies that – with the exception of Lord Hill's chairmanship – the director-general in practice made most of the other senior appointments.[6]

Who then runs the BBC? The emphasis placed in most discussions may well exaggerate the importance of the director-general; there is sometimes a tendency to see the director-general as a latter day combination of John Delane, the legendary editor of *The Times*, and Louis B. Mayer, the legendary Hollywood mogul. Some directors-general have certainly been good at presenting an image of themselves which was not totally in keeping with the more complex reality. John Reith presented ? masterful image to the world and a different one to his diary. But since the 1930s there has been an enormous increase in the quantity of output and the complexity of the BBC.

Even the common picture of Sir Hugh Carleton-Greene, as the director-general (1960–9) who firmly led the BBC into pastures new, may well involve more image than substance. Hugh Greene's term of office coincided with the Pilkington Committee and ITV's forced retreat from total commercialism; the BBC then had the benefits of BBC2, increasing revenue from higher colour licences, low inflation, and a low level of polarisation between the major political parties. Operating in this favourable climate Hugh Greene made a lot of both wise decisions and mistakes. But if putting a suitable human face on to the impersonal BBC is one of the DG's main functions, Hugh Greene was excellent. This mildly eccentric, mildly radical, brother of the famous novelist, former *Daily Telegraph* foreign correspondent, was an ideal BBC spokesman.

Increasingly both the director-general and the chairman of the governors have mainly looked outwards towards broadcasting legislation, renewing the Charter, raising the licence fee. With the future importance of satellite and other technology/policy issues, this trend will probably continue. Ultimately neither the chairman nor the director-general may be as powerful as might appear. The main power lies outside the BBC in the political/policy sphere and inside the BBC within the upper and upper-middle echelons of producer-managers.

Independent Television: bargaining barons

In contrast to the unitary BBC, independent television is pulled in several different directions. It does have advertising revenue; it has public companies with shareholders; it has a dominant trade union (ACTT) whose origins lie in another industry – film. ITV also has regional roots as well as a London presence. It is ruled over, not by 13 governors, but by an Independent Broadcasting Authority which roughly duplicates the engineering side of the BBC, but lacks the BBC's major activity of programme production. ITV is most of all a federal system of 15 regional companies amongst which the networking companies that make most of the peak-time programming – initially four, but from 1968 five, companies – are dominant. Then there are the ten lesser companies. Their trade association is ITCA (Independent Television Companies Association). Also important are ITN (the separate news organisation), the breakfast television company, and the second ITV channel (which is controlled via a

FIGURE 18: THE ORGANISATION OF INDEPENDENT BROADCASTING IN BRITAIN, 1983 ONWARDS

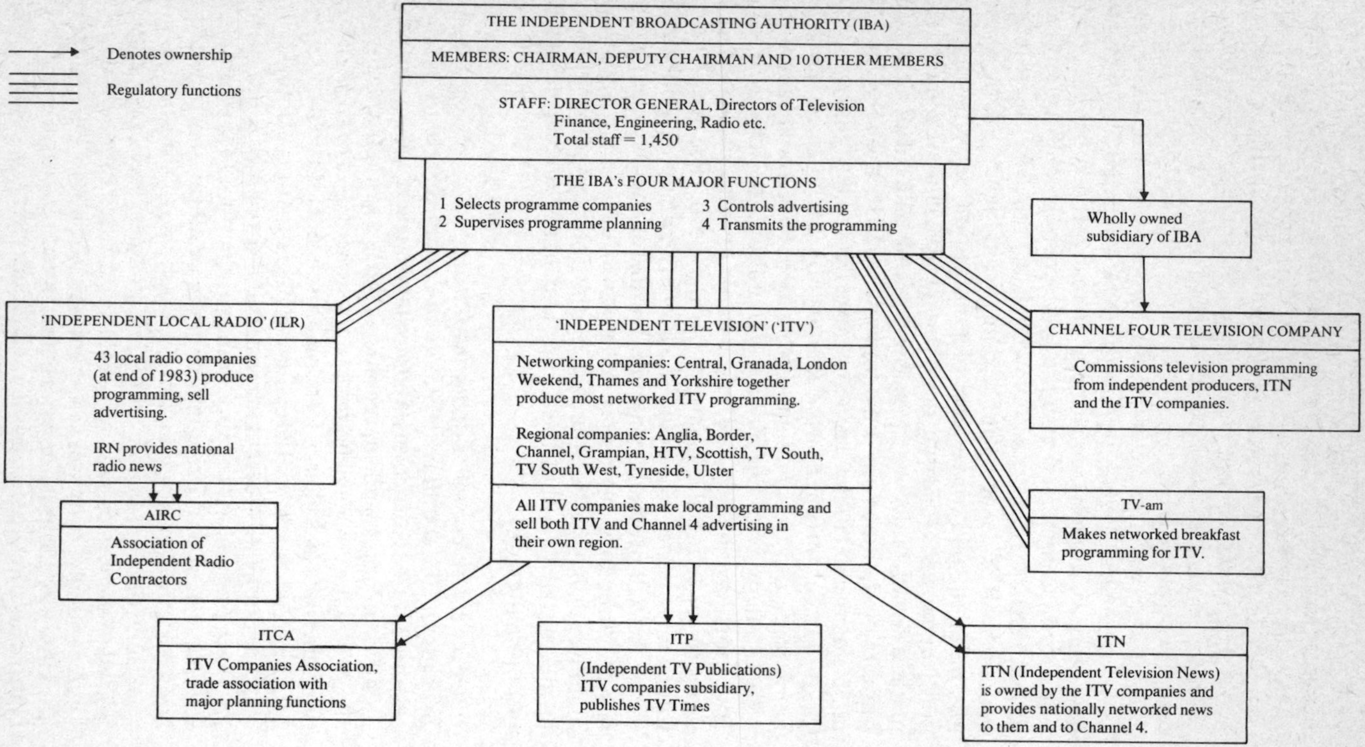

Denotes ownership

Regulatory functions

THE INDEPENDENT BROADCASTING AUTHORITY (IBA)

MEMBERS: CHAIRMAN, DEPUTY CHAIRMAN AND 10 OTHER MEMBERS

STAFF: DIRECTOR GENERAL, Directors of Television
Finance, Engineering, Radio etc.
Total staff = 1,450

THE IBA's FOUR MAJOR FUNCTIONS

1 Selects programme companies
2 Supervises programme planning
3 Controls advertising
4 Transmits the programming

Wholly owned subsidiary of IBA

CHANNEL FOUR TELEVISION COMPANY

Commissions television programming from independent producers, ITN and the ITV companies.

TV-am

Makes networked breakfast programming for ITV.

ITN

ITN (Independent Television News) is owned by the ITV companies and provides nationally networked news to them and to Channel 4.

'INDEPENDENT TELEVISION' ('ITV')

Networking companies: Central, Granada, London Weekend, Thames and Yorkshire together produce most networked ITV programming.

Regional companies: Anglia, Border, Channel, Grampian, HTV, Scottish, TV South, TV South West, Tyneside, Ulster

All ITV companies make local programming and sell both ITV and Channel 4 advertising in their own region.

ITP

(Independent TV Publications) ITV companies subsidiary, publishes TV Times

ITCA

ITV Companies Association, trade association with major planning functions

'INDEPENDENT LOCAL RADIO' ('ILR')

43 local radio companies (at end of 1983) produce programming, sell advertising.

IRN provides national radio news

AIRC

Association of Independent Radio Contractors

separate board by the IBA). Figure 18 is an attempt to depict this.

Along with the five networking companies perhaps should be listed the Fourth Channel, ITN and the IBA itself – eight main barons. Then there are the five middle-rank ITV mini-barons and TV-am, finally the five smallest ITV companies. With Independent Television Publications (*TV Times*) this makes 20 entities constituting 'Independent Television'.

The prevalent style is one of bargaining. Initially the bargain was between the four networking companies. The central bargaining concerns the construction of the ITV schedule by the networking companies. The transaction is essentially a bargain in which the networking companies each agree themselves to make approximately one-fifth of the networked programmes and to show the other four-fifths in their own regions. However in detail the bargaining has always been much more complex – and acrimonious – than this description implies. One reason is that in fact the regions are not the same size (Table 22) and there are thus quite sizeable adjustments over a system of five equal fifths. Each network company has something close to a veto – it can refuse to accept a show offered by one of the others. There is thus very protracted horse-trading over particular schedule slots in which particular network companies are interested.

The bargaining between barons began in 1955 in a life-or-death atmosphere with the two London companies (AR and ATV) struggling for dominance first in the Midlands, then in the North. In the early years the ITA was not directly involved. The IBA has long since been involved in the two layers of meetings – strategic meetings of chief executives every two months, weekly detailed meetings of programme controllers. In the 1960s the ITA began to exert its legal powers to 'mandate' – in line with Pilkington recommendations – increasing quantities of 'balanced' or serious material. By the mid 1970s there were on any typical weekday evening of the year several fixed and immovable slots – the national news at 10–10.30 p.m.; typically one mandated current affairs, documentary, sport or drama item; early evening local news at 6 p.m.; usually also one 'banker' programme – a super popular serial like *Coronation Street* or *Crossroads*. This meant that on many nights of the week there was only one good slot available – with several rival candidate series being prepared for the slot by different network companies.

After the arrival of the second IBA channel in November 1982 the networking log-jam was somewhat eased, because of the big increase in available time. But in other respects the log-jam is even greater; there are now much bigger amounts of output, much more temptation to repeat popular series, more financial anxiety – but

TABLE 22

INDEPENDENT TELEVISION COMPANIES, 1983

	Net percentage of ITV homes %	IBA rental 1983 £ thousands	Fourth Channel subscription 1983 £ thousands
THE NETWORKING MAJORS:			
Thames	} 19·9	8,927	21,672
London Weekend		5,183	16,440
Central	15·2	6,911	17,148
Granada	11·8	7,487	19,770
Yorkshire	9·9	5,759	13,614
Total . . . 56·8			
THE MINI-MAJORS			
TV South	8·3	5,616	15,408
Harlech	8·3	3,311	8,124
Anglia	6·3	2,375	7,830
Scottish	6·2	2,375	6,828
Tyne Tees	5·9	2,304	8,193
Total . . . 35·0			
THE MINOR COMPANIES			
TV South West	2·8	719	2,109
Ulster	2·3	431	222
Grampian	2·0	72	495
Border	1·1	58	120
Channel	0·2	14	9
Total . . . 8·4			

Sources: Young and Rubicam for Net Homes (as opposed to Gross Homes which includes overlap areas); IBA press statement, 23rd December 1982.

still only the same number of peak slots on the one main ITV channel.

Numerous accounts of the networking arrangements exist. The Annan Committee gave a clear and simple account in 1977. In numerous articles and memoirs various senior ITV persons have given rather more vivid accounts – stressing the extremely aggressive style of bargaining and the high level of acrimony.[7] There seem to be some similarities to the European Economic Community and its bargaining-cum-veto arrangements (in which case the choice of

Lord Thomson – a former EEC Commissioner – as IBA Chairman in 1982 may be appropriate).

A key aspect of this quickly established pattern is that initially only two companies were involved – Rediffusion and ATV which shared London (Table 23). Five months later in February 1956 ABC began operating in the Midlands at the weekend only. Not until May 1956 – seven months after the birth of ITV in London – did the fourth company, Granada, start to operate. Moreover Granada began initially only in Lancashire because the Yorkshire antenna was not ready; for this reason and because it was in any case financially weak, Granada entered into an unequal bargain with Rediffusion, by which Rediffusion supplied Granada with very generous quantities of programming in return for even more generous slices of Granada's early profits (which were massive).

These arrangements established several important rules about the core bargaining. The bargaining placed the four networking companies in the forefront of ITV; the ITA was still small, mainly involved in engineering and passive on programme issues. Moreover the bargaining was not between equals. The battle to get ITV on the road was largely fought in those early months in London and the Midlands; only an agreement between the two key companies – Rediffusion and ATV – allowed the networking arrangements to develop. Despite its supposedly regional basis ITV continued to be London-Birmingham dominated. After 1968 the key company was no longer Rediffusion but Thames (a combine of Rediffusion and ABC); the second – or first equal – company (until 1982) was ATV, operating in the Midlands seven days a week but in fact making much of its programming in London at Elstree.

Granada was initially the number four company in ITV and a client of Rediffusion; only after 1968 did it move up to number three. The new boys were London Weekend and Yorkshire. Since 1968 three of the five networking companies have still been based in London and Birmingham; about two-thirds of the network programming came from these three, and over half of the networked programmes (including the news) was produced in London.

This pattern of bargaining on a London-Birmingham axis had consequences in many fields, for example in the industrial relations practices of ITV. First, while the trade unions did not attend the network bargaining sessions, the belligerent style of bargaining which prevailed there was widely known and was quickly adopted by the unions themselves. ACTT, the main union, was determined itself to be a baron, and to bargain with full baronial belligerence. Secondly the London-Birmingham axis, and the fact that even after 1968 some of the 'Birmingham' output was made in London, established ITV's labour practices on a fully metropolitan basis –

TABLE 23

ITV NETWORKING COMPANIES

	1955–1968	1968–1981	1982–
LONDON			
Weekday	Associated-Rediffusion	Thames (Rediffusion and ABC)	Thames
Weekend	ATV	London Weekend (including Friday from 5 p.m.)	London Weekend
	(Began: 22 September 1955)		
MIDLAND			
Weekday	ATV	} ATV	Central
Weekend	ABC		
	(Began: 17 February 1956)		
LANCASHIRE AND YORKSHIRE			
Weekday	Granada	LANCASHIRE Granada	Granada
Weekend	ABC	YORKSHIRE Yorkshire TV	Yorkshire
	(Began: 3 May 1956)		

comparable to those of the metropolitan BBC, but more extra-vagent in manning and more generous in payment.

ITV after 1962: Practising Pilkington
The *Report of the Committee on Broadcasting 1960*, chaired by Sir Harry Pilkington, was published in June 1962 and it marked the end of ITV's opening phase. The days of massive profits and a passive Independent Television Authority had to end. In 1964 the government levy began, not on ITV profits, but on net advertising revenue – rising to a top rate of 45%. For the next few years the levy removed about a quarter of total revenue.[8] While there was thus much less financial motive to maximise revenue, the ITA began to mandate more and more serious, (unpopular) programmes; the BBC acquired its second channel.

For the programme makers this inevitably had to mean greater power. A whole array of different forces compelled the ITV companies to focus more upon 'good' programming; whatever 'good' programming might mean it was good news for producers, for BBC executives wanting to make their way in ITV, for actuality programming, and for serious drama.

For the battling barons who had built ITV in its early days, all this meant that their most heroic days were now over – at least *within* ITV. In the years of peak profit around 1960 some of them had already begun to diversify into other things – to broaden their base against the insecurities of the franchise, and in anticipation of the inevitable taxation of the embarrassingly high profit levels. Thus the businessmen could now turn their attention to consolidating these much wider portfolios of now much larger companies. Lew Grade (of ATV) became increasingly interested in foreign sales. Sidney Bernstein (of Granada) was diversifying into book publishing, catering, and television set rental while devoting quite a lot of time also to some amusing law suits. Roy Thomson got on with buying up newspapers, and entering the travel business.

With programming left largely to producers, to the ITA and to the network schedulers, what else was there for businessmen to do? The engineering was taken care of by the ITA, so nothing there. The selling of advertising time might appear to be the only remaining challenge and a good deal of senior businessmen's time certainly went into this. But selling television advertising time in Britain is a rather unusual type of selling. The quantity is rigidly limited (seven minutes per peak hour and six minutes overall), and each contractor is a monopolist more or less (especially after 1968). The demand is extremely strong in general, but highly unstable in particular (dates, times, scheduling and budgeting). Harry Henry[9] has described these conditions as an auction in which price is determined by demand and demand only. Certainly this is a neat explanation for the extraordinary variety of special prices (ranging from far below the norm, to far above, for immediate bookings on the day) which prevail. Harry Henry is exaggerating a little – the sales people have enticed new advertisers into television – but his basic point is surely correct. Demand in the short term is the only important variable, and being a monopoly seller of television advertising does not present a difficult challenge to the salesman; this is unlike trying to syndicate your wares to American television, for example, which is more difficult and can be more rewarding.

While the power of the programme makers increased, and while that of the businessmen within ITV decreased, the Independent Television Authority was flexing its muscles for a massive demonstration of power. The ITA chairman was Lord Hill – already proving to be an exceptionally active chairman at the ITA before moving to the BBC to repeat the performance there. The key changes, affecting the network companies, are shown in Table 23. All of the networking regions were altered. The split weekend/weekday arrangement was dropped except in London. The northern region – previously split by weekend and weekday – was now re-divided into two regions, Lancashire and Yorkshire. The major company, the General Motors of ITV's first decade, Associated-Rediffusion, was penalized – although allowed to retain half of the new joint company, Thames. And further carnage ensued elsewhere. One of the mini-barons – Television West and Wales (TWW) – was removed to be replaced by Harlech.

There was, however, one major mistake – the famous London Weekend Television disaster. This consortium had a galaxy of programme talent led by Michael Peacock who was billed as the BBC's youngest and most dazzling programme chief so far. LWT incorporated all of the ITA's hopes for 'better' programming. Its birth was a disaster. The ACTT deployed its brutal bargaining tactics – pulling the plug on the opening night. The BBC, with many months in which to prepare its assault, was ready to switch roles; while LWT put on its serious programming, the BBC answered each weekend with a formidable battery of popular entertainment shows. LWT's supposedly dazzling programme talent began to depart *en masse* and at one point it looked as though Rupert Murdoch, owner of the *News of the World*, would add LWT to his weekend attractions.

By bringing in new people, and failing to meet many of the promises which won the franchise, London Weekend eventually survived and prospered. But the LWT events nevertheless pointed to enormous weaknesses in the Authority's position. It could and did shuffle the franchise-holders, but the LWT events showed that the programming changed rather less. The slow drift towards more serious programming partly resulted from other forces – the Pilkington Report, and the government's decisions on BBC2 and the ITV levy. Just how important were the ITA's reactions to these events remains unclear.

Even Lord Hill's massive interventions only tidied up some of the major weaknesses of the early 1954–56 decisions – notably the weekday–weekend split. By retaining this split (and two of the now five dominant companies) only in London, the ITA was re-inforcing both London dominance and regional monopoly; it was acknowledging that its earlier preference for competition within ITV and its opposition to networking were both impractical. And while the ITA had its stick with which to force some regional programming, it failed – and still fails – to provide some significant carrot which would give the companies a financial interest in more regional programming.

The ITA in 1966–8 made only one major geographical change – the splitting of Lancashire and Yorkshire. The IBA has remained stuck with a split into 14 regions, which is basically the previous BBC regional system, with a few 1955 vintage alterations. Although some of the regions appear capable of alteration, the investments in transmitters and the interests which are now entrenched – mainly local politicians and unions – have discouraged changes or mergers.

Moreover the masterful power-wielding of Lord Hill carried with it several implicit warnings which the Authority later ignored. These events showed that the primary power of the Authority only existed at franchise time; there was thus a temptation – seen again in 1980–82 – to make too many changes all at one time. The departure of Lord Hill (willingly to the BBC) immediately after the franchise allocation indicated another unsatisfactory element – the Authority chairman handed out the franchises afresh and then stepped aside, leaving another, novice, chairman to pick up the pieces.

Lord Hill demonstrated the importance of political skills and understanding – which the IBA later ignored. The London Weekend events also demonstrated that the Authority's staff had a weak grasp of the core essentials of ITV – both programming and advertising. Finally the financial panic of LWT's early months showed that the ITA – supposed by some to be the very pulpit of capitalism – had a weak understanding of finance in general and of relations with financial institutions in particular.

The Authority also seemed to be extraordinarily sensitive to press comment and remarkably concerned with creating images – for example of regional virtue. The Authority certainly had a dilemma in its press relations – an initial legal requirement to involve press elements and consequent vulnerability to critical comment from rival press elements – which in turn might alert politicians, alienate advertisers and perplex programme makers. London Weekend Television had major press participation and became the object of savage press criticism.

Granada illustrates the point about imagery. Sidney Bernstein, with his cinema background, was aware of the vital importance of press publicity. His key appointment here was an astute one: Gerald Barry, who had been editor of the *News Chronicle*, 1936–48. Granada's adept public relations strategy was aided by two secret weapons: it had a reputation for being pro-Labour, and, as the only major company with a left-of-centre image, Granada had already achieved virtual total security. But secondly Granada was based in Manchester, where the London establishment could not see its local programming; an impression was created – for which there is no reliable evidence – that Granada's local programming was of superior quality.

Granada (despite its South of England origins) was able to present itself to politicians and journalists in London as authentically and virtuously northern. *Coronation Street* with its Manchester accents helped; *What The Papers Say* flattered journalists; some innovations in local election coverage flattered politicians; annual public lectures on communications with weighty speakers filled the Guildhall in London.[10]

IBA's concern with imagery – sometimes at the expense of substance – has become notorious; this weakness of the IBA is frequently on display, and not least at franchise time. The kind of procedures introduced in the 1967 franchise decisions – Lord Hill's influence again – stress future promises, performance at the interview, and what appeals to those IBA members who happen to be serving at franchise time.[11] The image comes first, the substance comes some months later.

The IBA in 1980–82

The Independent Broadcasting Authority was faced with a new franchising round and the launching of its second channel all in the same period of 1980–82. (The IBA was also launching new radio stations and ignoring government Space Satellite policy.) But despite apparently holding in its hands all the key powers – not only in ITV but in British broadcasting in general – the IBA only managed to demonstrate that, while it might reign, it did not rule.

The IBA's dilemmas derived partly from the powers conferred on it by legislation and the difficulty of realising ambitious legislative plans during a major down-swing in the economy. Some of the IBA's problems, however, arose from the amateurism, not only of its part-time members, but also of its full-time staff.

These weaknesses were all too evident when the ITA became the Independent Broadcasting Authority and launched local commercial radio. One major problem was the Act of 1973, which, in converting a television authority into a *broadcasting* authority also called for newspaper participation in a network of 60 radio stations; this target was heavily cut back by the Labour government in 1974. Even so, the IBA unwisely accepted that few changes were necessary in its own composition in order to handle radio. Its first Director of Radio, although an experienced print journalist, had little experience of either radio or television. Commercial radio in Britain had one of those disastrous openings for which new broadcasting ventures in general, and commercial ones in particular, are justly famous. Once again the opening was of two companies in London, one the news sheet anchor (LBC) the other a popular music station (Capital); once more there were disastrous losses, departing executives, rebellious and strike-prone employees, massive disaster story coverage in the press, and the IBA anxiously dithering on the sidelines. However, ILR eventually was pulled around key roles in the rescue being played by several former BBC radio men. However all of this had happened back in 1973–4 and meanwhile ITV had been on its best behaviour during the 1974–7 life of the Annan Committee.

Then with the change of government in 1979, an increasingly active and assertive IBA found itself entrusted with the fourth channel as well as the franchises. Let us briefly summarize some of the key decisions and their implications.

1. *Of the 15 ITV contractors two were removed altogether* – in the South West and South-South East regions. The IBA's formal statement on the decisions[12] is extremely short on explanation. But Westward Television (Plymouth) had recently become notorious for a slogging boardroom battle between its founding father, Peter Cadbury, and Lord Harris. The IBA seemed determined to rid itself of both of them and their squabbles by awarding the contract to a new company, Television South West.

From the other English south coast region, which borders London to the East, South and West, the IBA decided to expel Southern Television and install a new group, TVS. Possible reasons may have included TVS' ambitious plans greatly to increase local programming and Southern's ownership by major press groupings (which the IBA had long been trying nationally to cut down). However, a more probable reason was that one major execution was thought necessary. Execution of one of the Scottish or northern companies might have left the

IBA vulnerable to accusations of South of England imperialism. The South and South East region, as not only the most 'Southern' but also the most affluent of the mini-baronies, was an ideal place *pour encourager les autres*. Minimum risk to the network and maximum impact in the press was assured because so many London journalists and TV producers commute from the Southern region. One reason stated by the IBA was that 'In the dual area of South and South-East England there were three times as many new contenders for the franchise as in any other area.' This resulted in part from the IBA's own preference for applicants with substantial television experience who also were local residents. The winning application was apparently concocted by some TV executives who commuted into London together on the train from Hastings.

2. *The new Breakfast Television contract* went to a company called TV-am. This company was offering an incompatible mixture of show business and serious analysis with the former likely to triumph. The company was heavily national, and its choice seemed to conflict with ILR's ratings success at breakfast time. Breakfast television also puts the IBA once again into an awkward relationship with the press. Its novelty attracts press interest, but by competing against the national newspapers for both audiences and advertising it is also vulnerable to press enmity.

3. *In the Midlands television area* the IBA decided (echoing the surgery on Rediffusion in 1967) to chop in half the interest of its most venerable remaining network contractor – ATV Network, a subsidiary of Lord Grade's Associated Communications Corporation. Since ACC in its *Raise The Titanic* phase was short of cash, being forced to sell off 49% of ATV was probably not unwelcome. The IBA also wanted to make the Midlands into a 'dual region' by closing ACC's London (Elstree) base and opening, as a counter-weight to Birmingham, a major new East Midlands studio in Nottingham by using its transmitter at Waltham and building; the intention was to raise the additional finance in the East and West Midlands.

These IBA plans all fell apart, however, by 1982. Instead of a Midlands company controlled from and based in Birmingham and Nottingham, ACC was in fact bought by an Australian, Mr Holmes à Court, in a takeover battle involving maximum acrimony and several legal actions. The IBA's traditional share arrangement – of a small number of voting shares held by approved persons in order to prevent takeovers – was shown to include the worst aspects of 'undemocratic' share control, without the intended security against takeover.

Whereas the IBA's intention was to get more Midlands involvement, Midlands people from both East and West failed to buy the remaining 49% of shares when offered. In fact the biggest slice of shares was picked up by D. C. Thomson (of Dundee), the absentee landlords whom the IBA had recently kicked out with Southern Television. Next biggest takers were Ladbroke's, a company which had recently been held unfit to hold a gaming licence in London. Another big block of shares went to companies controlled by Mr Robert Maxwell, a businessman with a highly controversial reputation of the sort (perhaps wrongly) not normally approved by the IBA.

The IBA was legally obliged to remove the now existing foreign (Australian) control; in 1983 another change of ownership occurred, with the arrival of Sears' (British Shoe Corporation and William Hill betting shops). D. C. Thomson, Ladbroke's, Sears', and Maxwell (Pergamon/BPCC) now held 74% of voting shares.

When Central at last went on the air there was the usual get-the-boot-in strike, over the delicate issue of moving ACTT members from London to Nottingham. Despite the IBA's brave intentions, then, midlands ITV was still to be dominated by one national trade union and by a consortium whose interests were national and commercial rather than regional and media.

4. *The Fourth Television Channel.* The full implications of this channel both for ITV and for the BBC will be only revealed during the rest of the 1980s. But a few comments can be made. This is a *national* channel, which, along with the other decisions, redefines ITV along increasingly national lines and sharpens competition both with the BBC and with the national press.

This channel is much more directly dependent upon the IBA than the previous channel has been, and this is bound to produce tensions as well as bringing the IBA more and more into the centre of controversy. From the viewpoint of the existing ITV companies the fourth channel is a compromise – it is not a commercial competitor; old ITV is the main subsidiser and a major supplier of its programming, but at risk to its profits.

What general conclusions can be drawn from the IBA's performance in 1980–82? A major impression is of IBA decisions which do not lead to the intended consequences. The IBA's constitutional position requires that its members are amateur; its chairman who presided over the franchise allocations, Lady Plowden, then stepped aside – handing on the unintended consequences to her successor. The IBA has relatively few senior staff outside engineering.

That some of the sorts of weaknesses indicated above might indeed exist was implied by the surprise appointment in 1982 of Mr John Whitney as the new IBA Director General. Mr Whitney – in addition to having run Capital Radio, once said to be the 'world's most profitable radio station' – had wide experience of many other relevant things: writing and producing TV series, making programming for Radio Luxembourg, successful political lobbying in the setting up of commercial radio, experience as chairman of the ILR companies' trade association (AIRC) and finally an active interest in space satellites.

The Whitney appointment marked the end of the reign of the cultural bureaucrats at the IBA. The original cultural bureaucrats were the then Sir Kenneth Clark (ITA chairman 1954–7) and Sir Robert Fraser (ITA Director-General for the ITA's first sixteen years). These two men had met when they both held senior positions in the wartime Ministry of Information. Kenneth Clark was, of course, an eminent art historian and art administrator – he was Director of the National Gallery 1934–45 – and combined his chairmanship of the ITA with chairmanship of the Arts Council.[13] Sir Robert Fraser – the dominant single personality in the first sixteen years of the ITA – had been a journalist but his main qualification was having been since 1947 Director General of the Central Office of Information.[14]

The second Director General of the ITA (later IBA) who held the post from 1970 to 1982, was Sir Brian Young; he was another cultural bureaucrat – classics scholar, public school headmaster and head of the Nuffield Foundation.

It can be said of this remarkable 28-year incumbency of just two cultural bureaucrats that under their direction the ITA/IBA had an unsure touch in nearly all of the key areas of television and radio administration – finance, programme planning, industrial relations and advertising. The IBA's supervisory functions placed it in an awkwardly negative 'censorship' role in both programming and advertising; in finance and industrial relations it was always at one remove from the real scene of action. Nevertheless, Fraser and Young – the two cultural bureaucrats – together with their shorter stay chairmen, had by 1982 built independent broadcasting into something comparable to the BBC. If the IBA had lost some of the internal battles, it had done rather well in the external political wars.

Producer power and trade union power

The real winners from the events of 1980–2 are the related groups of producers and programme makers and secondly the trade unions. Much of the battle over the Fourth Channel was fought around the concept of 'Independent Production'. This appealed to Lord Annan's colleagues including the two former television producers on his committee; it is the sort of idea that appeals to almost anyone, until you look at it closely. American network television depends on independent production by companies in Hollywood. A key point about independent production is that once it becomes successful in such an expensive field as television it is quickly dealing with seven-figure sums (one hour per week even at Channel Four's low average starting cost of £30,000 per hour would total £1·56 million per annum). Successful independent producers must in practice quickly become biggish. The larger programme budgets in fact initially went to a handful of production teams with established track records and of course to the existing ITV regional companies and to ITN.

But if 'Independent Production' summons up false images of television as cottage industry, these images have not only been good public relations but also helpful to programme makers in general. Any new channel which sets out to make a mixture of popular and less popular programming means a lot of new work and opportunities for programme makers.

The new television channel was initially populated at the top with just two main kinds of people – television programme makers and, once more, quite a number of those rank outsiders without whom no IBA project would be complete.

The other grouping that has done well out of Channel Four and out of the other 1980–2 decisions, and which is a powerful influence over British broadcasting is, of course, the trade unions. The pace-setter here is ACTT (the Association of Cinematograph and Television Technicians) which is the main ITV union and has organized most of the new jobs created by the new TV channel.

The BBC did not even have a house union until 1945. The next big step in unionism involved the start of ITV in 1955. ACTT, a film union, stepped in and organized the ITV workers.[15] This union had over its years in the film industry managed to establish very generous levels of manning – partly because movie production also is vulnerable to union strength and partly as an agreed method of relieving the insecure and casual nature of film employment. ITV in 1955 looked equally uncertain and the generous manning and pay levels were carried across into ITV, where ACTT ever since has been the dominant union – not only for technical staff but also for producers and directors.

These developments in ITV galvanized the BBC house union into much more vigorous existence; within a few years not only had ABS become much more militant, but the BBC also recognized four other Unions – the NUJ for journalists, NATTKE (another film union), EETPU (the electricians' union) and SOGAT (a print union). ITCA also recognized the first three of these (while IBA employees themselves are mainly ABS members). Both BBC and ITV recognize British Actors' Equity and the Musicians' Union.

Consequently BBC and ITV each recognize and negotiate with some half dozen extremely active trade unions, which have a predominantly craft flavour. In specialized areas these unions play a large part in determining programming – for example the Musicians' Union in the entire BBC music output. Equity and the Musicians' Union work together and these two major talent unions are especially active in the field of secondary payments for repeats of both programming and advertisements across the entire range of TV-radio-video. Equity once again showed its muscle by depriving Channel Four, at its launch, of much of its advertising revenue.

Tom Burns argues in his book *The BBC* that the trade unions (especially the ABS) permeate all activities; managers and producers complain – often bitterly – about the restrictive climate. But this may partly be because the unions in practice – as in the press – are doing some of the administration. Moreover if television is overstaffed, it is possible that this overgenerous level of manning does also contribute to high technical standards.

Trade Union pressure is fundamental to the basic policy of making 86% of programming in Britain; there were in fact in 1982 some relaxations in the small print of the 14% import limits. But the unions, having obtained a Fourth Channel to their liking could afford minor concessions. Crucial to this 14% quota level – which operates across British television – was a 1955 'Gentleman's Agreement' between the original ITV companies, and all the television and talent unions.[16]

The trade union interest is also extremely important in all questions to do with regional programming and ITV and ILR franchises. A major reason why the IBA has largely stuck to the early areas is that, for example, trying to close a studio in London for transfer to Nottingham leads to some very fierce bargaining responses; major relocations also tend to be achieved at such a price as to make any management victories distinctly pyrrhic.

The ACTT has some similarities to the National Union of Journalists – its militant tactics are designed partly to hold together an increasingly varied membership; ACTT has members not only in feature films, film laboratories and television, but also in television commercials, independent local radio and the new video fields. The

ABS similarly deals with a huge range of occupations within the BBC. Both ACTT and the ABS are, however, unlike the NUJ in being essentially London unions. The ABS has its roots in Broadcasting House and radio, the ACTT in the film industry of North and West London. One reason why the IBA has made so little progress in really getting television out of London is that the unions like London, its glamour, its high rates of pay and its range of electronic media employment.

The ACTT, especially, shows its militancy from time to time in strikes. ACTT was on strike for 11 weeks in August, September and October 1979. Some argued that this strike was worth-while in terms of the benefits gained; others believed the strike to show that people as well paid as television technicians could survive a long strike. Another cynical interpretation was that the government in effect financed the strike via lower profits and thus lower levy. Certainly ITV's share of the advertising cake shrank in 1979. But another interpretation of the ACTT strike was that it was fundamentally a *macho* demonstration – a kind of thumping of the chest before the franchise carve-up of 1980.

Certainly the *macho* quality is strong in television production. This is a craft field, which means a predominantly male set of occupations – which in turn means *de facto* discrimination against both women and ethnic minorities.

Two excellent studies, one by ACTT and one about the BBC, document the dominance of white males.[17] There are two major career ladders in television – one of these is in engineering and technical fields and very few women indeed are found here. The second main area is the rough career ladder which involves such jobs as floor manager, director, producer, senior producer; with this 'producer' career ladder there is the need to persuade or command the troops on the studio floor – camera, sound and the other craft skills. This requirement falls especially on the floor manager, the man (almost invariably) who walks about the studio floor receiving instructions from the gallery above and passing them on to 'crew' and performers. This task is believed to require leadership or masculine qualities; the people who believe this are the men who run television.

Women do, of course, work in television in quite large numbers but according to the ACTT study there is just one area which they dominate – Production Assistant/Secretary. About half of ITV programme researchers are women and more than half of all vision mixers – but this latter job offers little prospect of advance. Even in Design the great majority are men, and similarly in editing. In 1982 ACTT had 342 members who were directors, producers, or producer/directors. Forty-two of these, or 12%, were women.

The BBC study of women in senior posts suggests that in the 1970s the position of women in some respects actually worsened. Women in senior positions are – as in some other occupations – heavily concentrated in certain fields (such as children's programming). Television is a field in which some people ascend very rapidly – they enter as graduates, become directors at say 24 and are senior producers in charge of major programmes by their early thirties. Some of these precocious producers then go to top BBC jobs, or to very senior posts in ITV companies by their early or mid-forties. But these very rapid upward careers nearly all belong to men. Women move upwards more slowly at all stages. A woman may become a director at 30 but not at 25 and so on upwards. Those who leave to have children seldom return at the same level, and those few women who reach senior positions mostly do not have children.

These factors which discriminate against women are of course common to other occupations, and especially in crafts and professions. Television broadly speaking is a craft area, with professional overtones at the senior levels. These are well paid jobs for which people compete actively. The factors which discriminate against women also discriminate against blacks and Asians.

Conclusion

This chapter has suggested that in terms of power *within* British broadcasting communicators (producers) come first, then trade unions, then businessmen, then the 'public' amateurs – the BBC governors and IBA members. But these groups are fairly evenly balanced, and their comparative strength can vary. The essential point will still remain – that power in television is widely spread between a number of occupational categories and baronial outposts. But power is much more narrowly shared in that these occupations and outposts are primarily manned (literally) by white males of middling years and highish income mostly resident within commuting distance of Shepherds Bush, West London.

The fourth television channel broadly illustrates this argument. In the long history of the channel's emergence the idea of 'independent production' and the general interests and arguments of producers have usually been paramount.[18] Secondly, the trade unions have every reason to be pleased with the new channel – it provides much new work especially for ACTT members, and once again mainly at generous rates of pay and in the London region. Equity, the actors' union, staged the traditional strike-at-the-opening, about the crucial question of advertising repeat payments for actors in a small audience channel.

The interests of businessmen were not entirely ignored – the ITV companies had to subsidize the new channel, but they do receive its advertising revenue in return; their existing monopoly of TV advertising remains. Nevertheless Channel Four could scarcely be described as an example of tooth-and-claw capitalism.

Finally, on internal power, the IBA members are not in a strong position to influence Channel Four because – apart from their continuing amateur dilemmas – there is a much more professional-looking Board interposed between the IBA members and the Channel Four staff. The Channel Four Board's ultimate significance will only become evident over a period of years, but creative film and television producers and directors appear to constitute its largest single grouping.

Ultimately, of course, much of the power lies outside the broadcasting industry in the world of politics and policy. Later we consider those areas in more detail, but now one final word on the position of producers and other programme makers: whatever the technological and policy future may bring, and whether the BBC and the IBA survive into the next century, the position of producers and programme makers is unlikely to be weakened. Hardware is vital, but software – the programming which will attract audiences – is even more vital.

The position of broadcast producers is similar to that of the senior print journalists. Moreover the technological revolutions which will confront both producers and journalists are likely to bring their work even closer together. This may propel some two thousand 'producers' and another two thousand or so 'journalists' into an even more powerful position.

CHAPTER FIFTEEN

The regions

Previous chapters have argued that the media in Britain are predominantly national; with only a few exceptions the facts of the economies of scale and the facts of political power and prestige combine together to minimise both regional and local media offerings.

But this varies somewhat between regions of Britain, and it also varies according to where you live within that region. Table 24 shows that Scotland is the main exception. Scotland gets somewhere

TABLE 24

REGIONAL AND LOCAL TELEVISION, RADIO
AND NEWSPAPERS, CIRCA 1982

	BBC TV	BBC Radio
English major regions e.g. Midlands, North-West	Produce for network. 3–4 hrs per wk for own region.	20 hrs per wk for network. No regional radio BBC local stations.
English lesser regions e.g. East Anglia, North East	Nil for network. 3–4 hrs per wk for own region.	Nil for network or own region. BBC local stations.
Wales	2–3 hrs per wk for network. 16 regional hrs per wk (7 in Welsh).	2 hrs per wk for network. 140 regional hrs per wk. Opt-out local stations.
Scotland	2–3 hrs per wk for network. 10 hrs per wk for own region.	5 hrs per wk for network. 125 regional hrs per wk. Opt-out local stations.

Sources: BBC Annual Report and Handbook 1983; IBA Annual report and Accounts Media Digest Sept/Oct 1982.

near to being, indeed, a separate 'nation', in the media, and especially in its newspapers. The next exception is Wales, especially in both its television and radio.

Less well provided with regional and local media are the English regions; this is especially true, of the heavily populated industrial areas such as the Midlands and the North West. Paradoxically these areas have the largest 'regional' media, but in both press and broadcasting they are primarily only satellite printing and production centres for London.

However within each region there is another exception; while the most *regional* media are weak, the media in each of the main regional cities are comparatively strong. The larger urban centres each have their daily newspapers and typically these have high readerships within the core area of the city. For example in 1981 the *Leicester Mercury* went each evening into 75% of all households in the city of Leicester. In the cities also the 'local' radio stations are based; BBC tradition, union insistence and IBA guide-lines all favour the model of a fairly large local radio station which in turn requires an urban centre of population.

IBA TV	IBA Radio	Regional press	City press	Paid for weeklies	Free sheets
8 hrs per wk network. 8 hrs for own region.	ILR stations	None	Strong	Weak	Strong
Very little for network. About 10 hrs per wk for own region.	ILR stations	Some	Weak-ening	Weak	Strong
Very little for network. 11 hrs per wk for Wales (7 in Welsh).	ILR stations	Some	Weak	Mixed	Weak
Very little for network. 11 hrs per wk own region.	ILR stations	Strong	Mixed	Strong	Weak

While the 'local' media tend in fact to be *city* media, so also do the 'regional' media. Very few newspapers have a real regional spread. (Two exceptions are the *Northern Echo* in Darlington and the *Eastern Daily Press* in Norwich.) Moreover the same applies to 'regional' television – in practice such television mainly reflects the city in which it is based. The IBA is trying to do something about this latter situation by developing sub-regions such as the *East* Midlands (around Nottingham) and South-West Lancashire (around Liverpool).

The Scottish and Welsh media, to at least some extent, probably do both reflect and re-inforce the sense of a Scottish and a Welsh nation. But the media in the North West of England or the Midlands do little or nothing to create a regional loyalty; the local media which exist in England do, however, reflect and buttress urban loyalties – not to the North West but to Oldham or Bolton, not to the Midlands but to Nottingham, Coventry or Wolverhampton.[1] Along with this pattern often seems to go a resentment against the big regional city – against Manchester and against Birmingham.

Provincial media: Inter-war decline, revival to 1975 . . . 1980s more decline?

London dominance of the British media has not always existed. Indeed in 1920 (Figure 3) the provincial daily newspapers outsold the Fleet Street national mornings. It was only in the 1920s and 1930s – while provincial daily sales remained stable – that Fleet Street morning sales almost doubled. Something similar happened to radio in the 1920s. The early BBC (Company) favoured local programming but later in the 1920s and 1930s BBC radio came to be increasingly national and London based.

The third quarter of the century, however, saw some reversal of this trend. In contrast to the centralizing trend of 1925–50, the third quarter of 1950–75 seemed to mark a trend back towards provincial media. From 1955 the ITV system led for the first time to television production in significant quantities outside London. Provincial newspaper sales boomed in the 1950s and advertising followed; the years 1970–75 were the most prosperous ever experienced by Britain's provincial press. By 1973 the BBC's first batch of 20 local radio stations were completed and by 1976 these had been joined by 19 ILR commercial local stations.

But around 1975 this apparently strong trend towards the provinces seemed to falter. Further growth of local radio was stopped (until 1980). The provincial press got into major difficulties; around 1980 not only the IBA, with its new franchises and new channel, began to re-emphasize national television, so also did the BBC.

Local and regional press, television and radio, all seem to face further hard times in the later 1980s, while the 'new media' – satellites, cable, home video – will in practice be dominated by non-local programming.

National Press v. provincial press

A cyclical change of fortune between provincial and national papers has a long history in Britain. London newspapers were strong in the years before 1855 (because of penal taxation) and in the years around 1900 – as Northcliffe pushed 'his' revolution out of London towards Manchester. But the provincial press also had its periods of strength – the later eighteenth century was the first; in the 1870s the electric telegraph was partly responsible for a boom in provincial dailies.

The provincial press was extremely volatile at certain times and its history even in a single city quite complex. For example in Wolverhampton 29 different daily and weekly papers were published between 1850 and 1950. But 12 of the 29 lasted less than a year. Briefly in 1884 there were three evenings in competition, until by 1915 the *Express and Star* emerged as the sole winner.[2]

But the 'revival' of the provincial press in the 1950s and 1960s took place against a number of historical, geographical and other British peculiarities which together favoured a *national* press. The Liberal press was extremely significant in the late nineteenth century and it served a stepping-stone function in allowing London owners subsequently to buy provincial dailies.[3] With the decline in the early twentieth century of the Liberal vote, some Liberal owners of provincial dailies found themselves anxious to sell to a financially well-endowed Liberal company, such as the Westminster Press.

Fleet Street was, compared with other countries, early in adopting the *Joint Stock Company*. Northcliffe pioneered joint stock status with voting control retained in family hands.[4] This pattern combined central control with access to capital for expansion by Londoners into provincial newspaper operations. The London-owned chains of provincial dailies, which allowed rationalization and helped to reduce managerial eccentricity, played a key role in the emergence of London dominance.

The Press Association, when it first appeared in 1868, favoured provincial dailies against nationals. But in the longer run the news agencies placed the provincials at the receiving end of a one-way flow of cheap uniform news. The increasingly similar supply of national news for all provincial dailies contributed to the decline of competition within particular cities.

The provincial mornings found in the 1920s that especially with better *roads*, they were losing the battle not only against the provincial evenings but also against the national mornings. This

change forced the provincial daily press into a popular evening role
– and one increasingly seen as subordinate to the Fleet Street daily.

Fleet Street consolidated its pattern of satellite printing plants,
with the *Daily Mail* printing first in Manchester in 1900. By 1930
four Fleet Street populars were printing in Manchester[5] and the
Daily Express was printing also in Glasgow. Fleet Street in the 1920s
further strengthened its grip on the provinces through the establishment of London owned provincial chains. The 1920s saw a sharp
drop in competition in provincial cities and the rapid rise of chains.
By 1929 44% of provincial dailies were already owned by just five
national chains.

The previously formidable category of English provincial mornings shrank steadily – from 66 in 1900 to 18 in 1939 – into a small
beleaguered group led by the *Manchester Guardian*, the Leeds
Yorkshire Post, the *Glasgow Herald*, and *The Scotsman* (Edinburgh). Many provincial dailies found themselves as part of chains,
which in turn were subordinate to national daily newspapers owned
by the same company in London. Within a company such as
Kemsley (later Thomson) or Northcliffe – the goals of the national
and provincial dailies were differently defined. The Fleet Street
daily was fiercely competitive, and spent lavishly in pursuit of
political influence, general prestige and newspaper machismo; the
chain of provincial dailies under the same ownership tended increasingly to be monopolies, to make big profits via advertising in
good years, while cutting costs in bad years, and were dedicated
to commercial success, keeping out of trouble and newspaper
sobriety.

These historically based differences continued after 1950. The
revival which followed was primarily a revival of advertiser, much
less reader, interest. Some of the provincial chains – especially those
such as Thomson and Associated each with several large dailies –
were enormously profitable. These profits were often taken out of
the provincial dailies and invested in other more prestigious activities, including the subsidization of loss-making Fleet Street dailies.
A few companies, such as the family owners of the *Wolverhampton
Express and Echo* – who lacked any national titles – reinvested their
profits in new equipment, new editions, more news, more journalists and a better service to readers.

But most provincial dailies remained vulnerable to any turn-
down in the lavish advertising of 1965–75. After 1975 they were hit
with multiple problems. Job advertising shrank dramatically; the
profitable weeklies were hit by a savage burst of competition from
freesheets; many traditional paid-for weekly titles were converted
to freesheets. As free local newspapers become more numerous and
of better quality the less people may want to buy weekly or daily

ones. Local radio offered further competition. Provincial dailies with less advertising and hence fewer news pages, had to raise their cover prices – thus seeming to constitute a still worse bargain as against a free local or a more exciting brash national tabloid. The 'management revolution' on which some regional newspaper executives prided themselves was revealed as being narrow-minded, too concerned with advertising revenue and perhaps rather cynical about provincial news and provincial audiences. Thomson Regional Newspapers – the group which had pioneered the 'new' style of chain newspaper management – suffered especially severely.

The electronic media

The first of the 'new media' was the film and this was located largely in and around London. It was attracted to London by the theatrical and entertainment industries and by proximity to a market. Eventually it moved to the north-west suburbs and, when it declined after the 1950s, left big studios at places like Elstree, Ealing and Pinewood, which were used by American film makers and British television companies

The BBC began in the heart of London at Savoy Hill, off The Strand. As its transmitters spread across the country, it initially seemed natural that major centres of population should also originate their own programming. But 1926 was a turning point for the BBC in several ways, including the start of a policy which gave a lesser place to its lesser provincial centres (Newcastle, Bournemouth and Aberdeen) and also held back the major provincial centres (Birmingham, Glasgow, Cardiff and Belfast). In the late 1920s a policy evolved that regional BBC producers should not attempt to do what London could do better, but should focus on what they could clearly do better than London. Asa Briggs[6] describes the evolution of this attitude into a 1929 BBC doctrine of 'centralization'. This doctrine derived from a combination of financial and engineering arguments – plus the administrative convenience of concentrating 'the brute force of monopoly' at a single point.

Despite many small twists and turns, the BBC's regional policy has not greatly altered since. The BBC in the 1960s agreed to local radio as part of the political deal involved in outlawing the pirate ship radio stations. This forced the BBC to rethink the structure into which local radio would fit. What then emerged was one policy for Scotland, Wales and Northern Ireland and another for the English provinces.

The BBC created three major centres in England – Birmingham (Pebble Mill), Manchester and Bristol – which would make some programmes for the national networks (Table 25). Bristol, for

Media industry

TABLE 25

BBC: NATIONAL, REGIONAL AND LOCAL HOURS OF
TELEVISION AND RADIO OUTPUT, 1981–82

| | Television | | | Radio | | | |
	Net-work Hours	Re-gional Hours	Total Hours	Net-work Hours	Re-gional Hours	Local Radio Hours	Total Hours
Programmes produced in London	5,270	—	5,270	25,467	—		25,467
Programmes produced in							
Birmingham	513	179	692	1,018	—		1,018
Manchester	545	177	722	919			919
Bristol	224	175	399	689	—		689
Norwich	2	174	176	—	—		—
Newcastle	7	179	186	—	—		—
Leeds	10	175	185	—	—		—
Southampton	15	175	190	—	—		—
Plymouth	9	176	185	—	602		602
Scotland	129	512	641	256	6,457		6,713
Wales	135	840	975	116	7,110		7,226
N. Ireland	30	317	347	65	4,508		4,573
Total programmes produced in regions	1,619	3,079	4,698	3,063	18,677		21,740
British and foreign feature films and series	1,530	—	1,530	—	—		—
Local radio	—	—	—	—	—	86,587	86,587
Open University	1,243		1,243	859	—		859
TOTAL hours of Broadcasting	9,662	3,079	12,741	29,389	18,677	86,587	134,653

Source: *BBC Annual Report and Handbook, 1983* pp. 115, 117.

example, specialises in natural history programming. These three
centres plus five others would also each make about 175 hours of TV
a year (primarily half an hour of daily local news).

In radio the BBC has almost completely abolished English *regional* output as such. Its three major satellite centres make radio
for the national networks (mainly Radios 3 and 4). Otherwise radio

for audiences within the regions is left to BBC Local Radio.

ITV despite its supposedly regional nature, in its early years did little local programming. After twenty years, the network companies in whose areas the majority of the British population lived were each putting out about four and a half hours of *local* output per week. During the life of the Annan Committee this increased a little, and by the early 1980s network companies were transmitting about one hour a day – mainly local news plus a little current affairs/documentary/sport – to four regions each of which averaged some eight million people.

Of course regional television is expensive in relation to the audience reached and local worthies such as MPs will be quite happy to be on for a few minutes per month. Consequently both the IBA and the BBC have in practice decided to settle for a television compromise in the English regions. They each put out only semi-token amounts of regional material (half an hour a day for BBC regions and an average hour a day for ITV regions) but they schedule this regional material into key peak time slots, such as early evening.

However the bulk of city and local coverage is left to local radio operations. By mid-1982 Independent local radio passed the point of being available to three-quarters of the whole British population; according to JICRAR research, in these areas just over half of all adults listen to ILR at least weekly and a third of all radio listening is to ILR (Table 6). BBC local radio has a significantly smaller audience, but the combined local radio audience compares well with that for regional daily and local weekly (paid for) newspapers; the main exceptions are rural areas and this distinction will steadily disappear.

Does local radio provide a satisfactory local service? Clearly there is a local *flavour* to ILR – the disc jockeys, phone-ins and 'other speech' all have this. Some of the advertising is local and ILR stations average around 3 minutes of national and 3 minutes of local news per hour. But ILR stations typically have very small staffs of about 10 journalists[7] – comparable to the staff of a *weekly* newspaper; their effort typically is concentrated into one main news package at breakfast time and smaller news packages at mid-day and early evening. BBC Local Radio has similar problems of small budgets and staffs; in view of its heavy radio network provision of music, the BBC Local Radio stations focus more heavily on local talk and news; this BBC programming policy is known to – and duly does – produce older and smaller audiences than the more music and youth-oriented ILR obtains. Little public research exists, but in view of the size of staffs it is perhaps hardly necessary. One detailed study of the output of the three London local stations complained that they carried little local news, but a lot of traffic reports, interviews with entertainers and authors, and similar 'publicity' material.[8]

Scotland: Britain's only media region?

Scotland is perhaps the exception to the major rule of Britain's national media audience; it has a much more distinctively regional pattern of media – especially in the press. Fleet Street's attempt at imperialising the Scots newspaper reader was left very late – mainly to Lord Beaverbrook who began a separate Glasgow print of the *Daily Express* in 1928. The main Fleet Street effort in Scotland coincided with the mid-century inflation of Fleet Street sales and sales promotion, and it subsided in the 1960s. .

In 1935 Beaverbrook's *Scottish Daily Express* was read by 20% of Scots adults; the *Daily Herald* was read by 10%; Fleet Street dailies were read by 43%, but 60% read a Scots morning paper, quite apart from the Scots evenings.[9] By 1943 the *Daily Express* was read by 28% of Scots but the other Fleet Street dailies had fallen back to only 12% combined. 48% saw a Scots morning and 55% saw a Scots evening every day.[10] After 1945 the Fleet Street dailies tried another assault, with the *Daily Mail* deciding to print in Edinburgh – an eccentric choice of beach-head. (It eventually gave up its Edinburgh effort in 1968.)

But the paper which finally triumphed in the Scottish market was the *Daily Record*, a popular Glasgow morning paper on which Northcliffe had sharpened his skills in 1895. The *Record* was, and is, a Scottish paper owned from London. In 1947 it was still owned by the Kemsley group with a sale of 374,000, second to the *Scottish Daily Express* with 536,000.[11] Glasgow with in 1947 (in addition to the *Express*) three mornings and three evenings was the scene of perhaps the most ferocious British newspaper sales war of all time. Very slowly the *Daily Record* overtook the *Scottish Daily Express*; the *Express* finally conceded defeat only in 1974, when the Glasgow print was closed as a result of losses in London and the *Scottish Daily Express* went back to print in Manchester. In the 1960s both *Record* and *Express* had been read by almost half of all Scottish adults; after 1974 the *Express* fell back sharply. The *Daily Record* advanced from 528,000 in 1970 to 740,000 in 1982. It is a highly Scottish version of *The Sun* and *Daily Mirror* combined. It is of course a stable-mate of the *Daily Mirror*.

Scottish daily newspaper sales have thus long been split into three main divisions:

1. The Fleet Street dailies, none since 1974 printed in Scotland. The steep decline of the *Scottish Daily Express* has only been

partly balanced by the rise of *The Sun* and thus Fleet Street's
sales share is still declining.

2. *The Daily Record*, which since 1974 has been read by just over
    half of all Scottish adults.
3. Roughly equal in sales to the *Daily Record* is the rest of the
    Scottish daily press. Big declines in evening paper sales have
    occurred especially in Glasgow and also in Edinburgh. But
    these have been matched by increases in the sales of the
    already strong Scottish mornings. The *Glasgow Herald* is
    by general consent the leading provincial morning paper in
    Britain; *The Scotsman* (Edinburgh) plus the morning
    papers in Dundee and Aberdeen – together with the *Daily
    Record* – gives Scotland a regional morning press with sales
    of over one million copies. There is still also a substantial
    group of six evening papers with (unusually for Britain)
    total sales only a little higher than the regional morn-
    ings.

Scotland also has its own successful pattern of Sunday papers, with
the incredible D. C. Thomson *Sunday Post* read by over two-thirds
of all Scottish adults, and the *Sunday Mail* (*Daily Record* stable)
also very strong. The *Glasgow Herald* stable also produces the
prestige *Sunday Standard*.

In press terms Scotland is then largely a region apart, at least in
terms of content; with this press goes stronger audience interest
than in any other British region.[12] In fact all of its main four
newspaper publishers are British national as well as Scottish
'national' companies in one way or another; even D. C. Thomson –
the eccentric and secretive owners of the two Dundee dailies –
are national producers of comics and women's magazines with a
presence in London.

Scotland seems to have acquired a separate press pattern mainly
for reasons of distance and population. Because of the distance
from London, Fleet Street groups went to print in Scotland. But for
the *Express* and the *Mail* this proved too costly a venture for a
region of only five million people. This number of people – plus the
distance of 400 miles from London, plus a somewhat different
political and social system – seems to match with the semi-national
press pattern found in Scotland.

However in broadcasting Scotland has a much less distinctively
Scottish pattern. The demand for Scottish broadcasting appears to
be strong – for example the ILR station Radio Clyde (Glasgow) was
from the outset the most successful of the big city local radio
stations. But the 'national' Scottish service provided by the BBC
talk channel is less successful. Scots, it seems, can be very critical

not only of certain Scots accents but also of certain Scots programming.

Scottish Television and Grampian are the ITV stations serving
central Scotland and the North East. They are fairly typical of ITV
stations of their size; Scottish Television averages about 90 minutes
of the usual mainly news, actuality and sport per day and shows the
network material like any other ITV mini-major. Grampian (Aberdeen) originates about one hour of television each day. For the
BBC, Scotland is a 'National region'. This means in the case of
television that BBC Scotland makes some 3 hours per week for the
two BBC networks and another 10 hours a week for Scotland alone.
Thus viewers in Central Scotland can see over 20 hours per week of
Scottish-made television, although over 90% of all available TV
output comes from outside Scotland.

The BBC's big Scottish effort is in radio, primarily for the whole
of Scotland – some 130 hours a week of it, mainly on 'Radio
Scotland' (which substitutes for BBC Radio 4). This effort has quite
a troubled history and a far from enormous audience; inevitably
there are major problems in running a radio service on a single radio
channel to a 'nation' as complex and in some respects as non-
national as the Scots.

The third line of BBC attack in Scotland is the local radio stations,
but not separate local radio stations on the English pattern. These
are 'opt-out' stations which add local hours to the 'national' material
of Radio Scotland. Three of the first five of these local opt-out
stations were in the islands, and one is heavily committed to
Gaelic.

Altogether this BBC effort is quite considerable in scale and – in
contrast to the English regions – it is more ambitious than the IBA
effort. While BBC confines the Scottish national approach to
radio, ILR sticks to its City radio approach. ILR was at first limited
to stations in Glasgow (1973) and Edinburgh (1975), but in 1980–2
added radio stations in Aberdeen, Ayr, Dundee, Perth, and Inver-
ness. All of this amounts to a lot of radio and enough television to
enable a light viewer to watch little but Scottish programming. But
what happens in fact? Something like two-thirds of all newspapers
read in Scotland are published in Scotland; probably about 40% of
all radio listening is to Scottish stations – but much of that will be
music. Scotland also offers something not available elsewhere in
Britain – a choice of either a strongly popular or a more up-market
selection of regional media. There is the *Daily Record* and Radio
Clyde, or the *Glasgow Herald* and the BBC's Radio Scotland.

Wales
The Welsh media are much less Welsh than the Scottish media are

Scottish, with the exception that Wales now has one television channel which is not only dominated by Welsh-made programming, but also devotes its prime evening time to specially made Welsh-language material.

Wales' population is smaller and less conveniently placed from a regional media viewpoint. The main centre of population, in the south, is only two to three hours by train from London and it receives the same regional Fleet Street editions as go to South West England.

The Welsh press is extremely English; there are only three daily newspaper centres – Swansea, Cardiff, Newport – which are all in the South and the papers are all now owned by London groups (Associated, Thomson, Fleet). The population centre in North East Wales is close to Liverpool and gets the same English newspapers. The hilly lowly populated area of central Wales gets English newspapers not only from Liverpool but from Wrexham and Chester. Even among the weekly press the Welsh language element is nearly extinct.

The Welsh language itself has long been in decline and the 1971 and 1981 censuses show a big drop in Welsh speaking since 1961. Why then a special television channel for some half million Welsh speakers, most of whom also speak English? The answer is, of course, political. Broadcasting is subject to political pressures and on this issue Welsh Members of Parliament of all parties constitute a voting block; they want to preserve Welsh culture, the core of which is the Welsh language.

Wales has an idiosyncratic broadcasting history. The BBC radio tradition was to broadcast some Welsh-language material, and this tradition was carried over into BBC television and ITV.

ITV has had a bumpy history in Wales. No less than two Welsh ITV companies have ceased to operate. One of these was a station called Wales West and North (WWN); against the ITA's better judgement WWN began transmitting to the Wales West and North hillsides in September 1962; it was a failure for various technical, cultural and financial reasons, but not least because most of the (small) potential audience were already receiving ITV from either Cardiff or Manchester.[13]

The Cardiff ITV station was in fact based in Bristol as well; it was called Television West and Wales (TWW) – and reflected the IBA's initial view that the small Welsh population plus engineering convenience required a station to serve both coasts of the Bristol Channel. TWW had thus to face three ways – and to make programming for – the West of England around Bristol, the English speaking majority in Wales and the Welsh speaking minority. Having given TWW this arduous task the ITA concluded in 1967 that it had been unsatisfactorily performed and Harlech took up the triple burden in 1968.

As the Fourth Channel's arrival grew closer, at least four different committees (including Annan) all concluded that in Wales the new channel should carry Welsh programming. However, when the Conservative government in early 1980 announced their plans for an IBA fourth TV channel, they also announced a change of mind on the Welsh-language channel. Mr Gwynfor Evans, leader of the Welsh nationalist party and previously its first Westminster MP, announced that he would commence a fast unto death if the government did not change its mind by October. Delegations of Welsh worthies visited London to emphasize that the existing gentle campaign of civil disobedience (e.g. switching off transmitters and refusing to pay the licence fee) would undoubtedly become violent. Even such non-violent disobedience was worrying enough. The government, realizing that Mr Evans would make a formidable martyr, relented.

Thus came about the Welsh channel – with Welsh programming made partly by the BBC, slightly less by Harlech and even some by 'independent producers'. The initial 23 Welsh hours were slotted for peak time with other English-language Welsh items added on. Both those who liked Welsh programming and those who disliked it were happy to have it all on one channel.

When the Welsh Fourth Channel (SC4) began in November 1982 it quickly surprised many sceptics, by showing that large fractions of the entire Welsh-speaking public would indeed watch Welsh-language programming. The year 1982 had been taken up with the many crucial and awkward details. There was a new Welsh Fourth Channel Authority (WFCA). While the BBC seemed to be reasonably happy (just one more complex burden to add to so many others) the necessary co-operation for the joint BBC-IBA enterprise was less easily achieved.

The IBA, the ITV companies through ITCA, and the employees through ACTT were all sceptical – as was Harlech, the regional IBA company directly involved. There were other doubts about the number of people in Wales who pointed their antennae towards English transmitters; the highish level of Cable (20%) in some parts of Wales was also said to be explained less by hills than by attempts to avoid Welsh-language programming. There were also doubts about the supply of Welsh-speaking actors and the undoubted past and probable future inadequacies of audience research.[14]

There was, however already evidence that Welsh programming which aimed to be popular could indeed be popular.[15] The Welsh Fourth Channel has sacrificed culture in the interests of culture. Not

only is some three hours of Welsh-language programming scheduled on to one channel but into peak viewing time. The initial 22
hours per week may not seem an enormous increase over the 14
Welsh-language hours (7 BBC, 7 Harlech) previously transmitted,
but the 14 hours were scattered about, mainly out of prime time.
Had Gwynfor Evans indeed starved himself to death he would have
been not so much a television martyr, as a television *scheduling*
martyr.

Nevertheless even the previous 14 hours a week, of more educa-
tionally oriented and lower budget Welsh-language programming,
was obviously a strong basis upon which to build towards 22 hours of
news-drama-entertainment programming with higher budgets.
There has in recent years also been a fairly smoothly executed
trebling in the Welsh-language hours on BBC radio.

Wales in some respects is the media mirror image of Scotland.
Wales has a much more English press; but in both radio and
television and in both English-language Welsh programming and
also Welsh-language programming, the Welsh have a uniquely rich
set of regional offerings; these include the usual ILR pattern of local
stations, plus a planned BBC pattern of small 'opt-out' stations
linked to 'national' Welsh radio.

But perhaps the IBA were right to be sceptical. The ITCA
companies, the BBC and the government (via the levy) are paying
for Welsh-language programmes, which will cost between 10 and 20
times as much per viewer as do television programmes in Britain at
large. Is this a dangerous precedent, the more successful in audience
ratings the more dangerous?

Just as some Welsh people turn their TV antennae towards
transmitters in the English Midlands, some people in the Midlands
can receive SC4. What if they demanded the same kind of thing for
the English Midlands?

The English Midlands

As discussed in the previous chapter, the IBA had already become
increasingly anxious about the demands of members of parliament
and others in the East Midlands; a powerful transmitter located
between Nottingham, Leicester and Lincoln had enabled the IBA
to cast Nottingham into the role of sub-regional ITV Midlands
capital.

Such a move, however, created many new problems. A glance at
Map 2 illustrates the problem. This area has a population of around
9 to 10 million, about the same as Scotland, Wales and Northern
Ireland combined. As defined on this map – which conforms
roughly to the area reached by the Central ITV company, including

some overlaps with other ITV regions – there are 2 morning daily newspapers, 17 evening dailies, one Sunday, 8 BBC local radio stations and 7 ILR stations. But there are many other possible ways of defining the Midlands. And in many cases the local preference is to look away from, rather than towards, Birmingham. Oxford has little in common with Birmingham; Nottingham and Lincoln share little with either Birmingham or Oxford.

The real local loyalties are indeed *local*, not regional. There is some evidence of genuine ties between Nottingham, Derby, Leicester and Lincoln – and BBC local radio stations in these cities have pooled some programming quite successfully.[16] But the strongest loyalties seem to be very local indeed – not to the Birmingham-West Midlands conurbation but to one of the twenty localities within it. The evening papers in lesser cities are probably the largest media which closely match such local loyalties. And the sale of the *Coventry Evening Telegraph*, for example, was in 1982 about the same as in 1960.

The great success story of Midlands newspapers is the *Wolverhampton Express and Star* which doubled its sales between 1947 and 1980. This was done with a combination of heavy investment, good luck and wise planning. The good luck was that Wolverhampton was at the western end of the conurbation adjoining an area whose population greatly expanded with post-war re-housing. But in addition to their exurban satellite daily, the *Shropshire Star*, the Graham family invested lavishly in news appealing to the ultra local loyalties of the 'Black Country'.

This led to punishing circulation wars in border areas with the *Birmingham Evening Mail*. But the Birmingham group were faced with other problems, because of their continuing commitment to *regional* news – with the *Sunday Mercury* and the prestige morning *Birmingham Post*. The role of the regional morning newspaper is especially hard in the Midlands, which had five morning dailies after 1945 and only two struggling survivors by 1980. Birmingham's two mornings sold together 160,000 in 1947; 35 years later the *Birmingham Post* was down to less than a quarter of that level. In trying to be the newspaper for the West Midlands businessman, the *Post* felt the full competitive blast of the London dailies.

Seen from Fleet Street, the Midlands is more than a shapeless mess – it is a highly accessible market neatly placed along the main railway lines from London and bisected by a modern road network. The northern part of the area is equally convenient for Manchester-printed editions. After sending its first editions to the far-flung locations, Fleet Street garnishes its second or third editions with Midlands football, car industry stories and the odd Midlands tragedy. In the eyes of Fleet Street the main Midlands cities are the

destination for newspaper trains and the locations of local correspondents and 'stringers'.

Local radio is eccentrically distributed but quite strong in audience terms. BRMB's lack of political coverage of West Midlands
politics enhances its popularity. It has a Birmingham accent without
the ultra local detail. BBC Radio Birmingham is very much less
popular. Indeed one BBC study has shown that Wolverhampton's
Beacon Radio also was better known in Birmingham than was BBC
Radio Birmingham.[17] It is easier to achieve a regional sound than
regional substance.[18] According to JICRAR data the most popular
local radio station in the Midlands is Mercia Sound in Coventry;[19]
this underlines again the *local* nature of loyalties because Coventry
is, like Wolverhampton, close to Birmingham and has a strong
evening newspaper.

In view of this rather un-regional Midlands region, was the IBA
being fair in penalizing ACC/ATV for not providing enough Midlands or sub-regional television? Certainly the BBC does no better,

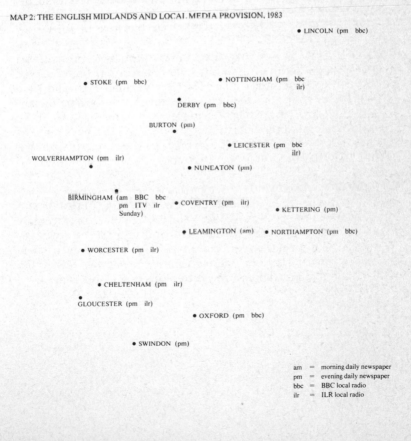

MAP 2: THE ENGLISH MIDLANDS AND LOCAL MEDIA PROVISION, 1983

● LINCOLN (pm bbc)

● STOKE (pm bbc)   ● NOTTINGHAM (pm bbc
                                          ilr)

● DERBY (pm bbc)

BURTON (pm)

● LEICESTER (pm bbc
                 ilr)

WOLVERHAMPTON (pm ilr)

● NUNEATON (pm)

BIRMINGHAM (am BBC bbc
            pm ITV ilr   ● COVENTRY (pm ilr)
            Sunday)   ● KETTERING (pm)

● LEAMINGTON (am) ● NORTHAMPTON (pm bbc)

● WORCESTER (pm ilr)

● CHELTENHAM (pm ilr)

GLOUCESTER (pm ilr)

● OXFORD (pm bbc)

● SWINDON (pm)

am = morning daily newspaper
pm = evening daily newspaper
bbc = BBC local radio
ilr = ILR local radio

using Birmingham as a satellite production centre and leaving Midlands coverage to eight rather ineffectual local radio stations.

There was perhaps more image than substance in the failures of ACC/ATV. Lord Grade certainly made plenty of mistakes, not least in believing that a man in his seventies can judge the film tastes of people 50 years younger. Lord Grade was perhaps too good at Hollywood and London public relations, and less good with the media in the Midlands. He also failed to court local politicians, and Lord Windlesham – a Conservative peer – was not an obvious choice as chief executive for a mainly Labour area.

But as to the actual charge of failing on local and regional programming, ACC/ATV seems to have been selected on the basis of image, rather than substance, to play the role of networking scapegoat. ATV had an image as a producer of glossy 'mid-Atlantic' series aimed at the export market, and that criticism is repeated in the Annan report. But this was the national *network* output. In its last full year of output ATV produced more local programming than required by the IBA 'and only 12 minutes a week less than the biggest network provider of local output, Granada'.[20] At least one detailed outsider's account was highly appreciative of ATV's regional output.[21]

Nevertheless a 'region' like the Midlands seems to produce not much less media acrimony and bitterness than do the better served regions of Scotland and Wales. The Birmingham Post and Mail group has been subjected to much abuse not only by local politicians but also by its own journalists during several bitter strikes. Of the other main potential regional media providers it is perhaps remarkable not that the ITV Midlands company has been so criticized but that the BBC has been so little criticized.

No regional media policy

Behind all this lies the fact that there is no such thing in Britain as a coherent media policy. The Welsh Fourth Channel is an extremely instructive case; the many government indecisions and revisions illustrated clearly that the only areas which do have even some semblance of partial regional media planning have achieved it as the direct result of political pressure exerted on central government.

Media policy

CHAPTER SIXTEEN

Media policy and fragmentation

British traditions: minimalist legislation and the voluntary principle
Both British press tradition and Anglo-Saxon legal tradition have
favoured a minimalist approach to legislation. In the press the
tradition has always been that no special press law is required. In
broadcasting it is impossible altogether to avoid legislation, but
even so the tradition is of the *minimal* legislation required. Broadcasting laws and related legal instruments are in fact quite frequent,
but, because of the British tradition of minimal legislation, these
legal documents are extremely brief. The document which extended
the BBC's life for another 15½ years (August 1981 to December
1996) contained 14½ pages of text.[1]

Another example is the connection between this minimalist
tradition and the issues of access and redress against unfair coverage. Clearly under such a tradition these rather difficult and detailed
issues are, along with much else, regarded as 'not suitable for
legislation'. But more positively they are thought suitable for the
voluntary approach. In this tradition, giving the Press Council penal
powers, say, to fine editors – or even to compel them to print replies
or retractions – such powers, or 'teeth', are widely regarded as
undesirable. The British way to settle disputes of any kind – legal,
industrial, or anything else – is, if at all possible, to try the *voluntary*
approach. Editors of newspapers, producers of programmes and
complaining citizens should be able to settle their disputes via some
voluntary mechanism, such as correspondence.

Thus the British Press Council, the Advertising Standards
Authority and the Broadcasting Complaints Commission all work
on a primarily voluntary basis, although the latter two are in
practice equipped with enough teeth to allow if not a big bite, at
least a small sharp nip.

This tradition, which stresses voluntarism and minimalist legislation, is consistent with the equally loosely drawn arrangements by
which 'amateur', but often distinguished, persons preside over the
BBC and the IBA. Somewhat similar sets of public persons are also
drawn into running the Press Council, the Advertising Standards
Authority and the Broadcasting Complaints Commission. Beyond
this, the BBC and IBA have pressed into service numerous 'advisory committees' of suitably amenable citizens – some 'professional',
but most amateur.

Not for Britain, then, the common West European approach of mass media policy being located within a single government department such as 'communication' or 'culture'. Nor even for Britain the American approach which locates the media largely in three Washington agencies – dealing with all telecommunications (the FCC), with trade (FTC), and with anti-trust (Justice).

Britain's telecommunications monopoly dates back to the early 1870s, a tradition re-inforced in the early 1920s with the radio monopoly conferred on the then British Broadcasting *Company*. But despite, or perhaps because of this telecommunications tradition, Britain now has a well-established tradition (although like many British 'traditions' of fairly recent origin) of hostility towards a single media ministry, or a single set of strategic national media goals.

Table 26 (p. 244–5) indicates that some thirty public bodies are involved in setting and carrying out British media policy. This figure of thirty is somewhat arbitrary; one could argue that the real figure is higher because this list leaves out all the business ownership-trade association bodies and all of the trade unions which effectively make policy in certain important areas. Alternatively one could argue that the number of *major* bodies is less than thirty. But whether the total is as high as fifty or as low as fifteen, the main point is that the number is much higher than one, two or three.

This superfluity of policy agencies leaves a lot of sorting out and co-ordination to be done at the commanding heights of the civil service and political apparatus. The departments which in British political tradition are regarded as the senior ones – Treasury, Foreign Office, Home Office – are all deeply involved in media policy. So are the three main economic/finance departments – not only the Treasury, but also both Industry and Trade. Consequently 'Downing Street' in practice becomes the main locus of British media policy-making. Media policy is largely made in Britain by senior ministers in and around major Cabinet committees – one of the most private areas of British public life.

Policy in this very public field is largely made privately. A policy tradition which rejects a single media department, and prefers a more democratic practice of policy fragmentation, paradoxically in fact centralizes media policy-making. Fragmented policies require co-ordination and this is done by Prime Ministers. Britain's nearest equivalent to a Minister of the Media is the Prime Minister. Harold Macmillan was the first Prime Minister (1957–63) to be confronted with an integrated media industry – a successful ITV and many press closures – which required a succession of sensitive media policy decisions. In 1961, for example, Macmillan personally decided the government response on the key Odham's merger issue (which led to IPC).[2] He also took an active part in finally resolving the disputes within the Conservative party over the introduction of the ITV levy.[3] Subsequent Prime Ministers – especially Harold Wilson and Margaret Thatcher – have been even more eager to play the role of Minister of the Media.

Public: Separate broadcasting, film and press policy traditions
Central to this whole problem are the differences between the main media; only in mid-twentieth century did it start to become apparent that 'the media' – an American advertising agency term – constituted in many respects a single field.

By this time separate policy traditions existed. Radio around 1920 appeared to be completely separate from film and press, and thus radio was established within the separate policy framework of the Post-Telephone Authority. Since 1922, broadcast policy has been the most coherent, and the pattern of media policy cycles, each of about twelve years (Chapter 3) is primarily a broadcasting policy cycle. It has focused upon three components – technological innovation, new channels, and Broadcasting Committees. These components have matched more or less neatly, at least until the third post-1945 cycle of the Annan Committee (1974–7) and the allocation of the fourth TV channel.

The film industry has had a quite different policy tradition. A long series of narrowly focused enquiries have mainly looked at highly specific aspects of the finances – and financial disasters – of the British film industry, despairingly putting a finger in the dyke while the Hollywood imports flood over the top. These enquiries have not been ignored, but they have been largely ineffective.

The press has another and much more successful policy tradition. This is the policy of having no press policy. The unintended consequences of broadcasting committees and policies (notably ITV in 1955) have had a bigger impact on the press than have the three grandly titled, but largely impotent, Royal Commissions on the Press. In contrast to the committees which have invariably attempted to control market forces in the cases of both broadcasting and film, the members of Royal Commissions on the Press have been intensely aware that any attack on, or interference with, press market forces is not on the national agenda. Press Commissions have been acutely sensitive to two jealous veto groups – a pugnacious press itself and an acquiescent Parliament – both of which define the task of Press Royal Commissions as being to minimise interference in the press, to keep 'press freedom' (however defined) on the national agenda and press legislation off the national agenda.

Public: Royal Commissions and Committees

Broadcasting Committees and Royal Commissions on the Press, no less than the various official enquiries into film and other aspects of the media, are manned (and to a smaller extent womanned) mainly by members of the articulate occupations. They tend also to be people from the South East of England (plus the inevitable Welsh and Scottish representatives) and the audience they have in mind tends to be Parliament, the civil service and the communicators – rather than the mass national audience.

The members of these Committees are not paid; some of the most prominent members probably attend fairly infrequently. The bulk of the sifting of evidence, questioning of witnesses and commissioning of research (if any) is done by the chairman, the secretariat (consisting of civil servants on loan from their departments) and those few members who can afford more than a token amount of time. Academics, journalists and broadcasters, lawyers and businessmen tend to be prominent. The chairman has few sanctions over the members; and in areas as publicly available and ideological as the media, the committee members (who represent a range of political views) must be expected to have plenty of things to disagree about. Thus media committees, probably more even than most others, tend to operate on a basis of compromise and vague consensus.

These professionally articulate, mainly London-based, public persons go for forms of consensus and compromise which are highly predictable. They, themselves national, tend to favour the national media. They also prefer the serious to the popular; they have a love/hate relationship with the BBC and a dislike for (or at least lack of interest in) commercial broadcasting, entertainment, and popular newspapers.

These Royal Commissions and Committees appear to spend a great deal of time surveying the field, while the report is drafted and then re-drafted fairly rapidly towards the end. This seems to lead to some major contentious issues being little discussed and to major internal inconsistencies between chapters in the same report.

For example the McGregor Royal Commission on the Press favoured the preservation of Fleet Street, but disapproved of state subsidies. It did not, however, draw the obvious conclusion that Fleet Street would thus require subsidy from elsewhere – in practice from the conglomerates which were rapidly tightening their grip on Fleet Street during the Royal Commission's 1974–7 existence.

The Annan Committee on Broadcasting was also guilty of certain strategic inconsistencies. Its biggest problem was allocating the fourth television channel. However, its recommendation that the fourth TV channel should go to the Open Broadcasting Authority

(OBA) was very vaguely worded, and its financial basis totally unexplained. So inadequate was the description of this OBA proposal that the Committee by default made a second commercial channel probably more likely than had the Annan Committee never existed.[4]

Annan lacked the courage of the Pilkington Committee (1960–2) which came close to equating popularity in television with lack of virtue. For Pilkington the hugely popular ITV was vulgar and irresponsible – living proof that the much less popular BBC should get the third TV channel.

Private: Thirty separate policy agencies

The term 'private' is used here in the sense of two American political scientists who studied Britain's Treasury.[5] This is the *secretive*, rather than absolutely secret, Whitehall style. But media policy-making is also 'private' in another, slightly different, sense. With thirty or so agencies involved, it is quite unrealistic to expect that more than two or three of these agencies could – even if they wanted to – attract much public (media) attention for their policies. Some agencies do try – and it is a common, if bizarre, complaint of media bodies that they cannot attract adequate publicity. But in practice the bulk of publicity is focused at any one time on just one or two of the thirty agencies; broadcasting committees are exceptionally public and well publicized.

Media policy-making is also sufficiently fragmented that even the policy-makers themselves in one agency typically have little idea of what most of the other agencies are doing. It is unusual to find anyone – civil servant, journalist, politician, academic – who has even read the major public documents in both the press and broadcasting. One of the few exceptions has been Anthony Smith who in 1974 produced two edited books of extracts one of press documents, the other of broadcasting documents.

Democratic ideals, administrative realities and other dilemmas

The traditional British ideals in this field all sound excellent. But freedom, objectivity, pragmatism and voluntarism are ideals of such a high level of abstraction as to give little practical guidance. Behind such ideals may lurk the privilege of a few controllers, the occupational interests of a few thousand 'professionals', the incompetence or simple ignorance of 'amateurs', and – rather than pragmatism – the *status quo* of muddle and chaos.

Other industries have unclear or multiple goals, relate to several government departments, have highly complex labour forces and systems of finance, touch society at several delicate points, and are the victims of short-term political interest. The peculiarity of the media industry seems to be not that it is fragmented in these ways but that it is so comprehensively fragmented and that media policy has so many dilemmas and polarities: one media policy, or several or many? Should policy be left to politicians, or 'professionals' or 'amateurs' or to civil servants, to managers or to unions? What do terms like 'professional', 'responsible' and 'accountable' – so widely used in the media – actually mean? Does accountability to a public mean anything outside a market response? Is it possible to combine education, entertainment and information without doing each badly or incompletely?

One particularly obvious policy dilemma concerns the weight which should be given to Britain's *national* and international media performance as opposed to its *local* and regional performance. Everyone outside London is aware that most British media are really London media; everyone is aware of a sharp distinction between the local press and radio and regional television as against the London variety. In the early days of new television channels, for example, the British public outside London and Birmingham knew that those two centres got the new things first. People in mountainous and hilly areas are aware that the new media reach them last of all, although they may not be fully aware of quite how many times more costly – and hence subsidized – are transmitters in hilly areas. With cable and satellite such policy dilemmas will become even more severe. Yet, astonishingly, there is no tradition of national debate about the priority which should go to regional media. Most policy agencies ignore such issues as irrelevant; others pursue vigorous regional policies – because it is in the Act and it is an old BBC custom anyway to take the word to the remoter corners. But nobody considers that Wales and Scotland may be heavily subsidized while in practice a similar number of people in the Midlands are footing the bill.

In administrative reality media policy is located in the central government departments indicated in Table 26. Here, the ultimate purpose or logic is often unclear: for example the location of general broadcasting policy in the department which also deals with the police is an oddity.[6] But at least the actual functions to be performed are relatively clear in this case – because laid down in Broadcasting legislation.

In the second column of Table 26 are listed the operational bodies which can loosely be described as nationalized industries. All of these could be said to be less typical nationalized industries than coal, or gas, or rail. The BBC is unusually independent; the IBA (previous to Channel Four) was only a regulatory agency dealing with its brood of commercial programme companies; British Telecom (formerly the non-postal wing of the Post Office), Cable and

Wireless (the ex-colonial telecommunications body) and British Aerospace (now important for satellites) are all in turn somewhat special cases of nationalized industries. But at least each of these bodies – even if its future looks rather unpredictable – has a lot of hardware, buildings, and specific operational activities. Even if not quite sure where it is going, British Telecom does at least know that it is running a telephone system.

These half-dozen nationalized industries, of course, are formally not policy-making bodies; but in practice they do make policy, they lobby their 'parent' departments about their future roles and finance, and they are likely still to be there after today's politicians are gone. It is from this hardware and telecommunications category of relatively large, centralized and modern-looking media policy-makers that the press is so conspicuously absent.

In the context of the press as an industry prone to obsolescence and monopoly, this is important. The traditional British solution for basic industries which suffer from excessive concentration or decay has tended to lie in nationalization. The Conservatives may see state ownership as a phase before a return to commercial virtue, while the Labour party sees it as a final virtuous destination. But while both these parties have long thought that nationalization had its place in the overall scheme of things, the press has always been an exception. Past tradition and present ideology forbid press nationalization and force the press to soldier on in the heat of commercial competition or at least under the protective wings of eager conglomerates.

The third type of public body is described in Table 26 as 'Specialized State Agencies'. These typically are quite small, have only one or two narrowly defined functions, and not surprisingly – in a media industry where goals and policies are so fragmented and chaotic – these bodies often exhibit quite considerable evidence of identity crisis. The Television Advisory Committee is perhaps an exception – an extremely important committee which advises on technical telecommunications questions and includes representatives of the major interests. The Broadcasting Complaints Committee is discussed below (p. 269). The Central Office of Information is the government's publicity agent for both domestic and foreign publicity – a somewhat uncomfortable combination, which requires the COI to be beholden to the Foreign Office for overseas publicity but to home departments for health, road safety and similar good works campaigns at home.

The British Council is the cultural wing of British overseas publicity – a task which some MPs think could be handled in other ways. The Printing and Publishing Industry Training Board was set up in 1964 as one of a series of such Boards and abolished by the

TABLE 26

PUBLIC BODIES INVOLVED IN BRITISH MEDIA POLICY

Central government department (main areas of responsibility)	State Industries	Specialized state agencies	Major voluntary bodies
Home office National broadcasting policy – TV, Radio, Cable – Licences cinemas	– BBC – IBA	– Television Advisory Committee – Broadcasting Complaints Commission	
Foreign office – Overseas broadcasting – Foreign publicity	– BBC External	– Central Office of Information – British Council	
Treasury – IBA levies – BBC licence fees – VAT Zero Rating, press.			
Department of industry National and regional industrial policy and state industries, telecommunications	– British Telecom – Cable and Wireless – British Aerospace	– (Printing and publishing industry training board)	
Department of trade Commercial policy, international trade, monopoly law and consumer affairs – Newspapers and publishing – Film industry – Advertising consumer affairs – Industrial property, copyright		Monopolies Commission	– Press Council – British Board of Film Censors – Advertising Standards Authority

TABLE 26 – *cont.*

PUBLIC BODIES INVOLVED IN BRITISH MEDIA POLICY

Central government department (main areas of responsibility)	*Specialized state agencies*	*Major voluntary bodies*
Department of employment Employment, industrial relations, trade unions	– ACAS	
Department of education and science Education, Arts	– Open University – British Film Institute – National Film School	NCTJ CAM
Ministry of defence – Broadcasting for British forces based overseas	– British Forces Broadcasting Service	

Thatcher government. The Monopolies Commission we will come to shortly. The Advisory, Conciliation and Arbitration Service (ACAS) presumably is a potentially important media body – if, as many claim, labour problems bedevil the media industry – but its achievements in this area are few.

Grouped under the Education Ministry are several bodies whose media activities (at least) are not easy to justify. The Open University's television and radio programmes have since 1971 been put out on BBC national networks, but they are the part of the OU's activities which seem least easy to justify. The British Film Institute is dedicated to the notion of film as art and education; the BFI's rate of expansion and the British Film Industry's rate of decline have recently suggested that the BFI could itself become larger than the industry and the BFI has wisely moved towards television – an industry with a lot more dying still to do. The National Film School is yet another oddity – an expensive, nationally subsidized film school, whose products have mostly gone into television. The British Forces Broadcasting Service is now greatly reduced in size, and has, like the rest of the list, an uncertain purpose and future.

It is, however, the 'voluntary' bodies in the final column of Table 26 which have the narrowest functions, the most idiosyncratic histories and the most extreme identity problems. They come in two main categories. The first group operate systems of 'voluntary' censorship or self-denial to which we return below. The final grouping are educational bodies – the National Council for the Training of Journalists (NCTJ) and its advertising and marketing equivalent (CAM). These are beleaguered bodies indeed – offering 'professional' education to industries whose enthusiasm for such education is not great.

After winning the General Election in June 1983, Mrs Thatcher announced that the Departments of Trade and Industry would again be merged. As Table 26 shows, the merger does concentrate many aspects of media policy. However, the major potential reduction in policy fragmentation was balanced by increases elsewhere. Plans to privatize British Telecom and to set up a special Cable Authority promised two new major independent players in the media policy game.

CHAPTER SEVENTEEN
Foreign media policy

Fragmentation in policy-making also exists in relation to media imports and exports. There is a similar superfluity of different agencies each pursuing its own pet objective. There is the same mixture of commercial and political objectives; there are similar official committees of investigation – for example into British overseas representation and the BBC Overseas Services – which once again are narrowly focused and ill-co-ordinated.

A central dilemma is that Britain has come to see herself as a media *exporter*; but if you set out to engage in media exports you may also become a big media importer. Moreover the salience of technological and hardware considerations, highly important in domestic media policy-making, is yet more marked in the foreign sphere. For while software trade – programming – may be the glamorous aspect, the sums of money to be earned by exporting for example television programming are small. The big money is in the *hardware*. British policy-makers have long been aware of this and for example in the late 1940s much of the policy debate on television focused on the hope of exporting television sets.[1] In each new round of technology – from radio receivers in the 1920s to Direct Broadcast Satellites in the 1980s – Britain has hoped to export the hardware, and these ambitions play a large part in Britain's pride in its technological innovations in television and related fields. But in practice Britain's export successes tend to be in software – which earns a lot of prestige, but relatively little money. Japan, of course, does the reverse.

Throughout British foreign media policy-making there are a few consistent themes. There is a near obsession with the *American* market, even though since the 1920s the realistic prospects for major earnings from exports into the USA have not been good. Another consistent theme – perhaps the most consistent – has been the determination of trade unions to protect their interests in media importing and exporting. Talent, film and TV unions of course want work; they discourage imports (unless these provide work at home) and favour exports. In this way trade unions have played a major part in achieving widely supported national media policy goals – at least in relation to software.

Another continuing theme is the notion of London as a world media centre. London is not only a focus for media exports and imports. But it is also a half-way house, an entrepot in various ways, which conflicting policies and policy-makers have tended to favour: London as an outpost of Hollywood film-making; London as a location for foreign correspondents, export publications and external broadcasting; London as a monitoring post for world media trends. All of this matches with national pride and mythology which see the British press and broadcasting as the world's 'least worst'. This in turn is linked to domestic media realities and (implicit) policies. The focus on London as media (mainly software) exporter, importer and entrepot goes along with the idea of the inevitability of London dominance in British domestic media and the casting of Birmingham and Manchester as branch offices of London national media.

The fragmentation of domestic media policy-making is probably exacerbated by the other fragmentation of foreign media policy-making. The two are closely linked by short-term political considerations in general and in particular by the short-term political interest of Prime Ministers in media and media policy on both the domestic and foreign fronts.

Many of these strands – encompassing both publicity of a highly flamboyant kind and also tight-lipped Whitehall silence – are present in the old but still popular game of the 'special alliance' between the USA and Britain in general and between American Presidents and British Prime Ministers in particular. From Churchill and Roosevelt, Attlee and Truman, Eden and Eisenhower, Macmillan with Ike and JFK, Wilson and Johnson, to Thatcher and Reagan, British Prime Ministers have been able to present themselves as world leaders, exchanging ideas apparently as equals – with the 'most powerful man in the western world'. This imagery is carried around the world by the world's media – in which the British again play a flatteringly large part, in some respects not far behind those of the USA – and of course all of this goes around the world and back, via the domestic British media, to the electorate. The number of occasions on which British Prime Ministers do these big diplomatic/summit/media appearances has increased with membership of the European Common Market – and here again the strength of British media in Europe adds an extra touch of flattery and potential political benefit domestically.

Another potential beneficiary of prime ministerial performances on the world media stage is the Foreign and Commonwealth Office – because its task is to stage manage both the diplomatic performance and its media presentation. This is a useful time also for other members of the political-diplomatic-media worlds; this kind of trip provides a chance for lobby correspondents to get out of their cramped and unpleasant quarters at Westminster and to fly off to exotic places holding firmly on to the Prime Minister's coat-tails.

These prime ministerial media-bathed summits are only the visible tip of a deeper relationship involving the Prime Minister, the foreign policy machine and the media. The Foreign and Common-wealth office – along with the Treasury – has a special part in the higher reaches of the political-administrative machinery, such as in the structure of Cabinet committees. The Prime Minister along with the Foreign Secretary receives a full supply of the most important cables from embassies abroad (while other ministers receive fewer). Certain foreign issues, which might cause embarrassment if subject to the usual Cabinet leaks, are deliberately held back from Cabinet discussion to be settled in smaller meetings of senior ministers. The Prime Minister meanwhile always has a private secretary specially seconded from the Foreign and Commonwealth Office (and another from the Treasury).

This has some important consequences for media policy or rather for the deliberate lack of media policy. The Prime Minister gets the lion's share of this most patriotic, and most politically beneficial, media publicity. Appearing on the world media stage is important for Prime Ministers, because superior access to massive publicity is one of the Prime Minister's major prerogatives. Another, of course, is superior access to all the most sensitive information from all the key fields (foreign, defence, security, economic, party political) which no other single minister receives.

Being the diplomatic media superstar helps the Prime Minister to cement the superiority which the office confers. Inevitably this must cause some envy and disquiet even within the Cabinet. The Prime Minister may seem to be distanced excessively from party sup-porters in the House of Commons by these twin false gods of inter-national diplomacy and media stardom. These FCO stage-managed media diplomatic appearances potentially raise awkward questions as to whether the Prime Minister is in fact using the supposedly neutral Foreign Ministry for party political advantage. These 'deli-cate' aspects all derive from the rather vague doctrines of the Constitution as to the responsibilities of Prime Ministers and Cabinets towards each other and to Parliament.

In another form of delicacy the media are more directly involved – much of British imagery abroad is carried through commercial media or public broadcasting over which the Prime Minister and the Cabinet have both in theory and in fact little or no control. For maximum impact perhaps there should ideally be some kind of coherent British media policy encompassing not only the FCO and its embassies, the Central Office of Information and the BBC overseas service, but also commercial media such as Reuters and commercial phenomena such as television exports. 'Ideally' perhaps, but the commercial media would never accept such government dictation.

The peculiarities of the British Constitution, which in any case favour a discreet lack of policy over strategic media issues, are re-inforced by short-term political facts which prohibit any 'policy' interference with the media areas most important on the world scene. The Prime Minister and the government thus have a political incentive to avoid the politically explosive area of 'imposing government curbs' – as the media world sees a media policy. They inevitably fall back on trying by the usual processes (granting interviews, dispensing flattery, leaking documents, and doing a little implicit bargaining) to try to get the best publicity from the media structure which exists. Rather than trying to impose a comprehensive media export-and-import policy, or to tamper with the existing media in any way, Prime Ministers are content to proclaim that 'British media still lead the world' so long as they themselves still lead the British media.

What is Britain's foreign media policy?

A major sub-theme within the continuing debate about a foreign policy for Post-Imperial Britain has been the question of what kind of public relations and media effort Britain should make abroad. Following a report of the Central Policy Review Staff ('Think Tank') – which called for big cuts in embassies and a massive cutback on British government publicity especially in the United States[2] – a government statement in 1978 on United Kingdom Overseas Representation identified relevant national objectives as follows:[3]

1. To safeguard the security of our country.
2. To promote its prosperity.
3. To uphold and extend the basic values and freedoms of our country.
4. To honour our commitments and obligations.
5. To work for a peaceful and just world.
6. To contribute to the achievement of the above objectives by providing assistance to developing countries.

Translated into information and media policies these comments seem to follow: The prime objective is security. The main application of this to media would be a continuing focus on BBC overseas radio towards the Soviet block and strategically significant areas such as the Middle East. 'Prosperity' means confirming the earlier change of overseas media emphasis to export promotion and related commercial goals. 'Upholding basic values' means promoting the democratic way in general, and promoting the English language (as the natural habitat and vehicle for such basic values). 'National commitments and obligations' is a catch-all category which presumably justifies support for Commonwealth and for European Economic Community ties, as well as those of NATO and the Atlantic alliance. General good works and support for third world countries have a low level of priority.

Clearly, despite the main priority given to 'security' and 'prosperity', this remains a very wide and rather vague list of national objectives, which, when translated into the information field, becomes no less wide and vague.

Some other countries operate a closely integrated information policy; the United States has a post-1945 tradition of running general publicity, external radio and external cultural efforts out of a single agency. Britain combines the principle of a 'lead department' – the Foreign and Commonwealth Office – with a policy of decentralization. Each of the four main strands of the information apparatus has a dual loyalty – to the FCO and to another government agency.

First, the *Foreign and Commonwealth Office* both in London and in its embassies abroad integrates information work into diplomacy; the job of liaising with the news media is handled by mainstream career diplomats. The FCO's News Department in London emphasises a traditional diplomatic and foreign correspondent's definition of 'news'. The same activist approach is evident especially at the United Nations – where the British delegation has a long and unique tradition of not only briefing all correspondents on a daily basis but in having these briefings done by a career diplomat. The same policy is adopted by British delegations at major international conferences.[4] But there is a contradiction between this HQ emphasis and what happens in most British embassies around the world – where official policy stresses that the commercial goal is normally supreme.

Secondly, the *Central Office of Information* is the main government agency handling routine British government foreign publicity both at home and abroad. The COI is responsible for liaising with foreign visitors as well as journalists – especially trade journalists on short special-interest visits. The COI also produces and distributes abroad large quantities of commercial publicity, such as industrial films, briefing kits, and other media material designed for immediate use. About 70% of this effort is commercial, but the 'lead department' remains the Foreign Office; the

Trade Ministry (which has the 'lead' role in exports) has little connection with the COI.

Thirdly, the *External Services of the BBC* receive their finance via the Foreign Office, which controls the allocation of effort to particular target countries and the overall strategy. But the detailed control lies with the BBC, a large and powerful organisation which places especial emphasis on its 'independence' from government.

Fourthly, the *British Council* is the government agency responsible for general cultural contacts, educational exchanges and similar aspects of overseas 'cultural' policy. Again there is a certain duality as between FCO control and primarily educational and cultural activities.

Britain is the base for Reuters – one of the four major western international news agencies. Although some major news media have their own foreign correspondents, and the American agency Associated Press has some part in supplying foreign news within Britain, Reuters is the leading provider of foreign news to the national British media and plays an even more dominant part in providing foreign news to British provincial media.[5]

But it is on the world scene that Reuters mainly operates. Many different studies confirm that the four western agencies play the major part in the gathering and transmission of news for media use around the world outside the immediate Communist block. Reuters is also part-owner – mainly with the BBC – of Visnews, which is the leading agency collecting and selling video news primarily to television stations around the world.

One consequence is that happenings in Britain, and perhaps London in particular, still receive a surprisingly large share of the content of the world-wide flow of news. In addition to Reuters – which, although very international, still contains a certain flavour of things British – London also is the location for major offices of all three other western 'world' agencies. Thus the business of building and maintaining an image of Britain on the world's news agenda is carried on 24 hours a day by one commercial agency in particular – Reuters – which responds largely to supply and demand factors in the world market for news and financial data.

During both world wars the British government exerted a powerful and direct influence on Reuters. This, however, led Reuters after each world war to attempt to emphasize especially sharply its independence of the British government. This 'independence' was essential to Reuters, since by the 1970s well over 80% of its revenue came from outside Britain.[6]

Throughout the 1970s there were complaints that media coverage of Britain around the world was 'unfair', placed excessive emphasis on Britain's economic failures and generally concentrated on bad news. But the chief carrier of this kind of news was none other than a British organization – Reuters – with newspaper, news agency, broadcast, stockmarket and banking clients in virtually every nation and territory on earth.

The dilemma of 'bad news' carried around the world by respected news organizations, in which a British agency, Reuters, took the lead, was exacerbated by two other factors. First, Reuters was a true child of Empire and of agreements made with foreign agencies from the late nineteenth century onwards. Thus Reuters was especially strong in those very areas where Britain had a special foreign policy interest – the white commonwealth, black Africa, South Asia, the Middle East and western Europe. Reuters was relatively weak only in South America. Reuters was especially strong in *financial* news. It had begun as a carrier of stock market news and from the 1960s onwards had diversified out of simple media news into a wide range of services more suitable for finance ministries, central banks, stockbrokers and currency dealers. Along with financial data-on-screens, Reuters also of course provides prose commentaries. Thus the details of British financial difficulties were and are transmitted around the world to the international business and financial community – and for substantial profit – by a British-based news agency.

When Foreign and Commonwealth Office spokesmen complained about 'one-sided' and unrealistically 'bad news' coverage of the British economy, they were swimming rather feebly against the continuing steady flow of coldly quantitative financial news which Reuters pumped electronically around the world 24 hours a day.

Foreign correspondents in London

London is a major centre for foreign correspondents. A study by David Morrison[7] shows that in 1980 there were some 400 foreign correspondents based in London. To an overwhelming extent their main source of information about Britain was the British media, especially the national newspapers. Each correspondent claimed to read six newspapers a day; they monitored the radio and watched TV news. Although correspondents based in London were also responsible for other areas, such as Scandinavia, Ireland or even the whole of western Europe, they still focused mainly on Britain. These correspondents had some contact – often rather frustrating – with British officials and politicians. But their major source of material was undoubtedly the ready supply of daily bad news with which Fleet Street dailies competed to attract the attention of the jaded British public.

Here once again, then, was a major mechanism in creating the

British image abroad, largely fed off the domestic media, media which were perhaps negative to an extreme degree more connected with the excesses of Britain's national press competition than with any genuine peculiarities in, for example, its trade union apparatus. In this respect the foreign correspondents based in London operated in parallel to Britain's own international news agency (Reuters) and Britain's own 'propaganda' radio (external BBC).

Press

Traditionally the press has been a closed industry, protected from foreign competition. Imports of actual publications are largely confined to a few American magazines. The most significant of these has long been the British edition of *Readers' Digest*. Two of the major women's magazines publishers are also American-owned. But Britain has also long been an exporter of magazines, and a number of magazines export a significant fraction of their circulation. In 1982 the total export circulation of British publications – mainly weeklies and monthlies – was around 5 million. The most obviously influential weekly was *The Economist* with a 140,000 export circulation. At least 32 publications each regularly sold at least 20,000 copies abroad. These included a number of technical magazines, women's weekly magazines, men's sex magazines, and several scientific and medical publications. Fifth largest export sales belonged to *Africa Now* – with a 66,000 export circulation. A number of smallish African, Asian, and Middle Eastern publications are based in London; many of these are political but some are technical with such titles as *African Water and Sewage* or *Middle East Electronics*.[8]

With air freight, and the boom in multi-centre electronic printing, the possibilities for imports and exports of newspapers have improved. The main 'imported' newspaper was for a long time the American *Herald-Tribune* which has a separate British printing. In the other direction the London *Financial Times* began a European edition, which printed in Frankfurt, and was exporting some 45,000 copies a day when the *Wall Street Journal* began its European edition in early 1983.

In respects other than simple sales of copies, foreign 'trade' played a significant role in the press. Notably a succession of 'friendly foreigners' put money into loss-making newspapers – Astor (1922), Thomson (1966), and Murdoch (1981) for *The Times*; Beaverbrook (1915) for the *Daily Express*; Murdoch for *The Sun* (1969), Atlantic Richfield briefly (1976–81) for *The Observer*. This foreign money helped to maintain an artificial number of titles, which in turn probably sharpened the pursuit of audience-enticing 'bad news', which was then taken out of the London media and relayed abroad around the world. Good news for London media employment, but more bad news about Britain.

Radio and television
Importing and exporting of radio and television take many different forms, but although both are areas where 'public service' principles might seem relevant, there is a remarkable shortage of explicit policy statements or guide-lines about either importing or exporting.

Direct imports of programming into Britain are normally discussed only in the context of television, but they do exist also in radio in the form mainly of recorded popular music. In television the standard formula agreed by all those involved – unions, government, BBC and IBA – is that only about 14% of programming shall be 'imported'. This is measured in time terms; but since there is a large potential supply of popular television and film material competing to squeeze into this 14%, in terms of audience time the real figure is probably somewhat higher. Probably equally or more important in Britain has been the importing and copying of formats – for example the borrowing of such genres as radio comedy, radio and television game shows, and the action adventure TV series.

Two further sorts of 'importing' have been relatively unimportant in Britain compared with some other countries. There has been little direct foreign ownership in broadcasting.[9] But there has been direct ownership of most of the largest advertising agencies from Madison Avenue which has presumably influenced British TV commercials and more subtly the programming and editorial content.

Another sort of 'importing' – widespread tuning into foreign radio and TV – has to date been fairly small; listening to foreign government-backed radio has also been small, with rare exceptions such as the early days of the Second World War.[10] Over longer time periods listening to Radio Luxembourg and other foreign commercial radio stations – land- and sea-based – has been more significant.

In the category of government-backed radio aimed at foreign audiences Britain has obviously been a much bigger exporter. In 1950 Britain was the world's biggest external broadcaster – certainly in numbers of hours (643 hours) per week. Britain has since then kept to roughly the same output. By 1982 Britain with 741 BBC external radio hours per week had fallen to fifth place behind USSR, USA, China and West Germany. For a long period there has been a heavy focus on certain areas – such as the Middle East, the Soviet Union and former colonial countries in Africa and Asia. In certain areas such as Nigeria, northern India, and Pakistan both audience research and general impressions suggest large audiences.

The direct exporting of television programming is another matter. The BBC and ITV companies have been fairly successful at selling their services in both developed and third world countries. At least 50 countries in the world buy more than token amounts of British programming, but in some cases the purchase seems to be of only one or two short series in a year. There is also a big contrast between numbers of *hours* sold and the prices paid per hour; huge sales in terms of hours took place in the United States in the 1970s but most of the material appeared on PBS, the 'public' system which paid low prices. Success in placing material on the American TV networks was much more rare. From 1981 the BBC decided to switch its USA outlet from PBS to Cable television.

BBC exporting seems to be carried on mainly for reasons of prestige. Gross income from such exporting is equivalent to about 3% of total BBC turnover, but the net income is much smaller. Since the programming has already been made, such activities only have to cover additional costs (such as those of salesmen and extra artists' fees); but more important in many cases probably is the calculation that exporting earns domestic plus marks for virtue – relevant to BBC licence fee increases and IBA licence renewal. The same is true for ITV, but an additional motive has to do with the financial advantages of incurring export artists' fees early which in effect reduces the amount of levy paid.

Whether these exports are indeed in the national interest is an altogether more complex question partly because different importing countries may see different messages in the same exported programme, and partly because different countries choose very different selections of programmes. Off-beat British humour and off-beat British sports (such as darts) are popular. Especially popular, however, are costume dramas. 38 countries have bought the entire BBC batch of all the Shakespeare plays. And in 1981 45 bought a full programme on Prince Charles[11] designed for showing just previous to his wedding. But whether a costume drama/Royal ceremonial/zaney comedy view of Britain is really a useful export from modern Britain is a question easy to ask but hard to answer.

Film and records
In the case of film the recent history of exports is a poor one; much of British film exporting since 1945 and even more since 1955 has been of films made in Britain but financed and distributed by Hollywood. British policies designed to encourage exports have been unsuccessful. In particular the traditional policies of modest subsidy and quota have been unco-ordinated with BBC and ITV policies of using films (mainly from Hollywood) as a cheap way of entertaining large audiences.

In the field of recorded music Britain has been much more successful and this is despite an almost total lack of any government policy. In the 1960s the British rock industry may have contributed to general British exports both by direct sales within the USA and by the popular glory reflected back on to (swinging) London, which in turn produced a second wave of exports of Hollywood-in-London films. In the 1970s both trends seem to have gone into reverse as many British rock stars and film directors settled in Hollywood.

They were followed also by British film producers – especially EMI and ATV, both of which had major interests in rock music and in British commercial television. Both EMI and ATV were briefly successful in the late 1970s as independent production companies based in Los Angeles; but, as is the way with such companies, their success ran out and financial losses followed.

Throughout all these twists and turns of failure and success the enormous following which British music achieved on the world scene – and which thus presumably played a large part in shaping Britain's international image – was ignored, or not even thought of, by Britain's official image-makers.

Fragmentation and passivity in foreign media policy-making

British foreign media policy is not unique in being fragmented, muddled and filled with self-delusion. Similar characteristics are found in many or most other countries.[12] Nevertheless Britain may be a little unusual in the extent to which it suffers from such a large number of major dilemmas and contradictions.

Perhaps the central difficulty in that policy fragmentation leads to *de facto* centralization in the Foreign and Commonwealth Office and 10 Downing Street. The FCO has many strengths and many weaknesses, but unfortunately media policy reflects too many of its weaknesses; diplomats are simply not the best people to deal with such questions. Similarly the Prime Minister acquires many powers over the media. In both cases – FCO and Prime Minister – media issues are seen as subordinate to other more important problems, and media policy is dominated by short-term diplomatic and political goals.

One paradox is that of political freedom against political in-fighting. There really is a lot of political freedom – for example in the BBC External Services; but along with this goes perpetual political guerilla warfare. The BBC External Services in return for their comparative freedom have had to pay the price of endless battles about cuts in particular language services, endless lobbying of backbench MPs and so on. The effort expended on cancelling a few hours in a particular language – and then restoring them a few years later – is out of all proportion to the cost of such services.

Another dilemma in foreign media policy-making is that the *hardware* implications tend either to dominate or to be misunderstood, or both. The BBC external services again provide many examples. The Government often finds itself making small savings in programming while at the same time engaging in vastly bigger capital expenditure for new transmitters on islands close to faraway continents.[13]

Basic British problems – whether Britain should align itself with the USA, the Commonwealth or with Western Europe – are exacerbated in this field. But a continuing source of error seems to be excessive concern with the United States and lack of interest in Europe (which shares most British media dilemmas).

The fragmentation in this field is all too clearly indicated by the official committees, which are numerous and narrowly focused. One BBC chairman has complained that the BBC external services were between 1952 and 1977 scrutinised by nine major committees.[14] Some of these documents are frankly of sub-standard quality.[15] These documents both separately and collectively fail to come to grips with such central dilemmas as the significance of the English language or the consequences of being a world media capital. (Does English teaching by BBC radio merely aid Hollywood? Is media notoriety the inevitable price of 'excessive' media attention?)

One of the main consequences of policy fragmentation – and the belief that having a media policy is unBritish – is a general *passivity*. Media policy is made, if at all, on an *ad hoc* basis in response to outside pressures. This was so in the 1930s when Britain was responding to German, Italian and Soviet propaganda initiatives.[16] When the war began the Ministry of Information reflected the indecision and lack of planning.[17]

Similar things were still happening fifty years later. In the early 1980s London's tradition as a media entrepot was enhanced by its new role as video piracy capital of the world; the components of this new role were all typically accidental. Britain has a high rate of VCR penetration domestically – a triumph for Japanese, not British, policy-making; London had direct flights from an especially large number of separate American cities making illegal importing of films especially simple; London had a big media software export trade to all parts of the world, thus enhancing its importance as a market. Finally in the early 1980s Britain had no effective policy or legislation in this field.

CHAPTER EIGHTEEN

Domestic media policy: past and future

The real policy problems of the 1970s
The early 1980s marked the end of the third major post-1945 round of British media policy-making. In 1982 Britain acquired its fourth national television channel. The Thatcher government produced a flurry of policy documents in 1980–82 with titles like *Information Technology*, *Direct Broadcasting by Satellite*, *Cable Systems* and *Report of the Inquiry into Cable Expansion and Broadcasting Policy*. Critics pointed out that each of these documents tended to be brief in length (average = 64 pages), narrow in terms of reference and the result of rather superficial deliberation. These genuine weaknesses, however, reflected to a large extent the inadequacies of the past, the irrelevance of many of the media policy issues which had concerned Britain in the 1970s.

Had the 1970s media policy debate focused upon the real policy issues what would these in fact have been? Had these debates taken place within a fuller understanding of what was happening not only in the USA, but in Europe, Japan and the third world, these might have been some of the main concerns:

1. The Electronic 'New Media' Revolution and the multiplication of channels.
2. The problem of the survival of 'old media' – such as newspapers, magazines, film, radio and books.
3. The issue of power both within and in relation to the media.
4. Media taxation and subsidy.
5. The balance of international, national and regional media.
6. Problems of excessive monopoly and excessive competition.
7. Public redress and access.

The remainder of this chapter will consider these seven points.

1. The Electronic 'New Media' Revolution and the multiplication of channels
The 'new media' revolution has many aspects, all of which were already separately evident in the 1960s. The electronic revolution in

the press – photocomposition and computer storage – was appearing in the British provinces in the mid 1960s. The original Communications Satellite Act passed the US Congress in 1962 and Direct Broadcasting Satellites were being debated later in the 1960s; there was a debate and vote on the DBS issue in the UN General Assembly in November 1972.[1]

But in 1970s Britain the main discussion about new television channels focused upon a fourth conventional television channel. The extent to which this topic had dominated discussion for some twenty years was shown in 1982 by the Independent Broadcasting Authority; so obsessed was the IBA with introducing the 20-year-old concept of a fourth channel that it scarcely noticed that the Government was allocating two Direct Broadcast Satellite channels to the BBC.

The significance of the electronic revolution, however, goes beyond the potential multiplication of new channels. In addition to making many video channels available, it ushers in a potential new era of information; the television screen, the telephone, the copier, video playback, the typewriter, and the computer all begin to merge. All of the 'old media' are affected. Old media-based concepts like 'news' may have to struggle in order to resist being subsumed into 'data'.

2. The problem of the survival of 'old media' – such as newspapers, magazines, film, radio and books

It was evident well before the 1970s that conventional television alone was having massive consequences for the old media. But a separate Press Commission and a Broadcasting Committee – despite having exactly the same life span, 1974 to 1977 – made no real attempt to consider the inter-relation of the two spheres.

The serious policy issues of the 1970s should have included the question of whether and how the 'old media' would survive. Would it matter if popular newspapers became, in effect, optional printed accompaniments to television? Or should some policy be evolved which would preserve at least middle-brow newspapers – such as the subsidies in Scandinavia for weaker papers or the American policy of *de facto* legalizing local monopoly daily newspapers aimed at the middle market? Should magazines be encouraged as a source of independent voices or should magazines be allowed to become incorporated into newspapers?

The impact of television on films was also evident long before the 1970s. It was fairly obvious that any 'solution' to the problems of film would also have to encompass television. Despite this a separate strand of British policy-making continued in the 1970s attempting to deal with films in isolation. Consequently Britain finds itself entering an age of Cable with very little domestic supply of feature films – Cable's most popular offering.

Not only are films dominated by television policy considerations, so also has radio been. In view of this fact radio policy – which broadly has been made alongside television – has been much more realistic than policy in the other 'old media'.

3. Issues of power both within and in relation to the media

Power over the media and power within the media are topics which attract a lot of popular attention. But most of this comes from the press and is presented through the usual journalist's device of personalities in conflict – the Prime Minister's clashes with the BBC, the press tycoon and the editor, the printing chapel father versus the newspaper cartoonist, the television producer versus the IBA censor. Press Commissions, Broadcasting Committees, the Press Council and the various Broadcasting complaints bodies have also been fascinated by such interpersonal conflicts.

In the meantime much more important structural features of media power were largely ignored throughout the 1970s. The Prime Minister's power is not merely power to bully individuals, but a power to determine – or more usually to prevent – media policies over a huge area. But other groups of politicians are important – small groups of backbenchers, especially Conservative back-benchers since it is their party which largely makes media policy. And it may well be that from this area – or perhaps a larger multi-party grouping of informed MPs – that more coherent and considered media policies may eventually come.

Two of the most significant developments in media power were almost entirely ignored in the 1970s. One of these was the *conglomeratization* (and the related *internationalization*) of British media ownership. Even though 1974–77 was a peak period for these developments neither Press Commission nor Broadcasting Committee considered them. Film Committees have long had to consider such things – in view of Hollywood – but they also have only looked at little bits of the phenomenon. The Monopolies and Mergers Commission in the 1970s – when it considered the media – looked mainly at proposed takeovers of groups of local weekly papers. It was not asked to look at the overall operations of the major media conglomerates involved in some of these same cases.

Secondly, the conventional wisdom has it that the trade unions are powerful in the media. This is true, but the unions whose power has the widest significance are the talent unions – whose policies enormously influence the music and drama output, plus the commercials. The growing power of a few thousand senior producers and journalists was totally ignored – although it appears to encompass the shaping of new TV channels, the preservation as independent entities of ancient newspapers, and the entire serious editorial output of the media. The new media will consolidate and expand this communicator power.

4. Media subsidy and taxation

If a government wanted to operate a coherent media policy, its strategic powers of taxation and subsidy are perhaps the most obvious ones to use. The reality, however, is highly haphazard – with each piece of the media looked at separately by its particular governmental guardian. If a medium seems to be making too much profit it may (or may not) attract special taxation, and if it seems to be making too big a loss it may attract a subsidy. Such policies give little regard to the fact that often a single multi-media organization is being specially taxed on some activities and specially subsidized on others. Subsidy and taxation policies in relation to the different media have varied as follows:

News agencies: For many years a deliberately low cable rate was operated within the Commonwealth which in particular acted as a subsidy to the British agency Reuters.
Press: During and after the Second World War newsprint rationing, which allowed newspapers to charge the same cover price for about a one-third size product, constituted a hidden subsidy. In the early days of ITV, official government blessing for press holdings in commercial television led to another *de facto* subsidy to the press. Later when Britain adopted Value Added Tax, the press used its political influence to acquire zero-rating, which amounts to a massive subsidy – in the early 1980s over £200 million per year.[2]
Broadcast: In its early days the Post Office on behalf of the Treasury kept a sizeable slice of the BBC's licence fee which, under the guise of a collection charge, was really a special tax. Later this tax was removed. The special levy on ITV profits (and later ILR profits) constitutes a special tax on television. However the funding arrangements for the second IBA channel involved the special tax being directed back into ITV as a subsidy to the new channel.
Film in its best days in Britain was subject to heavy entertainments taxation; later penal taxation was replaced by attempts at subsidy.
Advertising has been free of any significant special taxes on subsidies.
Foreign Office funds pay for the entire overseas operation of the BBC.

Other media – books have done best of all by winning exemption not only from Resale Price Maintenance legislation – which forces retailers to sell at prescribed publisher prices – but books are also zero-rated for Value Added Tax.

5. *The balance of international, national and regional media*

One of the worst consequences of British media policy fragmentation is that domestic media policy is separately considered from foreign media policy. Countries which are major media importers – most countries in the world – cannot make this mistake; all third world countries, and also the smaller wealthy countries (e.g. Scandinavia) do indeed consider the two aspects of media policy together. The one country in the world which is a major media exporter – the United States – can afford the luxury of carrying on apparently separate foreign and domestic media policies, partly because in practice there is a lot of co-ordination between a very few media trade associations and a very few Washington agencies.[3] (Britain incidentally – in addition to its numerous involved government agencies – has many different media trade associations; the press alone has five.)

Britain seeks to be a major media *exporter* and is a major media *importer*; Britain claims, with some evidence, to have especially strong *national* media. But Britain also, since the 1954 legislation setting up ITV, has formally encouraged regional media, and – with the birth of the Welsh Fourth Channel Authority in 1982 – Britain has an outstanding example of what regional/ethnic/vernacular television can look like. Such a country – in the absence of policy priorities – is certain to experience major anomalies.

There are many examples of these but one illustration may suffice. Lord Lew Grade in the ITV Midlands television region used his franchise to make programming which would appeal both to the British national public and to US and world audiences. For this ATV was given the Queen's Award For Export. Later, however, Grade was penalized by the IBA, but the new company – instead of becoming more British or more Midlands – came under the control of an Australian, before reverting to British national interests.

In the future such strains and conflicts are likely to become more severe, not least because multi-channel video, while apparently offering many local possibilities tends to be more *international*; this follows from its need for larger supplies of cheaper programming.

6. *Problems of excessive monopoly and excessive competition: Newspapers and the Monopolies and Mergers Commission*

Much criticism of the media is broadly to the effect that they are either too monopolistic or too competitive (yellow journalism, ratings war etc). In the media there is a tendency for extremes of monopoly and competition to go hand in hand – for example 'excessive' local monopoly and 'excessive' national competition. This tendency is likely to be exacerbated by the new media of the future; American experience in Cable television, for example, is that despite channel multiplication there is a local monopoly operator and a few dominant national suppliers.

Britain was during the 1970s subject to both of these problems. But British policy was as usual fragmented, minimalist and pregnant with unanticipated consequences. It applied only to certain very limited aspects of newspapers. It did not have anything to say about 'excessive competition' (although the Press Council to some extent attempted to handle some of its 'yellow' press consequences); it had no powers in relation to broadcasting; it also had no powers in relation to media conglomeratisation.

The majority of press cases which have been (and not been) referred to the Monopolies Commission have involved weekly newspapers. This has been because the main intention of the initial 1965 press monopoly legislation (following recommendations of the Shawcross 1961–2 Royal Commission) was to stop any significant purchases by one substantial press group of another.

As the third (McGregor) Royal Commission pointed out, between 1965 and 1976 no less than 50 cases arose. In forty cases consent was given because the purchase in question involved an average daily circulation of less than 25,000 copies. This was quite a loophole in itself, because it allowed – indeed focused attention on – the purchase of small weekly newspapers by major chains, often already owning dailies in the same localities. Between 1962 and 1976 the Westminster Press acquired additional weekly newspaper sales of about 620,000 copies per week (1976 circulation); seven other groups each bought over 100,000 copies per week of such local weeklies.[4] But if this was a loophole it was at least a public and legislatively more or less intended one.

Another major merger was allowed to take place – after a Monopolies Commission investigation[5] when Thomson bought *The Times*. The Monopolies Commission spent two months looking at the arguments; the new Thomson management gave evidence and public undertakings. However the major loopholes in the legislation and the opportunities for a decidedly 'private' phase of policy-making became evident only in a further series of major purchases of Fleet Street newspapers. Two of these purchases actually occurred during the life of the 1974–7 Royal Commission and well illustrated its impotence.

The loophole in the cases of *The Observer* and Express Newspapers was the same. In neither case was the purchaser an existing press company. No special press merger provisions discouraged a major press purchase, in the first case by a major American oil company (Atlantic Richfield), and in the second case by a conglomerate property-construction-shipping company (Trafalgar House).

The second loophole in the press monopoly law – revised into the Fair Trading Act of 1973 – was that the relevant government minister did not have to refer the case to the Monopolies Commission if he was satisfied that the publication was not economic as a 'going concern' and that the paper was in immediate danger of ceasing publication. This loophole was a massive invitation to private lobbying by the press interests involved, and gave to the Prime Minister and relevant Cabinet ministers decisive *de facto* and 'private' power to determine not only that a merger should go through, but to shape the entire 'public' presentation of a bid which was largely a *fait accompli*.

The second loophole – that the paper in question might die – is a particuarly brazen breach of the spirit (but not the word) of the relevant legislation. However the first loophole is equally significant in the degree of 'private' power it confers on the government; under the existing monopoly legislation, whether or not the government supports or opposes a merger is likely to be decisive – not only in the outcome but (via preliminary 'discussions') in whether the initial bid is made at all.

In five major cases of Fleet Street mergers since 1965 the Prime Minister and Cabinet of the day have been involved and have had their political motives for giving approval.

The purchase of *The Times* by Thomson in 1966–7 was pushed through the Cabinet by the Prime Minister (Wilson) and the minister concerned (Douglas Jay).[6] Wilson may have hoped that the Thomson management would feel some political 'gratitude', *The Times* which supported the Conservatives in 1964 had in fact withdrawn this support at the 1966 General Election.

The purchase of *The Sun* by Rupert Murdoch from IPC in 1969 was again approved by a Labour Cabinet under Harold Wilson. *The Sun* was a descendant of the old Labour-connected *Daily Herald* and it would thus have been an especial embarrassment to a Labour Prime Minister had it disappeared altogether. At that time there was every reason to believe that *The Sun* – with a heavily working-class readership – would continue to support Labour. It did so at the next year's (1970) General Election.

The Observer sale to Atlantic Richfield in 1976 was also approved by a Labour government. Again there were obvious political motives; the chairman of *The Observer* (Lord Goodman) was a close ally of Harold Wilson and other prominent Labour politicians. *The*

Observer was also the most Labour-inclined of the three prestige national Sundays.

The 1977 sale of three Beaverbrook newspapers to Trafalgar House may have been welcome to a Labour government since these papers had always been anti-Labour. However, in this decision, as in all others, pressure from printing unions, loyal Labour supporters – to 'save jobs in Fleet Street' – must have been important.

The sale of Times Newspapers to Murdoch in 1981 was perhaps the case in which 'private' power by the Prime Minister (Thatcher) and the relevant minister (John Biffen) was used to the greatest extent. Not referring this merger to the Monopolies Commission was a delicate decision because one paper, the *Sunday Times*, appeared to be not only economically viable, but actually profitable. There was an obvious political motive in that Murdoch's *Sun* had vigorously supported Thatcher's Conservatives at the 1979 election and Mr Murdoch was known both to be friendly with Mrs Thatcher, and also in the USA and Australia to have recently given vigorous support to politicians of the right.

The cases which were considered by the Monopolies Commission are also instructive in several ways. Four cases which came to the Commission in 1981–82[7] indicate problems of the 1970s which were not solved and which will continue in the future. In these cases the cost of new (electronic) plant looms large – its cost tends to discourage independent groups. In two of the four cases foreign ownership was involved – in each case one of the very few American press owners was selling papers back to British owners; in neither case was there any reference to policy guide-lines on foreign ownership – since none exist. In two cases a Scots or Welsh aspect appears; in one case the only remaining locally owned independent Welsh daily paper (the *South Wales Argus* of Newport) was being sold to a London group – and nobody seems to have found any inconsistency between this and the move towards more Welsh television. Another important continuing theme is the rise of free newspapers and also the power of existing major local newspaper groups to fight back – not least because they typically continue to control the lushest advertising and often many of the local retail newsagents as well.

The members of the Monopolies Commission have, of course, not been blind to the obvious inadequacies of their own powers. These reports include several gloomy comments to the effect that, though the particular case may be unobjectionable, the continuing trends in the local press are disturbing.

It could be argued that the excesses of monopoly – and the inadequacies of the Monopolies Commission's powers – have been corrected by competition in the form of free newspapers. In some localities the outcome may be satisfactory, but in other areas the local newspaper's monopoly is probably stronger than ever while the local voter gets less local news than ever.

Future monopoly policy must encompass competition as well, and must consider the broad range of media. In this area the experience of the 1970s can be useful, not least because the weaknesses of the Monopolies Commission are so obvious and so widely agreed.

7. Public redress and access: The Press Council

The Press Council in the 1960s attracted a great deal of British and international attention; as a voluntary court of honour dedicated to the elimination of bias and inaccuracy in the press – and especially when presided over by Lord Devlin as chairman (1964–69) – the Press Council was widely regarded as a shining example of British wisdom, common sense and pragmatism. In the 1970s, however, the Press Council seemed to slide downhill and it became difficult to imagine any visiting media policy-maker learning very much from such an eccentric and ineffectual body.

The Press Council under Lord Devlin was successful largely because it benefited from the King-Thomson led consensus as to the need for a more responsible press. Lord Devlin himself was an ideal chairman, unusually young and liberal for a former Judge, with a gift for popular communication and with good 'political' judgement. Under Devlin the Press Council continued the earlier work of hearing complaints, but it also issued several ringing general declarations. The first three chairmen had all come from the press and Devlin was the first lay chairman. It was at this point that the first research study on the Press Council was conducted; the Press Council was particularly well accepted by newspaper editors.[8]

But Lord Devlin himself was shrewd enough to recognize that the Press Council was a flimsy and vulnerable body. In his farewell address Devlin explicitly recognized the need for a total consensus of the major press groupings; he described Cecil King (of IPC and the *Daily Mirror* stable) as the 'architect of the Press Council in its present form'. And he said: 'But it must be remembered that a single great newspaper, if it chose to go its own way, could gravely weaken the basis on which the Press Council rests.'[9]

Devlin clearly had in mind Rupert Murdoch, who had recently bought *The News of the World* and had even more recently published in it the confessions of Christine Keeler. The Press Council itself in due course denounced this raking up of the old scandal of John Profumo.[10] Murdoch and his editor roundly denounced the Press Council in turn. The *Daily Mail* and the *Sunday Express* have also attacked the Press Council on occasion but the determined opposition of *The Sun* from 1970 onwards – together with Devlin's retirement – marks the end of the Press Council's period of success.

The Press Council idea originated in the PEP Report of 1938, which suggested a Press Tribunal chaired by an eminent lawyer or public man;[11] such Councils already existed in Scandinavia. The 'General Council of the Press' came into existence via the Ross Royal Commission and Parliamentary pressure in the form of a private member's bill. In its early years (1953–64) it was reluctantly, then increasingly, accepted by the national press, but the wide range of functions suggested by the original Commission had been pared down to only one major function – hearing complaints. The Council dropped the first major function – journalism recruitment and training – indicated by the 1947–9 Royal Commission; this was later taken up by the separate NCTJ. It also dropped the task of monitoring monopoly trends – this went in 1964 to the Monopolies Commission. The Ross Commission had seen the Council as the central professional body of the profession of journalism;[12] the Council saw itself as a much more modest body hearing complaints.

The commonest criticism has been that the Press Council is really a press public relations device for deflecting criticism. In view of the Council's early history this cannot easily be denied – it initially had an entirely press membership and it has always been financed (under-financed) by the main press trade associations.

Since its early days the Press Council has changed its activities very little, but it has changed its personnel. It started as a body with 100% press membership, but the lay element was introduced in 1964 and expanded on two subsequent occasions. When the NUJ withdrew in 1980 lay members made up 58% of continuing membership.

Another change was in the chairmanship. The three chairmen after Devlin were all prominent lawyers – but they lacked his unique gifts and the job has come to be seen as a part-time one; this is contrary to the original blue-print. Instead of a small body dominated by an eminent full-time energetic individual, the Press Council came to be run by its very small and rather anonymous full-time staff.

The main achievement of the Press Council each year is to adjudicate on some 60 complaints. Some are obscure or trivial; many of the successful complainants belong to the professionally articulate occupations or represent local church, trade union, voluntary, or political organisations. A recent study reveals that even successful complainants are highly critical of the Press Council's delays, its lack of a code or clearcut procedures, and what some of them still regard as its bias in favour of the press.[13]

But the Press Council itself is mainly significant, not for itself, but as an extreme case of the muddle, fragmentation – the sheer mess – which follows from an excess of pragmatism and voluntarism and a shortage of money, clear thinking, and explicit goals, procedures and powers.

The Press Council may meander onward but if it wishes to become a significant body it really has only two choices. First it could revert back to the kind of body outlined by the 1947–49 Royal Commission; it would then indeed play a major part in the press and in media policy. It would then need a professional staff – not only of journalists, but of lawyers, accountants and researchers – and a much bigger budget.

The other possibility seems to be that the Press Council should follow two other bodies, which exist in advertising and broadcasting, and should become a really efficient complaints body with narrow goals vigorously pursued. The Advertising Standards Authority was reformed in 1974 after a threat of legislation; the ASA's budget was hugely increased and it has gone into partnership with the consumer bodies to outlaw objectionable advertising. It is much more businesslike, efficient and quick and much less controversial than the Press Council. The ASA is given teeth by the agreement of the print media not to publish advertisements which it outlaws. It operates a genuine consensus – including an advertising industry which wants to be respectable; and since the ASA was reformed advertising has indeed come to be seen by the public as largely non-controversial.[14]

The Broadcasting Complaints Commission was set up by the Broadcasting Act of 1980; its five members were appointed by the broadcasting minister (Home Secretary); and the Commission has some teeth – it can compel either the BBC or the IBA channels to broadcast an agreed summary of an upheld complaint.

However, the Commission, like most British broadcasting innovations, contains many elements seen elsewhere – in the Press Council, and in complaints bodies previously established by both the BBC and the IBA. The BBC Programme Complaints Commission lasted ten years (1971–81) and the new body was modelled more upon it than upon the IBA body. The Broadcasting Complaints Commission's first chairman, Lady Pike, was a former Conservative junior minister. The five members included a familiar political balance, a trade union leader, a former senior BBC man, and a Scottish university professor with IBA connections. Their average age at the start of their five-year term of office was about 61. Possibly reacting to criticisms to the effect that it was armed with excessive and arbitrary powers, the Commission began extremely cautiously and in its first ten months upheld only three complaints.[15]

The Broadcasting Complaints Commission suggests that objections to a body 'with teeth' are greatly exaggerated.

The Press Council, of course, operates in a more difficult area. But it also ignores much that already exists, and not only the ASA and the BCC. At present the 'Letters to the Editor' columns in the newspapers provide much more effective and speedy redress and to many more people.[16]

The Press Council's 1983 report on the Yorkshire Ripper multiple murder case severely criticised the gross excesses of several national newspapers.[17] But the Press Council took two full years to condemn this indefensible press conduct; the prime culprit, the *Daily Mail*, quickly replied with a sharp denunciation of the Press Council; finally the report failed adequately to analyse the extent to which the publicity excesses of the police not only encouraged the press excesses but also had in turn been triggered by relentless and hysterical earlier press coverage of the police's failure to find the killer. Like the Press Council itself, this report was too narrow, too legalistic, too late, and ineffectual.

Future media policy

Will the policy cycle which began around 1982 be more or less haphazard than the previous cycles? All the signs – in both the early satellite and cable initiatives – point towards 'Downing Street' playing a decisive part. There are strong indications that European considerations of various kinds will be dominant in the satellite field, and important elsewhere. This may well increase the haphazard character of policy-making by increasing the number of participants beyond the present thirty agencies. It remains to be seen whether these developments will place yet more ultimate control in the hands of Downing Street or will transfer some to 'Europe'.

Haphazard media policy-making strengthens the tendency of media managers and editors to engage in image cultivation. Even names and titles are enormously important. 'Editor' is a magic word which seems for many otherwise sophisticated people to summon up visions of a degree of autonomy which never was. 'Independent' television long resisted the preferred BBC description of it as 'commercial' television; but either term seems remarkably successful at shifting public emphasis away from the fact that the ITV companies are also licensed monopolists of a service in keen demand – TV advertising. In 'Independent' local radio images are again important; are so many ILR stations named after rivers because such a name conveys the desired image of tranquil provincial virtue?

Journalists in general, and editors and factual radio/TV producers in particular, go in fear of the laws of libel and contempt of court. These and other legal areas cause anxiety partly because they seem to be deliberately vague, uncertain and – haphazard.

Equally haphazard is the scrutiny exercised by Parliament. In the 'public' style of policy-making, members of parliament grasp the public committee report in one hand and the proposed legislation in the other; during the formal legislative process some very detailed scrutiny does occur. But in the equally, or more, important 'private' mode of policy-making, members of parliament are left rather feebly putting down parliamentary questions and trying to find out what Downing Street is doing. Much of what is covered in the occasional short Debates and Questions tends to be constituency material (for example about a particular TV transmitter), or about a particular television programme having allegedly gone too far, or about the feared imminent death of another newspaper.

The excessive number of media policy-making bodies and their haphazard operation, plus the alternation of 'public' and 'private' phases of media policy-making, lead to excessive power being exercised by Downing Street and by a very few civil servants from the few major departments – who in turn negotiate with a small number of major media organizations, business interests and trade unions. The decisive struggle is typically between three or four senior ministers and their departments such as the Home Office making broadcasting arguments, the Department of Industry making hardware sales arguments, with the Treasury counting the cost. This struggle is refereed and eventually decided by the Prime Minister and then, quite probably, rushed through Cabinet and Parliament against an electoral timetable.

The most vital step towards a more coherent set of policies in this field would be a widespread recognition that the whole of the mass media do indeed constitute a distinct policy-making area. Until this is recognized there will be an increasing number of painful – and needless – surprises.

Notes and references

Chapter 1: National myths, media myths

1. 'Forty Years of Listening and Viewing in Britain', in *Annual Review of BBC Audience Research Findings 3*, 1975/6, p. 8.
2. Following the showing on both ITV and BBC TV in 1969 of the film *Royal Family* there was an increase in the proportion of the British public seeing the Queen as 'outspoken', 'powerful', 'approachable', 'lively'. BBC Audience Research, *The Effects of the Film 'Royal Family'*, October 1969, p. 4.
3. Jeremy Tunstall, *The Westminster Lobby Correspondents*, 1970, pp. 18–19.
4. Kathy K. Demarest, 'Royal Press Office – public service or public relations?' *Journalism Studies Review* (Cardiff), July 1980, pp. 19–23.
5. Christopher Griffin-Beale, 'Wednesday Morning Fever', *Broadcast*, 27th July, 1981.
6. *UK Press Gazette*, 18th May, 1981.

Chapter 2: Media made politics, politically made media

1. Colin Seymour-Ure, *The Political Impact of Mass Media*, pp. 140–3.
2. D. E. Butler and Richard Rose, *The British General Election of 1959*, London: Macmillan, 1960, pp. 75–97.
3. Jeremy Tunstall, *The Westminster Lobby Correspondents*, pp. 99–102.
4. This case has been argued on several occasions by Colin Seymour-Ure.
5. Robert M. Worcester and Martin Harrop (eds.) *Political Communications: The General Election Campaign of 1979*, London: Allen and Unwin.
6. Jeremy Tunstall, *The Westminster Lobby Correspondents*. See also the writing of Colin Seymour-Ure (bibliography) which place the Lobby arrangements in a wider context.
7. Jeremy Tunstall, *Journalists at Work*.
8. See James Margach, *The Abuse of Power*, London: W. H. Allen, 1978, and James Margach, *The Anatomy of Power*, W. H. Allen, 1979, pp. 125–55.
9. 'This is typical of Harold's (Wilson) handling of politics. He still thinks he can settle problems just by talking to the press'. Richard Crossman, *The Diaries of a Cabinet Minister*, Volume 1, London: Hamish Hamilton and Jonathan Cape, 1975, p. 161. See also pp. 165–6.
10. Annabelle May and Kathryn Rowan (eds.) *Inside Information: British Government and the Media*, 1982.

11. Patrick Gordon Walker, 'Secrecy and Openness in Foreign Policy Decision-Making', in Thomas M. Franck and Edward Weisband (eds.) *Secrecy and Foreign Policy*, New York: Oxford University Press, 1974, pp. 42.
12. Anthony Barker and Michael Rush, *The Member of Parliament and his Information*, London: Allen and Unwin, 1970, pp. 35.

Chapter 3: Politically made media policy

1. Tim Robinson (Madge), *The Nature and Meaning of Broadcasting Policy in the United Kingdom: 1945–1974*, unpublished PhD dissertation, City University, London, 1980.
2. H. Heclo and A. Wildavsky, *The Private Government of Public Money*, London: Macmillan, 1974.
3. *Report of the Committee on Broadcasting* (Annan), 1977, pp. 40–2.

Chapter 4: Television

1. 'Three American gameshows doing jolly well on British TV', *Variety*, 4th June, 1980.
2. The BBC in its 'Opera Month' of April 1979 had a total audience of five million for eight televised operas – enough people to fill Covent Garden for 2,000 performances. But this average audience of 600,000 achieves a rating of 1 (%). Source: BBC.
3. In 1954 the USA had 199 television sets per thousand population, the UK had 81, Canada 74; the highest levels in the rest of Europe in 1954 were 5 sets per thousand population in Belgium, and 3 in France. Jeremy Tunstall, *The media are American*, p. 293.
4. Asa Briggs, *Sound and Vision*, pp. 977–91.
5. For example: 'The BBC', *The Economist*, 29th June, 1946.
6. Lord Simon, *The BBC From Within*, 1953, p. 136.
7. C. F. Pratten, The *Economics of Television*, 1970, p. 14.
8. H. H. Wilson, *Pressure Group: The Campaign for Commercial Television*, 1961.
9. Tim Robinson (Madge), *The Nature and Meaning of Broadcasting Policy in the United Kingdom: 1945–1974*, unpublished PhD dissertation, City University, London, 1980.
10. *Report of the Committee on Broadcasting*, 1960 (1962), p. 46.
11. Gerald Beadle, *Television: A Critical Review*, London: Allen and Unwin, 1963.

Chapter 5: Networked radio, recorded music

1. BBC Broadcasting Research, *In-Car Listening*, BBC, April 1982, LR/82/82.
2. BBC, *Broadcasting in the Seventies*, 1969.

3. Simon Frith, *The Sociology of Rock*, pp. 97–102.
4. BBC Audience Research, *Old Grey Whistle Test*, BBC, 1980, VR/80/240.
5. 'The music press', in Simon Frith, *The Sociology of Rock*, 1978, pp. 139–56.
   'How the music press fights to hold a fickle readership', *Campaign*, 1st October, 1982, pp. 41–47.

Chapter 6: Film: long time a-dying

1. Jeffrey Richards, 'The British Board of Film Censors . . . in the 1930s', and *Historical Journal of Film, Radio and Television*, 1. October, 1981, pp. 95–116; and 2. March, 1982, pp. 39–48.
2. F. D. Klingender and Stuart Legg, *Money Behind The Screen*, London: Lawrence and Wishart, 1937.
3. Herbert J. Gans, 'Hollywood Films on British Screens', *Social Problems*, 1962, pp. 324–8.
4. Monopolies Commission, *Film: A Report on the Supply of Films for Exhibition in Cinemas*, 1966, p. 26.
5. Thomas H. Guback, 'American interests in the British Film Industry', *Quarterly Review of Economics and Business*, 7, 1967, pp. 7–21. Thomas H. Guback, *The International Film Industry*, Bloomington: Indiana University Press, 1969.
6. Monopolies Commission, *Films*, 1966, p. 31.
7. Twelfth Annual General Meeting, Odeon Theatres and Subsidiary Companies, *The Economist*, 3rd December, 1949, pp. 1266–7.
8. 'Films and the Future', *The Economist*, 12th November, 1949, pp. 1076–78.
9. The need for this was recognized later: Report of the Prime Minister's Working Party, *Future of the British Film Industry*, HMSO, 1976, Cmnd 6372.
   Report of the All Industry Committee of *The Film Industry 1977* (Chairman: Robert Bolt), London: Association of Independent Producers, 1977.
10. Recognized in 1981 by Fourth Report of the Interim Action Committee on the Film Industry, *Film and Television Co-operation*, London: HMSO, 1981, Cmnd 8227.
11. Iain Muspratt, 'The Home Video Perspective', paper for *Television '83* conference, 27th January 1983. This paper estimated the gross UK retail market in 1982 at £257m.
12. BBC Audience Research Department, *Film '79*, BBC, June 1980, VR 80/268, p. iv.
13. Young and Rubicam.
14. See, Open University, Mass Communication and Society course, Broadcasting Handbook 3, *The Making of 'The Spy Who Loved me'*, The Open University, 1977.

Chapter 7: Newspapers: slow fade

1. J. Edward Gerald, *The British Press Under Government Economic Controls*, pp. 34, 47–9.
2. Peter Clark, *Sixteen Million Readers*, 1981, p. 45.
3. For a trenchant and amusing account see Graham Cleverley, *The Fleet Street Disaster*, pp. 59–72.

Chapter 8: Magazines

1. Amalgamated Press in 1958, and Odham's in 1961 (Odham's itself having bought Hulton and Newnes in 1959).
2. Cynthia White, *Women's Magazines 1693–1968*.
3. W. D. McClelland, 'Women's Weeklies', *New Society*, 31st December, 1964, pp. 10–12.
4. Tom Hopkinson (ed.), *Picture Post 1938–50*, Penguin Books, 1970. Tom Hopkinson, *Of This Our Time*, London: Hutchinson, 1982.
5. 'The TV Programme Journals', *WPN and Advertisers Review*, 9th July, 1965, pp. 17–25.
   'How the newspapers have hit the *Radio Times*', *UK Press Gazette*, 23rd May, 1966, p. 11.
6. These ten fields had some 200 titles with total circulation of 8 million. See 'General and Special Interest Magazines', *Retail Business*, 294, August 1982, p. 37.
7. Graeme Hutton, 'How to avoid the pitfalls in the car ads jungle', *Campaign*, 5th March, 1982, pp. 24–31.
8. 'Trade and Technical Magazines', *Retail Business*, 295, September 1982, pp. 33–7.
9. Royal Commission on the Press, *Periodicals and the Alternative Press*, 1977, p. 30.
10. 'Who's Who in Computing', *Campaign*, 2nd April, 1982, pp. 37–42.
11. Martin Walker, 'Logs in the Intellectual Pulp Mill', *The Guardian*, 4th February, 1982.

Chapter 9: Audiences and content

1. 'Forty Years of Listening and Viewing in Britain', *Annual Review of BBC Audience Research Findings, 3, 1975/6*, BBC, 1977, p. 5.
2. *Annual Review of BBC Audience Research Findings, 3, 1975/6*, p. 9.
3. James Curran, Angus Douglas, and Garry Whannel, 'The Political Economy of the Human-Interest Story', in Anthony Smith (ed.), *Newspapers and Democracy*, Cambridge, Mass: M.I.T. Press, 1980, pp. 288–347.
4. Lord Hill, *Behind The Screen*, 1974, p. 39.
5. IBA Audience Research Department, *Audience Ratings of Television Coverage of the 1982 World Cup*.

'Television audiences for the World Cup 1978', in *BBC Audience Research Findings*, 6, *1978/9*, pp. 38–48.

6. In the second week of May 1982, BBC2 achieved 27% of the total audience, against 32% for BBC1. Nine of BBC2's top ten programmes were 'International Snooker', with audiences of between six and eleven million.

7. Jeremy Tunstall, *The media are American*, 1977.

8. Data compiled by John Williams for six weeks ending 17th December, 1981.

9. *BBC Broadcasting Research Findings*, 7, *1980*, p. 13.

10. Carrick James Market Research for Pye Ltd, *Children and Television: A national survey among 7–17 year olds*, Cambridge, 1978, Tables 21 and 22.

11. H. Hobson, P. Knightley, and L. Russell, *The Pearl of Days: An Intimate Memoir of the Sunday Times 1822–1972*, London: Hamish Hamilton, 1972.

12. Gerald Goodhardt, 'Beyond TV audience size', *Admap*, February 1982, pp. 103–6.

13. This distinction was made for both radio and television in a landmark 1974–5 survey of leisure activities conducted by the BBC: BBC Audience Research Department, *The People's Activities and Use of Time*, BBC, 1978.

14. Their unpopularity is charted and proposals made for reform in, Jay Blumler, Michael Gurevitch, and Julian Ives, *The Challenge of Election Broadcasting*, Leeds University Press, 1978. The unpopularity of PPBs in the 1979 election is reported in, BBC Audience Research, *The Coverage of the 1979 General Election Campaign on TV and Radio, Part 2*, BBC, 1981, VR/81/43.

15. 'The Coverage of the May 1979 General Election Campaign on Radio and Television', *BBC Audience Research Findings*, 6, *1978/9*, pp. 63–70.

16. 'Aquarius', IBA Audience Research Department, *Research Summary*, 26th March, 1976.

Chapter 10: Bias?

1. Peter Golding and Sue Middleton, 'Making claims: news media and the welfare state', *Media, Culture and Society*, 1, 1979, pp. 5–21.

2. Denis McQuail (ed.) *Analysis of Newspaper Content*.

3. Jay Blumler and Alison Ewbank, 'Trade Unionists, the Mass Media and Unofficial Strikes', *British Journal of Industrial Relations*, 8, 1970.

4. Glasgow Media Group, *Bad News*, 1976.

5. For such an attempt see, Jeremy Tunstall, 'The Problem of Industrial Relations News in the Press', in Oliver Boyd-Barrett et al., *Studies on the Press*, 1977, pp. 343–97.

6. John Hartley, *Understanding News*, London: Methuen, 1982, pp. 107–29.

7. J. M. Wober, *Television Coverage of Industrial Conflict*, London: Independent Broadcasting Authority, May 1979.
8. See Helen Baehr (ed.), *Women and the Media*, Oxford: Pergamon, 1980. Josephine King and Mary Stott (eds), *Is This Your Life?*, London: Virago, 1977.
   Robert Hamilton et al., *Adman and Eve*, London: Equal Opportunities Commission, 1982.
9. A. S. R. Manstead and Caroline McCulloch, 'Sex-role stereotyping in British television advertisements', *British Journal of Social Psychology*, 20, 1981, pp. 171–80.
10. J. M. Wober, *Television and Women*, IBA Research Department, 1981.
11. 'The Naked Civil Servant: what the audience thought', *Independent Broadcasting*, June 1976, pp. 24–5.
12. Jeremy Tunstall, *Journalists at Work*, 1977.
13. Geoffrey Robertson, *People against the Press*, Quartet, 1983.
    York: Oxford University Press, 1981.
14. The study was conducted by Bradley Greenberg, BBC Audience Research Report, VR/72/56.
15. Paul Hartmann, Charles Husband, and Jean Clark, *Race As News*, Paris: UNESCO, 1974, pp. 89–173.

Chapter 11: Inequality and ambiguity

1. David Morley, *The 'Nationwide' Audience*, British Film Institute TV Monograph 11, London: BFI, 1980.
2. For the combination of an aggressive tone with very modest demands, see, Philip Cohen and Carl Gardner (eds) *It Ain't Half Racist, Mum*, London: Comedia Publishing with Campaign Against Racism in the Media, 1982.
3. Made by James Curran in numerous publications and frequently repeated by trade union critics.
4. For views on the BBC see page 158 and note 8 below.
   For views on the provincial press of managing directors, council officials, head-teachers, councillors, and trade union secretaries – all on balance detected Conservative bias – see, Social and Community Planning Research, *Attitudes To The Press*, 1977, p. 218.
5. '*Till Death Do Us Part* as anti-prejudice propaganda', *BBC Audience Research Findings*, 1, 1973/4, pp. 26–35.
6. G. J. Goodhardt et al., *The Television Audience : Patterns of Viewing*, 1975.
   A. S. C. Ehrenberg and G. J. Goodhardt, 'The Audience of *Edward and Mrs Simpson*', *Independent Broadcasting*, April 1980, pp. 8–9.
7. Social and Community Planning Research, *Attitudes to the Press*, 1977, pp. 58–68.
8. NOP Market Research, *A Study of the Public's perception of the BBC and its services*, BBC, Audience Research Department, 1980. This

278   *Notes and References*

report is summarized in, 'The General Public's perception of the BBC and its role', *BBC Broadcasting Research Findings*, 7, *1980*, pp. 29–39.
9. Glasgow Media Group, *Bad News*, 1976, p. 1.
10. Channel Four from November 1982 has run a one hour television news on four nights a week, but its audience has been low.
11. *News Broadcasting in 1962*, BBC Audience Research, LR/62/1586, October 1962, p. 19.
12. Social and Community Planning Research, *Attitudes to the Press*, 1977, p. 35.
13. In a 1975 study *Panorama* was quoted by 19% of a national sample of adults as the current affairs programme they 'liked best' – against 40% who like *Nationwide* best. But 44% quoted *Panorama* as the TV current affairs programme they 'liked least' – against 10% who liked *Nationwide* least. *Current Affairs for the Under 35s*, BBC Audience Research, VR/75/570, October 1975, pp. 30, 32.
14. *News Broadcasting and the Public in 1970*, BBC Audience Research, LR/71/537, August 1971, p. 23.

Chapter 12: Finance, power, conglomerates

1. The Labour Party (Chairman, Lord Reith), *Report of a Commission of Enquiry into Advertising*, 1963, p. 55.
2. Royal Commission on the Press, *Final Report*, 1977, p. 54.
3. Monopolies and Mergers Commission, *Wholesaling of Newspapers and Periodicals*, London: HMSO, 1978, Cmnd 7214.
4. *International Thomson Organisation Ltd Annual Report, 1981*.
5. Monopolies and Mergers Commission, *The Berrow's Organisation Ltd and Reed International Ltd*, London: HMSO, Cmnd 8337, 1981.
6. *The News Corporation Limited Annual Report, 1982*.
7. *Reed International Annual Report*, April 1982.
8. *Advertising Age: 100 Leading Media Companies*, 28th June, 1982.
9. *Thorn EMI* Report and Accounts, 1982.

Chapter 13: Control in the Press

1. Jeremy Tunstall, 'Research for the Royal Commission on the Press, 1974–7', in, Martin Bulmer (ed.), *Social Research and Royal Commissions*, London: Allen and Unwin, 1980, pp. 122–49.
2. H. Yeo, *Newspaper Management*, London: John Heywood, 1891.
3. Political and Economic Planning, *The British Press*, 1938, p. 86.
4. K. Sisson, *Industrial Relations in Fleet Street*, Oxford: Blackwell, 1975. Roderick Martin, *New Technology and Industrial Relations in Fleet Street*, Oxford University Press, 1981.
5. Jeremy Tunstall, '*Editorial Sovereignty* in the British Press', in, Oliver Boyd-Barrett et al. (eds.), *Studies on the Press*, pp. 249–341.
6. Jeremy Tunstall, *The Westminster Lobby Correspondents*, 1970, pp. 12–14.

7. Jeremy Tunstall, *Journalists at Work*, 1971.
8. A detailed account of the administration of one London daily is, Edwin Samuel, 'The Administration of the Times', *Public Administration in Israel and Abroad*, 14, 1973, pp. 192–283.
9. Harry Christian, *The Development of Trade Unionism and Professionalism among British Journalists*, unpublished PhD dissertation, University of London, 1976.
10. Eric Jacobs, *Stop Press: The Inside Story of The Times Dispute*, London: Andre Deutsch, 1980.

Chapter 14: Control in television and radio

1. Tom Burns, *The BBC: public institution and private world*, 1977.
2. Lord Hill, *Both Sides of the Hill*, London: Heinemann, 1964.
   Lord Hill, *Behind the Screen*, 1974.
3. In his autobiography: Lord Simon, *The BBC From Within*, 1953.
4. Sir Michael Swann, 'A Year at the BBC', *The Listener*, 17th January, 1974.
5. Asa Briggs, *Governing the BBC*, London: BBC, 1979.
6. Charles Curran, *A Seamless Robe*, p. 49.
7. e.g., Howard Thomas, *With an Independent Air*, 1977, pp. 165, 181–2. Bernard Sendall, *Independent Television in Britain, Volume 1, Origin and Foundation 1946–62*, pp. 198, 251, 309–16.
8. National Board For Prices and Incomes, *Costs and Revenues of Independent Television Companies*, 1970, p. 19.
9. Harry Henry, 'The Commercial Implications of a Second (and Complementary) ITV Channel', *Admap*, October 1979.
10. An interesting document in this connection is, BFI Dossier Number 9, *Granada: the First 25 Years*, London: British Film Institute, 1981.
11. Lord Hill, *Behind the Screen*, 1974, pp. 37–61.
12. IBA, *ITV Franchise Awards, 1980*, 28th December, 1980.
13. Kenneth Clark, *The Other Half*, London: John Murray, 1977.
14. Bernard Sendall, *Independent Television in Britain, Volume 1*, 1982, p. 61.
15. Peter Seglow, *Trade Unions in British Television*, 1978.
16. Bernard Sendall, *Independent Television in Britain, Volume 1*, 1982, pp. 106–9.
17. ACTT, *Patterns of Discrimination*, London: ACTT, 1975. Michael Fogarty, Isabel Allen, and Patricia Walters, *Women in Top Jobs 1968–79*.
18. See Stephen Lambert, *Channel Four: Television with a difference?*, 1982.

Chapter 15: The regions

1. There is evidence to suggest that English local loyalties are even more local than this, stretching perhaps only two or three miles; Royal

Commission on Local Government in England, *Research Studies, 9, Community Attitudes Survey*, HMSO, 1969.
2. *Wolverhampton and Its Press*, Express and Star, 1950.
3. Alan Lee, *The Origins of the Popular Press, 1855–1914*, London: Croom Helm, 1976, p. 287.
4. Reginald Pound and Geoffrey Harmsworth, *Northcliffe*, London: Cassell, 1959.
5. David Ayerst, *Guardian: Biography of a Newspaper*, London: Collins, 1971, p. 488.
6. Asa Briggs, *The Golden Age of Wireless*, Oxford University Press, 1965, pp. 315–35.
7. IBA, *Annual Report and Accounts 1981–2*, p. 44.
8. Local Radio Workshop, *Local Radio in London*, London: LRW, 1982.
9. PEP, *Report on the British Press*, 1938, pp. 148–9.
10. Louis Moss and Kathleen Box, *Newspapers and the Public*, London: Wartime Social Survey, Ministry of Information, 1943, Table 22.
11. Viscount Camrose, *British Newspapers and their Controllers*, 1947, pp. 135–40.
12. Royal Commission on the Press, *Attitudes to the Press*, 1977, pp. 105–112.
13. 'WWN: bad news for Gwynfor', *Broadcast*, 22nd September, 1980, pp. 30–1.
14. For a valuable account of these and other problems, see, House of Commons Committee on Welsh Affairs, *Broadcasting in the Welsh Language and its implications for Welsh and non-Welsh speaking viewers and listeners*, HMSO, HC 448–1, 1981.
15. BBC Broadcasting Research, *Listening and Viewing Among Welsh Speaking People in Wales*, London: BBC and Welsh Fourth Channel Authority, January 1982, LR/82/10.
16. BBC Broadcasting Research, *Radio Nottingham: The East Midlands Experiment in Sharing 'Afternoon Special'*, April 1982, LR/82/84. Jamie Jauncey, 'Afternoon Special: a regional experiment', *Radio Month*, March 1981, pp. 28–9.
17. BBC Broadcasting Research, *Radio Birmingham: an awareness and image study*, September 1981, LR/81/201.
18. Anthony Wright, *Local Radio and Local Democracy*, London: IBA, 1982.
19. IBA Radio Division, *The Audience for ILR*, 1982, p. xx.
20. IBA, *Annual Report and Accounts 1980–1*, p. 36.
21. Bernard Davies, 'One Man's Television', *Broadcast*, 4th August, 1980, pp. 12–13.

Chapter 16: Media policy and fragmentation

1. *Broadcasting. Copy of the Licence and Agreement Dated the 2nd Day of April 1981 Between Her Majesty's Secretary of State for the Home Department and the British Broadcasting Corporation*, London: HMSO, April 1981, Cmnd 8233.

2. Harold Evans, *Downing Street Diary: the Macmillan Years 1957–63*, London: Hodder and Stoughton, 1981, pp. 136–7.
3. Reginald Bevins, *The Greasy Pole*, London: Hodder and Stoughton, 1965, pp. 85–114.
4. '. . . Annan brings nearer the very things he least wanted. Annan actually increases the chances of ITV-2. . . . In my view the likely consequence of Annan is that the fourth television channel will be a commercial version of BBC-2.'
Jeremy Tunstall, 'Annan in Wonderland', *Media Reporter*, Volume 1, 3, 1977, pp. 26–31.
5. H. Heclo and A. Wildavsky, *The Private Government of Public Money*, London: Macmillan, 1974.
6. Discussed in the Annan Report, pp. 50–1.

Chapter 17: Foreign media policy

1. This was reflected in a series of influential articles in *The Economist*. See for example, 'Television in a World Market', *The Economist*, 3rd September, 1949, pp. 517–19.
2. Central Policy Review Staff, *Review of Overseas Representation*, HMSO, 1977.
3. *The United Kingdom's Overseas Representation*, London: HMSO, August 1978, Cmnd 7308, p. 3.
4. Jocl C. Cohen, *British Foreign Policymaking and the News Media*, unpublished PhD dissertation, City University, London, 1981.
5. Oliver Boyd-Barrett, 'The Collection of Foreign News in the National Press', Oliver Boyd-Barrett et al., *Studies on the Press*, 1977, pp. 7–43.
6. This whole passage on Reuters relies heavily on, Oliver Boyd-Barrett, *The International News Agencies*, 1980.
7. David Morrison, *Foreign Media Correspondents based in London*, unpublished report, Department of Social Science, City University, London, 1981.
8. ABC, *Circulation Review*, January–June, 1982.
9. Previous to the control of ACC and Central Television from Australia by M.V. Holmes a'Court, various Canadian involvements in Independent Local Radio were the main example. See, Iain Murray, 'The Canadian Connection Revealed', *Campaign*, 8th July, 1977.
10. Robert Silvey, *Who's Listening?*
11. BBC, *Annual Report and Handbook 1983*, pp. 76–80.
12. Jeremy Tunstall, *The media are American*, 1977, passim.
13. Gerard Mansell, *Let the Truth be Told: 50 years of BBC External Broadcasting*, 1982.
14. Sir Michael Swann, *The BBC's External Services Under Threat*, BBC, 1978, p. 4.
15. For example, *Report of the Review Committee on Overseas Representation*, 1968–1969 (Chairman, Sir Val Duncan), London: HMSO, 1969, Cmnd 4107.

16. Philip M. Taylor, *The Projection of Britain: British Overseas Publicity and Propaganda 1919–1939*, Cambridge University Press, 1981.
17. Ian McLaine, *Ministry of Morale: Home Front Morale and the Ministry of Information in World War II*, London: Allen and Unwin, 1979.

Chapter 18: Domestic media policy: past and future

1. *Control of the Direct Broadcast Satellite: Values in Conflict*, Aspen Institute, Palo Alto, California, 1974.
2. The figure for 1975 was about £60m. according to the McGregor, *Royal Commission on the Press, Final Report*, 1977, p. 111.
3. Jeremy Tunstall, *The media are American*, 1977, pp. 222–31.
4. McGregor, *Royal Commission on the Press, Final Report*, 1977, p. 280.
5. Monopolies Commission, *The Times Newspaper and the Sunday Times Newspaper*, London: HMSO, 1966, HC 273.
6. 'Tuesday, December 20th (1966). Cabinet. The most interesting item on the agenda was the future of *The Times* . . . yet we never discussed the issue in principle. It went automatically to the President of the Board of Trade who automatically sent it to the Monopolies Commission and then made his personal report to Cabinet.' Richard Crossman, *The Diaries of a Cabinet Minister*, Volume 2, p. 172.
7. Monopolies and Mergers Commission, *The Observer and George Outram*, London: HMSO, 1981, HC 378. *South Wales Argus and Express Newspapers*, London: HMSO, 1981, Cmnd 8385. *Benham Newspapers, St Regis International and Reed International*, London: HMSO, 1982, HC 402. *Sheffield Newspapers*, London: HMSO, 1982, Cmnd 8664.
8. Paul B. Snider, *The British Press Council: a study of its role and performance, 1953–1965*, unpublished PhD dissertation, University of Iowa, 1968. Also reflecting the optimistic mood of this period is, H. Phillip Levy, *The Press Council*, 1967.
9. 'Between Devlin and the deep blue series', *UK Press Gazette*, 6th October, 1969, p. 3.
10. *The Press and the People: 17th Annual Report of the Press Council*, Autumn 1970, pp. 70–73.
11. Political and Economic Planning, *Report on the British Press*, 1938, p. 171.
12. *Royal Commission on the Press, 1947–1949 Report*, 1949, pp. 164–174.
13. Geoffrey Robertson, *People against the Press*, Quartet, 1983.
14. The Advertising Association, *Public Attitudes to Advertising*, 1980–81, London: A. A., 1981.
15. *Report of the Broadcasting Complaints Commission 1982*, London: HMSO, HC 478, July 1982.
16. Jeremy Tunstall, 'Letters to the Editor', Oliver Boyd-Barrett, Colin Seymour-Ure, and Jeremy Tunstall, *Studies on the Press*, pp. 203–48.
17. *Press Conduct in the Sutcliffe Case*, London: Press Council, 1983.

Annotated bibliography

ABC, *Circulation Review*. Published twice a year by the Audit Bureau of Circulations in London. Contains sales data on all significant magazines and newspapers, including local weeklies, with a very few exceptions.

Manuel Alvarado and Edward Buscombe, *Hazell: the making of a TV series*. London: British Film Institute with Latimer 1978. A private-eye short series made by Thames TV in 1977 receives well organized description and sane analysis.

Charles Barr, *Ealing Studios*. London: Cameron and Tayleur with David and Charles 1977. Examplary study of a British film production company (1938–58). Combines film critique, social history, organisational analysis. More revealing than the autobiography of studio head Sir Michael Balcon.

Joan Bakewell and Nicholas Garnham, *The New Priesthood: British Television Today*. London: Allen Lane, Penguin Press 1970. Two then young TV insiders present revealing extracts from 1969–70 interviews with top people in all sectors of BBC and ITV television. Still fascinating material.

BBC, *Annual Review of BBC Broadcasting Research Findings*. Published annually by the BBC since 1974 these reviews contain BBC data on the previous year's TV and radio plus reports on more specialized ad hoc studies.

BBC, *Annual Report and Handbook*. The most fact-packed annual volume on British TV and Radio; also prime example of BBC image-building.

Peter Beharrell and Greg Philo (eds.), *Trade Unions and the Media*. London: Macmillan 1977. The case that trade unions are maltreated by the media, argued in ten assorted articles edited from Glasgow Media Group stable.

Nora Beloff, *Freedom Under Foot*. London: Temple Smith 1976. Sub-titled 'The battle over the closed shop in British journalism'; supports the editors against the National Union of Journalists. The vituperation and bitter rhetoric of the 1974–5 'debate' also mar this account.

William A. Belson, *The Impact of Television*. London: Crosby Lockwood 1967. Many detailed findings from 1950s' BBC television survey research; less good on strategy and meaning.

BFI Dossier 15, *Tonight*. London: British Film Institute, 1982. Fascinating account of BBC's legendary early evening programme which began in 1957 and launched numerous television careers; most of this 'Dossier' was written by Deidre Macdonald circa 1970.

Jay Blumler and Denis McQuail, *Television in Politics*. London: Faber 1968. Sophisticated analysis of 1964 General Election survey of Leeds voters; main foci include Party Political Broadcasts and political knowledge gained via television.

Oliver Boyd-Barrett, *The International News Agencies*. London: Constable; Beverly Hills: Sage, 1980. Standard work compares the British Reuters and its specialized financial data services with the other three western 'world agencies'.

Oliver Boyd-Barrett, Colin Seymour-Ure and Jeremy Tunstall, *Studies on the Press*. London: HMSO for Royal Commission on the Press (Working Paper Number 3) 1977. Boyd-Barrett on Foreign News; Seymour-Ure on Science, Parliament, National Press and Parties; Tunstall on Letters, 'Editorial Sovereignty', and Industrial Relations News.

Andrew Boyle, *Only The Wind Will Listen: Reith of the BBC*. London: Hutchinson 1972. Excellent biographical account of the BBC's 'father' and his bizarre personality.

Russell Braddon, *Roy Thomson of Fleet Street*. London: Collins 1965, Fontana 1968. Light-hearted but revealing account of the Ontario advertising salesman who became a leading Scottish and then British media tycoon.

Brian Braithwaite and Joan Barrell, *The Business of Women's Magazines*. London: Associated Business Press, 1979. Two experienced magazine executives, who launched the British *Cosmopolitan* in 1972, are especially interesting on magazine launches, but also usefully over-view the post-1945 women's magazine field.

D. G. Bridson, *Prospero and Ariel: the rise and fall of radio*. London: Gollancz 1971. Outstanding autobiography of prominent BBC radio writer/producer (1935–69); strong on 1930s Manchester radio, early Third Programme, radio drama and poetry.

Asa Briggs, *The War of Words*. Oxford University Press 1970. Third volume in Briggs' monumental 'History of Broadcasting in the United Kingdom', unravels the BBC's 1939–45 war effort and its complex relationship with government.

Asa Briggs, *Sound and Vision*. Oxford University Press 1979. The fourth volume, 1082 pages on 1945–55. Briggs combines heavy use of documents with many astute insights. Inevitably, as an official history, a view of the BBC from the top down, but an outstanding example of the species. Ends with the birth of ITV in 1955.

Asa Briggs, *Governing the BBC*. London: BBC 1979. A 'short' (291-page) addendum on the BBC Governors 1927–77; excellent detail on crisis issues, with Briggs as usual reluctant to draw conclusions.

Charlotte Brunsden and David Morley, *Everyday Television: Nationwide*. London: British Film Institute 1978. Content analysis and 'reading' of BBC's national-regional news magazine show. Part revealing, part pedestrian.

Tom Burns, *The BBC: Public Institution and Private World*. London: Macmillan, 1977. The BBC as seen by eminent industrial sociologist; based on interviews with BBC producers and managers in 1963 and 1973. Strong analysis of unions and 'professionalism'.

Cabinet Office: Information Technology Advisory Panel, *Report on Cable Systems*. London: HMSO, 1982. 54-page report tells Britain to get itself cabled quickly.

Viscount Camrose, *British Newspapers and Their Controllers*. London: Cassell 1947. Then 'Controller' of the *Daily Telegraph* updates his 1939 pamphlet. This full-length book provides much more ownership detail than does the Ross Royal Commission on the Press.

Steve Chibnall, *Law and Order News*. London: Tavistock 1977. Popular newspaper crime reporting, 1945–75, is subjected to a textual critique.

Peter Clark, *Sixteen Million Readers: evening newspapers in the UK*. London: Holt, Rinehart and Winston, 1981. Brief useful summary of circulation and other statistical data on Britain's major non-national press sector.

Graham Cleverley, *The Fleet Street Disaster*. London: Constable 1976. Author combines experience as journalist, press manager, and business academic in devastating and amusing account of Fleet Street management.

R. H. Coase, *British Broadcasting: a study in monopoly*. London: Longmans, Green for London School of Economics 1950. A deftly sceptical economist's account of the BBC monopoly, which helped to undermine its intellectual justifications.

Stan Cohen, *Folk Devils and Moral Panics*. London: MacGibbon and Kee 1972. New edition, Oxford: Martin Robertson 1980. Analysing the 1960s' case of 'Mods and Rockers', Cohen sees them as an example of Folk Devils created to star in one of a continuing series of media-induced moral panics.

Stan Cohen and Jock Young (eds.), *The Manufacture of News*. London: Constable, Beverley Hills: Sage, 1973, revised edition 1981. Many more moral panics and entertainingly varied articles showing media love-hate of 'deviance' and the caricaturing of social problems.

Harvey Cox and David Morgan, *City Politics and the Press*. Cambridge University Press 1973. 1960s Merseyside politics were blandly and patchily covered by the Liverpool *Post* (a.m.) and *Echo* (p.m.) and their linked weeklies – say these two political scientists.

Hugh Cudlipp, *At Your Peril*. London: Weidenfeld and Nicholson 1962. The most relaxed and balanced of Cudlipp's four anecdotal books on popular newspapers; the *Daily Mirror* and its guru, Hugh Cudlipp, were still riding high.

Charles Curran, *A Seamless Robe*. London: Collins 1979. Sub-titled 'Broadcasting – Philosophy and Practice', the austere but thoughtful reflections of the BBC's director-general 1969–77.

James Curran (ed.), *The British Press: a Manifesto*. London: Macmillan 1978. A collection of pieces stressing press economics, power and policy. In part a left critique of the McGregor Royal Commission on the Press (1974–7) which is seen as do-nothing and conservatively biased.

James Curran and Jean Seaton, *Power Without Responsibility: The Press and Broadcasting in Britain*. London: Fontana 1981. Left critique focusing on 1930–60. Poor fit between Curran's revealing press audience analyses and Seaton's documentary research on 1940s' BBC. Outstanding bibliography with focus again on 1930–60.

Robin Day, *Day by Day: a dose of my own hemlock*. London: William Kimber 1975. Robin Day interviews himself about his first 20 years in political television. The 1961 version seemed highly original; this one contains much sage hindsight.

Jonathan Dimbleby, *Richard Dimbleby*. London: Hodder and Stoughton

1975; Coronet 1977. Son chronicles Father's pioneering work as radio news man, television commentator and personality; useful background on many clashes with BBC. An exception to the usual low quality of media biographies.

Direct Broadcasting by Satellite: report of a Home Office Study. London: HMSO 1981. The 'private' committee report which led in 1982 to the allocation of two British DBS channels to the BBC (option C out of 5 options indicated).

Richard Dyer et al., *Coronation Street.* London: British Film Institute 1981. Useful facts about Coronation Street's first twenty years, and, mainly Marxist, opinions about the significance of Granada's famous soap opera.

The Economist Intelligence Unit, *The National Newspaper Industry.* London: E.I.U. 1966. Consultant report documents the inadequacies of both management and unions in Fleet Street; illuminating details on particular publications and departments.

Philip Elliott, *The Making of a Television Series.* London: Constable, Beverly Hills: Sage 1972. Pioneer fly-on-the-wall account of a 1967 ATV documentary mini-series in production. Much insight, some humour, also an audience study.

Winston Fletcher, *Advertising.* London: Hodder and Stoughton, Teach Yourself Books 1978. Senior advertising man explains with brevity and wit how advertising works; excellent illustrations, many useful facts.

Michael Fogarty, Isobel Allen and Patricia Walters, *Women in Top Jobs 1968–1979.* London: Heinemann 1981. 'Women in the BBC' (one of four studies) reveals that in this decade women's chances of getting top BBC jobs failed to improve.

Simon Frith, *The Sociology of Rock.* London: Constable 1978. Sociologist and writer on rock music provides carefully documented account of all aspects of British pop music industry.

Simon Frith, *Sound Effects.* New York: Pantheon and London: Constable, 1983. Updated version of previous book including much comparative British/American material.

J. Edward Gerald, *The British Press Under Government Economic Controls.* Minneapolis: University of Minnesota Press 1956. Little known but important work describes massive exercise in press public policy via stringent newsprint rationing; the deep-freeze and slow thaw lasted 15½ years (1939–55).

Glasgow University Media Group, *Bad News.* London: Routledge and Kegan Paul 1976. Left critique of TV news coverage of trade unions; combines quantified analysis (22 weeks in 1975) with qualitative 'reading'. Many virtues and vices; superior to *More Bad News* and *Really Bad News* from same stable.

Grace Wyndham Goldie, *Facing the Nation: Television and Politics 1936–1976.* London: Bodley Head 1977. Austerely written but comprehensive account of the development of BBC political television by a pioneer who produced much of it.

G. J. Goodhardt, A. S. C. Ehrenberg, and M. A. Collins, *The Television Audience: Patterns of Viewing.* Saxon House 1975. Survey research focusing on repeat viewing; about 55% of viewers who watched this episode will also watch the next episode of the same series.

John Goulden, *Newspaper Management*. London: Heinemann 1967. Modest but revealing textbook on 1960s' newspaper management by manager with Kemsley, Thomson and United Newspapers experience.

Michael Gurevitch, Tony Bennett, James Curran and Janet Woollacott (eds.), *Culture, Media and Society*. London: Methuen 1982. Deriving from the Open University 'Mass Communication and Society' course, this mainly Marxist and theoretical collection includes pieces on media organizations, power, political effects, and race.

Stuart Hall, Chas Crichter, Tony Jefferson, John Clarke and Brian Roberts, *Policing the Crisis*. London: Macmillan 1978. Sub-titled 'Mugging, the State, and Law and Order', this lengthy and intricate analysis is the best single product of the Marxist Birmingham University Cultural Studies group.

James Halloran, Philip Elliott and Graham Murdock, *Demonstrations and Communication: a case study*. Penguin Books 1970. The London anti-Vietnam war protest of 27 October 1968; multi-faceted analysis of 'violent' media predictions and non-violent outcome. Perhaps the best Leicester University study.

Nicholas Hartley, Peter Gudgeon, Rosemary Crafts, *Concentration of Ownership in the Provincial Press*. London: HMSO for Royal Commission on the Press 1977. Cmnd 6810–5. Very fully documented account of declining competition in provincial morning, evening, Sunday and weekly press. Section on freesheets.

Harry Henry (ed.), *Behind the Headlines – the Business of the British Press*. London: Associated Business Press 1978. Derived from a series in ADMAP, an excellent if uneven collection covering the business and finances of the entire British press; edited by Lord Thomson's 1960s marketing guru, later unwisely banished to academe.

Alastair Hetherington, *Guardian Years*. London: Chatto and Windus 1982. Recollections of *Guardian* editor (1956–75), the last of the 'Sovereign Editors'; high points include Suez, leaving Manchester, and the vetoing of proposed merger with *The Times*.

Lord Hill, *Behind the Screen*. London: Sidgwick and Jackson 1974. The man who, as chairman of the ITA and BBC, put his mark on both, tells how he did it.

H. T. Himmelweit, A. N. Oppenheim and P. Vince, *Television and the Child*. Oxford University Press 1958. Classic study by team of social psychologists; incomplete spread of TV in 1950s allowed matching of TV users and non-users.

Fred Hirsch and David Gordon, *Newspaper Money*. London: Hutchinson 1975. Astute analysis of Fleet Street problems leads to eccentric remedy – the authors want a selective subsidy for the serious newspapers.

Dorothy Hobson, *Crossroads: the drama of a soap opera*. London: Methuen 1982. Researcher's 'inside' defence of long-running Midlands ITV soap opera focusing on 1981 decision to terminate key character. Criticizes 'elitist' view within ITV of popular mass programming.

Richard Hoggart (ed.), *Your Sunday Paper*. University of London Press 1967. This varied collection of articles is the best thing specifically on Britain's national Sunday newspapers.

Tom Hopkinson (ed.), *Picture Post 1938–50*. Penguin Books 1970. Splendid extracts from the magazine success of the 1940s by its then editor, Tom Hopkinson.

Charles Husband (ed.), *White Media and Black Britain*. London: Arrow 1975. Useful collection by academics, journalists and activists; most pieces accuse British media of exacerbating ethnic tensions.

Independent Broadcasting Authority, Annual Reports and Accounts. This is the serious report on its operations as a regulatory agency, published annually by the IBA. Much factual material on ITV and ILR.

Independent Broadcasting Authority, *Television and Radio*. The IBA's annual 'Guide to Independent Broadcasting' is aimed at the general public, combining sober material and glossy publicity.

Richard Ingrams (ed.), *The Life and Times of Private Eye*. Penguin Books 1971. The cartoons, brevity and wit of *Private Eye* are ideally matched to extracting as a Tenth Anniversary celebration. Lord Gnome wins again.

Ian Jackson, *The Provincial Press and the Community*. Manchester University Press 1971. Unpretentious but useful account of English (only) evening and weekly newspapers in late 1960s focusing mainly on their content.

Clive Jenkins, *Power Behind the Screen*. London: MacGibbon and Kee 1961. Originally something of a rag-bag of ITV ownership facts, now a useful historical document.

Simon Jenkins, *Newspapers: The Power and the Money*. London: Faber, 1979. Readable and brief introduction to Fleet Street's owners and trade unions in the 1970s; author was youthful editor of *Evening Standard*.

Terence Kelly, Graham Norton and George Perry, *A Competitive Cinema*. London: Institute of Economic Affairs 1966. Leans heavily on official reports and P.E.P. while expressing faith in relevance of free market solutions. One of the few reliable works on the British film industry.

H. V. Kershaw, *The Street Where I Live*. London: Granada, 1981. Anecdotal account of *Coronation Street*'s first 21 years by a former script editor and executive producer of the famous TV serial.

Stephen Lambert, *Channel Four: Television with a Difference?* London: British Film Institute, 1982. Scholarly history of the idea of a fourth television channel, ending with Channel Four's launch.

Brian Lappin (ed.), *The Bounds of Freedom*. London: Constable 1980. Transcripts of a Granada TV series, using prominent journalists, politicians and lawyers in 'hypothetical' discussions of media and privacy, contempt, rape, fairness, official information, terrorism.

Peter M. Lewis, *Community Television and Cable in Britain*. London: British Film Institute 1978. Useful account of half-hearted and underfinanced cable 1972–8 'experiments' in Greenwich, Bristol, Sheffield, Swindon and Wellingborough.

Peter Lewis (ed.), *Radio Drama*. Longman 1981. Collection of eleven authors, academics, producers, radio writers; focuses mainly on serious radio drama since 1950 but also covers historical origins and more popular fare.

H. Phillip Levy, *The Press Council: History, Procedure and Cases*. London: Macmillian 1967. Official account of British Press Council's birth and first 14 years, written at Press Council's high point (chairman: Lord Devlin). Largely a digest of complaints cases.

Annabelle May and Kathryn Rowan (ed.), *Inside Information: British government and the media*. London: Constable 1982. Comprehensive collection of extracts on unfreedom of information in Britain – official secrets, contempt, D Notices, public records, Prime Minister, Cabinet, Whitehall, Nuclear power, the Concorde project, Ulster, the Crossman diaries – by journalists, politicians, academics.

Denis McQuail (ed.), *The Sociology of Mass Communications*. Penguin Books, 1972. One of the first such collections of articles, this one includes British empirical pieces on television audiences, media organizations and race.

Denis McQuail, *Analysis of Newspaper Content*. London: HMSO for Royal Commission on the Press 1977 Cmnd 6810–4. Quantified content analysis of British national dailies, Sundays, provincial dailies, weeklies, also industrial relations, social welfare and foreign news – in 1975.

Gerald Mansell, *Let The Truth Be Told: 50 Years of BBC External Broadcasting*. London: Weidenfeld and Nicolson, 1982. Strong narrative history by BBC's 1970s Managing Director of External Services.

The Monopolies Commission, *Film: a Report on the Supply of Films for Exhibition in Cinemas*. London: HMSO 1966. Documents the Rank-ABC duopoly in cinema exhibition and Hollywood dominance in finance and production.

David Murphy, *The Silent Watchdog: the press in local politics*. London: Constable 1976. North of England local weekly press is unwilling and unable to unearth local political and planning malpractice; idiosyncratic account with Dickensian detail.

National Board for Prices and Incomes, *Costs and Revenues of Independent Television Companies*. London: HMSO (N.B.P.I. Report No 156) 1970 Cmnd 4524. Perhaps the most important of a number of media reports from the Prices and Incomes Board.

George Nobbs, *The Wireless Stars*. Norwich: Wensum Books 1972. Aimed at the market for 1940s' nostalgia, but a valuable account of radio stardom – Tommy Handley, Vera Lynn, Wilfred Pickles *et al*.

Grant Noble, *Children in Front of the Small Screen*. London: Constable, Beverly Hills: Sage 1975. A social psychologist's undogmatic and multi-faceted discussion of children and television in Britain.

Philip Norman, *Shout! The True Story of the Beatles*. London: Hamish Hamilton 1981; Corgi 1982. Scholarly research and lively writing make outstanding show business history; one of the few reliable books on popular music.

Marjorie Ogilvy-Webb, *The Government Explains*. London: Allen and Unwin 1965. As the title suggests, this useful account of the British governmental information apparatus has a Whitehall viewpoint.

Burton Paulu, *Television and Radio in the United Kingdom*. London: Macmillan 1956, 1961 and 1981 editions. Standard textbook by an American academic; both the 1961 and 1981 editions involved heavy re-writing. Some of the 1981 material is a trifle faded; the 1961 edition, *British Broadcasting in Transition* is excellent on the early days of ITV.

Guy Phelps, *Film Censorship*. London: Gollancz 1975. Complementing

John Trevelyan's autobiographical account, this is a more academic study, mainly of the British Board of Film Censors, circa 1970.

Wilfred Pickles, *Between You and Me*. London: Werner Laurie 1949. Britain's all-time most popular broadcaster shows that his many talents encompass autobiography; excellent on 1930s' and 1940s' radio.

Political and Economic Planning, *The British Press*. London: PEP 1938. The classic work on the British press; the anonymous authors, led by Gerald Barry (then *News Chronicle* editor), combine 'inside' and 'outside' views. The first Royal Commission on the Press (1947–9) is basically an update of the PEP report.

Political and Economic Planning, *The British Film Industry*. London: PEP 1952 and 1958. Another classic which documents the British film industry's period of greatest success as well as its chronic problems.

C. F. Pratten, *The Economics of Television*. London: Political and Economic Planning 1970. Brief PEP study containing valuable financial home truths about this costly medium.

The Press Council, *The Press and The People*. The Press Council's annual report, the core of which normally consists of adjudications on complaints. Also useful compilation of circulation data.

Simon Regan, *Rupert Murdoch: a business biography*. London: Angus and Robertson 1976. Anecdotal journalist's biography of press tycoon; but the best available so far on Murdoch up to his arrival in New York.

Report of the Committee of Privy Counsellors appointed to inquire into 'D' notice matters (chairman: Lord Radcliffe). London: HMSO 1967 Cmnd 3309. Detailed enquiry into 'crisis' in the voluntary editorial self-censorship 'D' notice system; also entertaining raw material on Fleet Street.

Second Report from the Select Committee on Nationalized Industries, *Independent Broadcasting Authority*. London: HMSO 1972. House of Commons 465. 400 pages of questioning by Members of Parliament provided most detailed account to that date of the IBA.

Report of the Committee on Obscenity and Film Censorship (Chairman: Bernard Williams) London: HMSO 1979 Cmnd 7772. Thoughtful report calls for scrapping of old law and old terms, to be replaced by new legislation.

Report of the Broadcasting Committee 1949 (Chairman: Lord Beveridge). London: HMSO 1951 Cmnd 8116. The document which, through its grudging backing for the BBC and Selwyn Lloyd's minority report, led to commercial television.

Report of the Committee on Broadcasting 1960 (Chairman: Sir Harry Pilkington). London: HMSO 1962 Cmnd 1753. Famous/notorious for its savage criticisms of ITV; its recommendation of a third TV channel to go to the BBC was implemented. Two fat volumes of written evidence were also published.

Report of the Committee on Broadcasting Coverage (Chairman: Sir Stewart Crawford). London: HMSO 1974 Cmnd 5774. Specialized report on technical coverage problems in the regions.

Report of the Committee on the Future of Broadcasting (Chairman: Lord Annan). London: HMSO 1977 Cmnd 6753. A readable account of British broadcasting and its dilemmas in 522 (unindexed) pages. Good on description. Weak on data, finance, future of telecommunications, and on conclusions. No evidence published. One short volume of *Appendices E–I* contains three useful papers by Blumler, Halloran and Croll, and Smith.

Report of the Working Party on the Welsh Television Fourth Channel Project. London: HMSO for the Home Office 1978. One of several reports which supported the idea of a Welsh Fourth TV channel.

Report of the Inquiry into Cable Expansion and Broadcasting Policy. (Chairman: Lord Hunt) London: HMSO, 1982, Cmnd 8679. Quick short report calling for go-ahead on Cabling Britain.

Royal Commission on the Press, 1947–9, (Chairman: Sir William D. Ross) *Report*. London: HMSO 1949 Cmnd 7700. One longish volume, mainly on national newspapers, then still newsprint-rationed. Evidence also published.

Royal Commission on the Press, 1961–2, (Chairman: Lord Shawcross) *Report*. London: HMSO Cmnd 1811. One shorter volume largely restricted to press as industry. Nine volumes of documentary and oral evidence also published.

Royal Commission on the Press, 1974–77, (Chairman: O. R. McGregor) *Final Report*. London: HMSO 1977 Cmnd 6810. The final report was accompanied by 12 other published volumes – some listed in this bibliography – these were mainly commissioned research; another 13 photocopied volumes of evidence are available in 17 libraries listed in this Report volume.

Royal Commission on the Press, 1964–7, Interim Report: The National Newspaper Industry. London: HMSO 1976 Cmnd 6433. Documents one of the low points of the Fleet Street roller-coaster.

Royal Commission on the Press (1964–7) Final Report Appendices. London: HMSO 1977 Cmnd 6810-1. Useful material on ownership and journalist's training.

Philip Schlesinger, *Putting 'Reality' Together: BBC News*. London: Constable, and Beverly Hills: Sage, 1978. Sophisticated analysis of BBC national news operation based on extensive direct observation and interviews in both TV and radio newsrooms in 1972–6.

George Scott, *Reporter Anonymous: the Story of the Press Association*. London: Hutchinson 1968. Centenary celebration leaves Britain's dominant domestic news agency still very little revealed.

Peter Seglow, *Trade Unionism in British Television*. Farnborough: Saxon House 1978. This 'case study in the development of white collar militancy', is an approving account of ACTT and its place in British commercial television.

Bernard Sendall, *Independent Television in Britain: Volume 1. Origin and Foundation, 1946–62*. London: Macmillan, 1982. First of three volume history by deputy director general of ITA/IBA during its first two decades. Certain to be the standard source of detailed information on the ITA/IBA. Less sure on the ITV companies and on analysis.

Colin Seymour-Ure, *The Press, Politics and the Public*. London: Methuen 1968. Standard work, equally strong on press and political sides.

Colin Seymour-Ure, *The Political Impact of Mass Media*. London: Constable, Beverly Hills: Sage, 1973. Linked essays on political system 'effects', parties and media, General Elections, *Private Eye*, *The Times* and Appeasement, Enoch Powell.

Milton Shulman, *The Ravenous Eye*. London: Coronet 1975. From his perch at the London *Evening Standard*, Shulman was for many years the fiercest critic of British television, accusing it of causing many of society's ills.

Robert Silvey, *Who's Listening: The story of BBC Audience Research*. London: Allen and Unwin 1974. Rather cautious autobiography by BBC's first head of Audience Research (1935–68).

Lord Simon, *The BBC From Within*. London: Gollancz 1953. Chairman of the BBC governors 1947–52, Lord Simon has many fascinating insights about the BBC in its last days of monopoly.

D. H. Simpson, *Commercialization of the Regional Press*. Aldershot: Gower 1981. Study of early 1970s provincial newspaper chain management decries increased emphasis on advertising and the decline of editorial.

William Smethurst (ed.), *The Archers: The first thirty years*. London: Eyre Methuen 1980, New English Library 1981. Excellent collection on long-running daily radio serial of country life; Smethurst, Archers producer from 1978, combines plot summaries with social history of the famous BBC Birmingham production.

A. C. H. Smith, *Paper Voices*. London: Chatto and Windus 1974. First (and non-Marxist) offering from Birmingham Centre for Contemporary Cultural Studies; detailed 'reading' of *Daily Mirror* (1937–45, 1964) and *Daily Express* (1945, 1964).

Anthony Smith (ed.), *British Broadcasting*. Newton Abbot: David and Charles 1974. Eighty-one short extracts mainly from comprehensive list of official broadcasting documents; some unofficial pieces as well.

Anthony Smith (ed.), *The British Press Since the War*. Newton Abbot: David and Charles 1974. Seventy short extracts mainly from official documents large and small, plus some personal opinion pieces.

Social and Community Planning Research, *Attitudes to the Press*. London: HMSO for the Royal Commission on the Press 1977. Cmnd 6810–3. Reports on three sample surveys – General public, local influentials, and editors.

John Spraos, *The Decline of the Cinema*. London: Allen and Unwin 1962. Economic analysis of British cinema's 1950s' downward spiral.

Walter Taplin, *The Origin of Television Advertising in the United Kingdom*. London: Pitman 1961. Survey research study of cautious approach by advertisers and agencies in early months of British television advertising.

Howard Thomas, *With an Independent Air*. London: Weidenfeld and Nicolson 1977. Entertaining autobiography of a key ITV pioneer.

Michael Tracey and David Morrison, *Whitehouse*. London: Macmillan 1979. A 'neutral' biography of Mrs Mary Whitehouse, leader of the National Viewers and Listeners' Association; this volume focuses on Whitehouse's Christianity rather than on NVALA membership.

Michael Tracey, *The Production of Political Television*. London: Routledge and Kegan Paul 1977. Producer interviews and crisis case studies make for useful, if rambling, account of dilemmas encountered in televising politics.

John Trevelyan, *What the Censor Saw*. London: Michael Joseph 1973. The Chief Film Censor, who presided during the 1960s' revolution in values, extends his highly individual approach into autobiography.

Jeremy Tunstall, *The Westminster Lobby Correspondents*. London: Routledge and Kegan Paul 1970. Interview and questionnaire study of 39 national political correspondents; also the 'rules' of this then highly secretive society.

Jeremy Tunstall, *Journalists at Work*. London: Constable, Beverly Hills: Sage, 1971. Based on interview and questionnaire data from 200 national specialist journalists covering: Politics, Labour, Education, Aviation, Football, Crime, Motoring, Fashion, Washington, New York, Bonn, Rome.

Jeremy Tunstall, *The Media Are American*. London: Constable, New York: Columbia University Press, 1977. Sub-titled 'Anglo-American media in the world' argues that American leadership in setting mass media patterns was assisted by British Empire, English language and lack of British media policy.

Jeremy Tunstall (ed.), *Media Sociology*. London: Constable, Urbana: University of Illinois 1970. This, the first British 'reader', contained empirical pieces on 1960s' British press, television, books and political media.

E. G. Wedell, *Broadcasting and Public Policy*. London: Michael Joseph 1968. Secretary of the Independent Television Authority, 1961–4, George Wedell presents the best overview of broadcasting policy between the Pilkington and Annan reports.

John Whale, *Journalism and Government*. London: Macmillan 1972. Perhaps the most successful of several pungent media books by ITN man in Westminster Lobby and Washington, before return to print journalism.

Cynthia White, *Women's Magazines 1693–1968*. London: Michael Joseph 1970. The basic study on British women's magazines. Strong on both early (1875 on) and recent history (early days of IPC magazine empire in 1960s).

Cynthia White, *The Women's Periodical Press in Britain, 1946–1976*. London: HMSO for the Royal Commission on the Press. (Working Paper Number 4) 1977. White updates her previous study with focus on early and mid-1970s' developments.

Raymond Williams, *Communications*. London: Penguin 1962. Eminent Marxist literary critic and historian makes some effective criticisms of British media but his solutions are nostalgic.

H. H. Wilson, *Pressure Group: The Campaign for Commercial Television*. London: Secker and Warburg, 1961. American social scientist sees the campaign for commercial television in the early 1950s as a vulgar commercial conspiracy.

Lord Windlesham, *Broadcasting in a Free Society*. Oxford: Blackwell 1980. Long regarded as an intellectual guru among senior ITV executives, Windlesham makes a disappointing guru but a sound writer of textbooks on British broadcasting.

Rex Winsbury, *New Technology and the Press*. London: HMSO for the Royal Commission on the Press 1975. Sub-titled 'a study of experience in the United States' this well conducted study led to Royal Commission false hopes.

Charles Wintour, *Pressures on the Press: An Editor Looks at Fleet Street*. London: André Deutsch 1972. For many years the London *Evening Standard*'s remarkably intellectual editor, Wintour here combines acute personal insights with routine Fleet Street critique.

Alan Wood, *The True History of Lord Beaverbrook*. London: Heinemann 1965. One of the few good Fleet Street biographies and the best on Beaverbrook as a newspaper publisher.

Robert Worcester and Martin Harrop (eds.), *Political Communications: The General Election Campaign of 1979*. London: Allen and Unwin 1982. Strong on advertising, polls and broadcasting in Mrs Thatcher's election. Weak on press.

Index